SINCE 1845

A History of
The Mutual Benefit Life
Insurance Company

Robert L. Patterson

SINCE 1845

A HISTORY OF
THE MUTUAL BENEFIT LIFE
INSURANCE COMPANY

by Mildred F. Stone C.L.U.

Rutgers University Press
The Mutual Benefit Life Insurance Company 1957

Library of Congress Catalog Card Number:
57–6226

DESIGNED BY LOUISE E. JEFFERSON

MANUFACTURED IN THE UNITED STATES OF AMERICA BY
BOOK CRAFTSMEN ASSOCIATES, INC., NEW YORK

This story of the Mutual Benefit Life Insurance Company is naturally based on much research. Also, it is the fruit of more than thirty years of unfolding acquaintance with the facts of the Company's history and close personal observation of top-level Company management. I have seen repeatedly the ideals of Patterson, Grover and Dodd given contemporary substance by Hardin and Rhodes, Stillman, Thompson and Palmer.

The more than a century of Company history reflects many of the important events and the economic and social developments of the United States. It is fascinating to see in our story the geographical and community growth of our country; the wars, epidemics and financial crises which have highlighted American history; the trends of business habits and operations. If one could really know the history of the Mutual Benefit Life, he would have a rich understanding of the United States.

Quotations from original sources have been used copiously in this book. These not only present necessary facts, but by their style and very words bring a sense of personality to the record. Hearing people who were there tell the story in their own words adds vitality to history.

In the earlier days of the Company specific developments were often definitely identified with one individual. In later years this has become much less true. With group and committee procedures and a much larger staff of officers it has seemed wise to put less emphasis in the later chapters on individual accomplishments. Many currently active Company officers and others of recent years have not been mentioned who undoubtedly will have their deserved place in a later history.

To all the officers and staff members who helped me so greatly with the factual material and with the physical preparation of this book, I want to express deep and sincere appreciation. Their ready cooperation has been heartwarming and typical of many happy experiences in my Company life.

To my mother and father who gave me what I brought to the Company, and to Jay Ream and Oliver Thurman who opened its doors of opportunity, I thankfully dedicate this book.

MILDRED FAIRBANKS STONE

CONTENTS

ILLUSTRATIONS

SINCE *1845*

A History of
The Mutual Benefit Life
Insurance Company

The Year of Beginnings

IN THE DAYS WHEN LETTERS WERE WRITTEN with quills, and candles lighted an office after dark, on January 31, 1845, the Governor of New Jersey signed a special act of the Legislature creating the Mutual Benefit Life Insurance Company of Newark, New Jersey. Few people then knew much about life insurance, and fewer appreciated its service. Estimates say that perhaps five thousand policies were owned in the whole country, and those mostly by the well-to-do. Many in those days felt that life insurance was wicked, a form of gambling and defying the purposes of Providence. Even a few years later an article in the *New York Times* stated: "He who insures his life or health must indeed be a victim of his own folly or of another's knavery."

When the Mutual Benefit Life was founded, Newark was a city of about twenty-five thousand population, already a center of industry and trade, with five thousand workers in its factories. Much commerce was done with the South which subsequently affected the Company's expansion. For instance, in Beaver Street in Newark were the factories making the broad-brimmed beaver hats bought by Southern planters.

The United States in 1845 included only twenty-six states. Texas was still the Lone Star Republic. California was a part of Mexico. The disputes with Great Britain over the boundary west of the Rockies were evoking cries of "54–40 or fight." An increasing tide of immigrants was pouring over the old Oregon Trail so lately surveyed by Fremont with his vision of a continental nation.

Railroads had only recently come into use and the wood-burning locomotives still struck terror to many timid hearts. Only a few months before, Samuel F. B. Morse had sent his historic message, "What hath God wrought," over the pioneer telegraph line from the Capitol in Washington to Baltimore.*

In 1845 letters were being mailed without adhesive postage stamps which did not come into use until 1847. Prepaid mailing charges were simply marked near the address. Many letters still in old Company files are a single page with the message written on one side, the sheet folded and sealed with red wax, and the address written on the other side.

The city of Newark was still largely rural. Even there people were just beginning to emerge from the self-sufficient, handcraft way of living. The problems of an industrial, money economy were only starting to be widespread enough to make public-spirited citizens feel a burden for doing something to help. In a community like Newark it was becoming a common occurrence to have a young father struck down in the prime of life, leaving his little family with no resources. As a worker in one of Newark's factories, he had supported his family from his wages. They had not depended on a home farm and animals for their living as in an earlier generation.

And so in Newark in Lewis C. Grover's law office, at Stewart's Hotel, under the sidewalk canopies of the business district, along the dusty tree-lined streets, and especially at Benjamin C. Miller's grocery store, on Broad Street just south of Market, tradition and imagination show us Robert L. Patterson talking about a new co-operative enterprise—mutual life insurance.

The story of the Mutual Benefit Life Insurance Company is the record of a community service which became a national institution. When the founding fathers of our Company talked together about their plans for a cooperative undertaking to meet the needs which they saw in the lives of their neighbors, they probably had little thought of operating over a far-flung territory. They chose the name of the Company with deliberate purpose. Their objective was to help people together do something for themselves and their families

---

* In the Company files is the first known Mutual Benefit telegraph message sent from Boston in 1851 to the New York office. The message is printed on a thin strip of paper about a yard long folded into a little three by five white envelope. The envelope carries the name "House's Printing Telegraph" with the address 8 Wall Street. This was just across the street from the Company's 11 Wall Street office. "10 min." noted in the corner may indicate the time required for delivery.

which no one could accomplish by himself. Their association was not a money-making enterprise but a service.

The founders recognized that they were pioneers. They gathered the best possible information and facts from the experience of others and then established their own plan of operation according to their judgment of what was right for a nonprofit, cooperative undertaking. Through the years we see a constant effort on the part of successive groups of officers to improve their stewardship for the members of the Company. The good of the present policyholders always appears as the strongest influence in Company decisions. This purpose has dominated the Company's development and has been the controlling factor in establishing a Company character.

The leading spirit in the founding of the Mutual Benefit Life was Robert Livingston Patterson, a vigorous gentleman then in his sixties, who had lived a colorful life and apparently had long been interested in life insurance. Of Mr. Patterson, Dr. William R. Ward* wrote:

> His grandfather was Robert Livingston, a name well-known and highly esteemed in Colonial history. Robert L. Patterson was born at the Manor of Livingston in New York State in 1776, the year in which our nation had its birth. As a young man, he appears to have been of a roving disposition with a fondness for the sea. In the course of time he procured a position on a sailing vessel as supercargo, an agent sent by the owners of the merchandise to sell it abroad and purchase a return cargo. Robert made several trips to England and, without doubt, during these voyages became impressed with the importance of marine insurance. It is also quite probable that while in London he acquired his first knowledge of life insurance. As he grew to maturity he became an importer and exporter of merchandise with an office on Wall Street, New York City. For many years Mr. Patterson carried on a successful business and acquired considerable wealth, but in the financial crash of the late Thirties he sustained severe reverses. Undiscouraged by this failure in business, he became interested in life insurance; and because of the paucity of material in this country, he went to England in 1842 to obtain first-hand information. At that time a voyage across the ocean was quite a formidable undertaking, and often sixty days were spent on the water. While in England Mr. Patterson interviewed the leading life insurance men and procured forms, prospectuses and other data bearing upon this subject. Upon his return to America he

---

* Dr. Ward, Company medical director and historical scholar, in 1932 wrote a history of the Mutual Benefit Life Insurance Company, *Down the Years*. That book is now out of print and will be quoted freely in this new life story of the Company.

endeavored to interest a group of men in the promotion of a mutual life insurance company.* In this endeavor he experienced considerable difficulty. The organization of the Mutual Life was then being promoted; and after a Charter had been granted to that company, the Legislature of New York was unwilling to grant a charter for another life insurance company. Undismayed by this difficulty, Mr. Patterson turned his attention to New Jersey; and in a comparatively short time he succeeded in bringing together a group of twelve men who were the incorporators of the Mutual Benefit Life Insurance Company.

The official Company seal for which a brass die was made early in 1845 is a perpetual reminder of Mr. Patterson. The design was borrowed from the Patterson family seal. It shows a "pelican in her piety," a very old symbol in heraldry for self-sacrifice. The symbolism is based upon an ancient legend that in time of famine a mother pelican will pierce her own breast and feed her babies with her blood. The pelican was very widely used in religious heraldry. One medieval writer spoke of Christ, "our pelican," who was sacrificed for us. There was a Pelican Life Insurance Company in England whose representative was operating in New York at the time the Mutual Benefit Life was organized. Its first American representative had been appointed in 1807, said to be the first life insurance agent in the United States.

Outstanding among Mr. Patterson's associates was a young Newark lawyer, Lewis C. Grover, then only 29 years old. He prepared the Company's charter and arranged for the necessary legislation by which the Mutual Benefit Life was incorporated.

Lewis C. Grover was born in Caldwell, New Jersey, the son of a lawyer and the grandson of Stephen Grover, who had served as a soldier in the American Revolution and subsequently became a Presbyterian minister in Caldwell. Stephen Grover was a beloved pastor and when he retired his young successor named his son *Grover* Cleveland. Today when one visits President Grover Cleveland's birthplace in Caldwell, it may stand as a tangible tie with Lewis C. Grover who was for nearly forty years a leader in Mutual Benefit Life affairs. Grover Cleveland became a Mutual Benefit policyholder.

Lewis C. Grover prepared himself for the law at night while

* Two of Mr. Patterson's grandsons stated to Dr. Ward that many years before they were informed that the formation of the Mutual Life of New York was materially aided by their grandfather's activities.

BENJAMIN C. MILLER

MARKET STREET, *Newark*

working as a clerk in the State Bank of Newark. He was admitted
to the Bar in 1839, and became recognized as an attorney of marked
ability and a leader in local Whig politics. Mr. Grover was an incorporator of the Company, the first attorney and counsel, and served
continuously as director from 1845 to 1881 and for the last nineteen
years of the period was Company president.

Again quoting Dr. Ward:

> Marcus L. Ward was another of the incorporators who was then a
> young man. He had just passed his thirty-second birthday. In the
> City Directory of 1845, he is listed as a "tallow chandler." This term
> has become quite obsolete; but at that time, when candles were one
> of the principal household necessities, a tallow chandler was engaged
> in a very essential business. His store was on Market Street between
> Broad and Mulberry. There he sold not only candles, but other
> household commodities. For many years Mr. Ward was a successful
> merchant, but in the course of time, greater responsibilities rested
> upon him. During the Civil War . . . his humanitarian efforts
> caused him to be known as "The Soldier's Friend." After the War
> he was elected Governor of New Jersey, which position he filled
> with great ability; and in 1872 he was elected a member of Congress.
> His biographer says of him, "Few men ever brought to public duties
> a greater amount of conscientious principle." The influence of such
> a man was a potent factor in establishing our Company upon prin-
> ciples of high public service, of equity, and of sound finance.
> Marcus L. Ward was unable to render a continuous service to the
> Mutual Benefit, largely because of official duties; but he served at
> intervals from 1845 until the date of his death, April 25, 1884.

Other incorporators were: Thomas V. Johnson, a wholesale
grocer; William Simpson, a merchant; Jesse Baldwin, a hardware
merchant; James L. Dickerson, a leather manufacturer; Henry
McFarlan, an iron manufacturer; Thomas B. Segur, a banker;
Charles S. Macknet, a harness and saddlery manufacturer; Guy M.
Hinchman, a banker and iron founder; and Samuel Meeker, a dealer
in carriages. The incorporators were all Jerseymen, but early shifts
in the directorate brought in some New Yorkers as will be indicated.
Early meetings of the directors were held variously in Newark or
New York (often at 3 P.M. on Saturday) at the Company offices or
at Stewart's Hotel in Newark at 12 M. where "room refreshments"
were paid for by the Company. (Mr. Stewart, the hotel proprietor,
became a policyholder, buying the $5,000 limit, Policy 14.)

In the first few months of the Company's existence, there were
many changes among the directors. One who was not an incorpora-

tor but who was elected in March 1845 and served helpfully until
his death in 1853 was Seth Low. He was a man of outstanding vision
and ability. He grew up in Salem, Massachusetts, son of a sea-faring
father. When that world-famous seaport, stricken by Jefferson's
Embargo and the War of 1812, was slowly dying, he decided to
join the migration of Yankee brains and moved to New York. There
he became prosperous and a leader in many enterprises, including
the China trade. He was one of the incorporators of Brooklyn. As
Mutual Benefit Life director he was particularly interested in
agency affairs, and in the construction of the first home office
building.

Seth Low sent his sons and daughters around the globe and to
live in foreign lands, though he himself, as indicated in his application for Mutual Benefit Life insurance and the subsequent claim
papers, was never out of the country. His youngest son and the
tenth of his eleven children was Charles Porter Low. Charles grew
up on Brooklyn Heights, prowled the South Street wharfs in New
York, felt always the call of the sea. Shortly before his father became
Mutual Benefit Life director, Charles had shipped for his first
voyage as cabin boy at age 18, at no wages, with fifty dollars from
his father to invest in China goods. They made Hong Kong that trip
in one hundred days.

Charles became the protégé of Captain Nathaniel Brown Palmer, America's greatest salt-water man. Captain Nat was the creator of the first clipper ships which made Americans the fastest sailors on the seas of the world.

At age 23 Charles Low was full-fledged shipmaster, the youngest clipper captain, commanding "the sweetest ship afloat." How he took it through a typhoon in the Indian Ocean that stripped it of rigging and stood it on its beam ends, but still brought it to port in China and home again to New York with a profit of $60,000 is only part of the fascinating story of the Low family.*

Charles later became a Mutual Benefit Life policyholder. In the application he identified himself as "shipmaster" and answered Question 5, "Has the Party resided abroad?" simply, "Have traded to China, California, South America and Europe." His story has been told in some detail to help recreate the times in which the Company was founded, to illustrate the kind of men who were interested in this new development—life insurance.

After the Company received its charter still much preparation for business was necessary. In March a permanent organization was determined. Robert L. Patterson was elected president and Benjamin C. Miller, secretary. Joseph L. Lord and John P. Lord were named representatives in New York City where much business was anticipated. Later these men (father and son) were designated respectively as agent and secretary.

The following salary scale was adopted:

President	$1,500.00 per annum
Secretary	800.00 per annum
Agent in New York	900.00 per annum
Secretary in New York	1,300.00 per annum
Assistant in New York	500.00 per annum

A plan of compensation for agents was also determined—5% of the amount of the first premium and 2½% on all renewals, but with the following limitation:

> When the business due to our agent at the regular premiums amounts to the sum of three thousand per annum, his commissions shall cease and the excess over and above this amount shall belong to the Company and shall be paid by the agent to the Company.

Limits for the amount of insurance were agreed upon: $5,000

---

* Told in a book *Tall Ships to Cathay* by Helen Augur.

on a single life at the start with increases gradually, as assets developed, to $15,000 when assets had been built up to $200,000, but "never for a larger amount."

"Necessary books and papers for commencing the business of the Company" were purchased and a special committee prepared a prospectus "in order to proceed to business." When the directors met on April 16, 1845, they agreed that all would be in readiness for the issuing of policies on the following Monday morning. The prospectus had been published, and newspaper advertising had been authorized in three New York papers—the *Journal of Commerce*, the *Evening Post*, the *Courier and Enquirer*—and in the *Newark Daily Advertiser*. It is interesting that the advertising committee later reported that the *Courier and Enquirer* rates were so high that they "declined advertising in it."

Tradition says that the first business of the Company was transacted in the back room of Benjamin C. Miller's grocery store. However, the 1845 Newark directory gives the Company address as 295 Broad Street. This was the southeast corner of Broad and Market Streets about opposite Mr. Miller's store. The rent for this office was $25 a month; the landlord, T. V. Johnson, one of the directors. The building in which it was located was three stories high and of red brick. It was known as the Daily Advertiser Building.

Dr. Ward gives us an interesting pen picture of this office:

From items in the cash book and from other sources, we can form quite an accurate picture of this first office. We know that a large sign indicated its position, for there is an item in the cash book of twenty-five cents for bringing this sign by freight from New York to Newark. We also know that the office was warmed by a coal stove and lighted by both an oil lamp and candles, for there are items of three dollars for a half-ton of coal and of eight cents and thirteen cents for "carrying in coal." We also observe items of seventeen cents and eighteen cents for candles and twenty-five cents for oil. The furniture of which we have knowledge consisted of a desk which cost twelve dollars and a stool which cost one dollar and fifty cents. At that time neither Broad Street nor Market Street was paved. Consequently in dry weather great clouds of dust arose from these streets; and so we find an item of one dollar for watering Market Street and two dollars for watering Broad Street, a much wider thoroughfare. That this office was kept clean is attested by the fact that one of the first items in the cash book is one dollar and fifty cents for "woman cleaning office" and also items of nineteen cents for a broom and twelve cents for a cake of soap. Steel pens had not as yet come into use and so we find an item of thirteen cents for quills. There is also an item of nineteen cents for shoveling snow from the sidewalk.

The Company also established an office in New York at 11 Wall Street, an address which is now the back door of the New York Stock Exchange Building. The office committee made their choice with instructions to pay not more than $500 a year for the New York rental.

The first medical examiners appointed were Dr. Joseph B. Jackson for Newark and Dr. James Stewart for New York City. Dr. Jackson agreed to work for $2 "for each policy" but Dr. Stewart received $3.

The first prospectus of the Company issued in 1845 read in part:

> The Mutual Benefit Life Insurance Company is authorized by its charter to make all and every Insurance appertaining to or connected with life risks . . . In this there is no Money Stock; the funds or capital arise from premiums paid in when persons make insurance, and these form the means to make payments on policies, grant loans, pay expenses and yield profits. All persons insured become members, and are not liable beyond the amount of the premiums to be paid by them. The books of the company are open to them, and the nett profits, at fixed periods, are divided among them. . . . The greatest portion of society, who by daily exertions of industry earn support, as artisans and mechanics, deriving livelihood from personal labor and skill, seldom resort to Life Insurance in any numbers for a future provision for their families, though to none is it as important as to those who by sickness and death may in a day leave those nearest and dearest to them in poverty. To those in *mercantile pursuits,* and those in *professional business* of every rank and class, Life Insurance is also of the utmost importance.

After outlining acceptable risks and limits of insurance to be issued, explaining the plan for financing premiums, promising payment of claims three months after proof of death, providing for "equitable" repurchase of policies (cash surrender values) and explaining proposed investments, the prospectus concludes:

> The observations and explanations above made on the principles of Life Insurance generally, and particularly the great and very superior advantages exhibited to the public by insuring in this Mutual Benefit Company; the credit which policies will give to men in trade, the gain it may be to all classes in their business vocations, and the duty of all to provide for their families, should induce every person to give this subject a careful consideration, remembering the injunctions of Scripture, that "If any provide not for his own, and especially

for them of his own house, he hath denied the faith, and is worse than an infidel."

The prospectus statement that the Company had no money stock and that funds were to arise from premiums paid by policyholders was literally true. The Company's earliest financial record is an old calf-bound cash book in which the first item is $52.25 paid on May 20, 1845, by Benjamin C. Miller for Policy 2. Of this sum $51 was the premium for the $1,500 life policy and $1.25 was a policy fee. This first policy on the life of the Company's first secretary had an unusual history. Mr. Miller served as officer, and later as a director, of the Company from 1845 until his death in 1900. In December 1898 he became age 96. He was still hale and hearty and in full possession of his faculties, although for insurance purposes, according to the American Experience Table of Mortality which the Company was then using, he had reached the limit of life. At that time the Company paid him the proceeds of his ordinary life policy, as it has done to many other policyholders since upon their attaining age 96. Tradition says that his associates gave him ninety-six red roses and hearty congratulations along with the Company's check. The next day he is reported to have appeared at the office as usual with the greeting, "Gentlemen, you must be surprised to see a corpse in your midst."

What about Policy 1? That was issued on the life of Horatio Holden, a Newark butcher, a life policy for $3,000. However, Mr. Holden lost his enthusiasm or his money or both, and did not pay the first premium. Hence, that policy was never in force.

Another strange circumstance is associated with Policy 2. Possibly it was not the first Mutual Benefit Life policy in force. The old policy register—another aging calf-bound book—lists each case with number, date of issue, name of insured and other items. For instance, there are: #1, May 6, 1845, Horatio Holden; #2, May 20, 1845, Benjamin C. Miller; and so on. Suddenly there appears a change: #51, April 25, 1845, Randall H. Greene; #52, April 28, 1845, Isaac H. Frothingham; and so on, listing six other policies before May 6, 1845, the date of the Miller policy.

At the time of Mr. Miller's policy payment at age 96, he was referred to in official records as the first Company policyholder. This may indicate that because of the way business was handled in those days he was technically the first man protected by Mutual Benefit insurance in spite of the question inspired by the policy register. Randall H. Greene who owned Policy 51 was a Brooklyn merchant. He served as Company director from 1848 to 1878. His policy was written through the New York City agency, where the Lords, father and son, were in charge of the Company's business.

Except for the record of their appointment as New York representatives, the Lords are not mentioned in the records of Company organization in the very early months. However, from implications of later references they must have been among the moving spirits in founding the Company. They must have been enthusiastic salesmen for nearly one-third of the 936 policies issued in the first nine months of business were on New York or Brooklyn residents. Joseph Lord was 55 years old and John was his son. They lived in Brooklyn and traveled back and forth to Manhattan of course by ferry. The master of the Brooklyn ferry became one of their policyholders. Answering the medical examination question as to daily habits, Joseph stated that he took "much exercise." That can be easily imagined from the results of his work. Selling at the rate of 400 policies a year on individual lives is a tremendous achievement today with the life insurance idea appreciated and accepted. A century ago that basic concept had to be promoted and the safety of the Company demonstrated before the actual sale could be made.

Dr. Ward gave us a brief review of early agency development:

In the beginning all the Company's business was procured through the efforts of the Home Office officials or through the New York agency, but, in a very short time, agents were appointed outside this limited area. Apparently the first agent thus appointed was Wolcott Huntington of Norwich, Connecticut, who began his work for the Mutual Benefit in July, 1845. A few months later James L. Howard was appointed an agent in Hartford, Connecticut, and served in that capacity for more than twenty years. James L. Howard was a leading citizen of Hartford, prominent in all that concerned the City's welfare and progress, and a promoter and supporter of many worthy enterprises. In later years he became Lieutenant-Governor of Connecticut. He died in 1906, at the advanced age of eighty-nine years. The following record appears concerning his insurance activities:

"An active campaign for policyholders was inaugurated. The idea of life insurance was so new that wide attention was given to it in a way little understood at present. Public meetings were held to discuss the question. All at once the novelty of life insurance became the talk of the town. The Mutual Benefit agent did a large business. The thought struck some Hartford business men that they could as well organize a home company. Three months after the appointment of the Mutual Benefit agent, which was in February, 1846, the Connecticut Legislature chartered the Connecticut Mutual Life Insurance Company."

Dr. Guy R. Phelps, a policyholder in the Mutual Benefit, was the creative spirit in the organization of the Connecticut Mutual. He was Secretary of that Company from 1846 to 1866, at which time he was elected President, serving in that capacity from 1866 to 1869.

Very largely the early spread of the service of the Mutual Benefit came as the immediate response of men who recognized it as a useful social institution, men who were actuated to further its cause as they would propagate a gospel of helpfulness. It may be recalled that this period of our country's life was preeminently idealistic. It was the time of social experiments, such as Brook Farm in New England and Robert Owen's New Harmony in Indiana. It was the birth era of many humanitarian enterprises such as special schools for the blind and the deaf, public hospitals for the insane, proper prison conditions for delinquents and criminals, slavery abolition movements. The principles of the Mutual Benefit were thoroughly in harmony with the spirit of the day. Its purpose of freeing men from anxieties and fears concerning their families' future support, of guarding old people and women and little children from the burden of poverty, of furthering the happiness and security of the American home through cooperative endeavor, found ready support among those who sought the amelioration of social ills.

It would be a difficult task to name in chronological order the men who represented the Mutual Benefit in its development. Consequently only a few will be mentioned. Reference has been made to the appointment of Wolcott Huntington in Norwich, Connecticut, in July, 1845. During that month the firm of Lawrence and Wright was appointed in Cleveland, Ohio. In August, 1845, Samuel Churchill was appointed in Utica, New York; Peter Conover in New Brunswick, New Jersey; and William A. F. Sproat in Taunton, Massachusetts. In September, Joseph C. Lewis was appointed in Washington,

D.C.; and in October, W. F. Holmes was appointed in Rochester, New York; Charles Mygatt and L. P. Warner in Columbus, Georgia; Augustus Robert in Augusta, Georgia; and John Neal in Portland, Maine. In November, E. W. Cobb was appointed in Nantucket, Rhode Island [*sic*]; Henry S. Campbell and Edmund Candler in Charleston, South Carolina; Thomas B. Church in New Orleans, Louisiana; George R. Babcock in Buffalo, New York; Samuel Page in Boston, Massachusetts; and in December, John Henley in Mobile, Alabama.

Many of the earliest agents in distant territories, such as Charles Mygatt of Columbus, Georgia, and Thomas B. Church of New Orleans, were established merchants in their home cities. Their names appear first in Company records as policyholders written in New York by one of the Lords. It is easy to visualize that these men came to New York on buying trips and there met the aggressive representatives of the Company who not only sold them personal insurance, but interested them in becoming representatives of the Company at home.

Some of these contacts apparently came through Edward Anthony, a 38-year-old New York merchant, who became a director in November 1845. Mr. Anthony was shown as "the applicant" on many early applications under which the person insured was a merchant from Ohio, Illinois or other distant places. "The applicant" in 1845 was the beneficiary and these cases were apparently business insurance.

Mr. Anthony was a firm believer in life insurance for personal as well as business reasons. In addition to insuring his own life, he bought a policy for his son Edward, aged 14. This was the Company's first policy on a child (Policy 105, issued June 2, 1845).

Mr. Anthony's philosophy is undoubtedly reflected in the following statement taken from the Company's prospectus for 1846.

> A gentleman of the City of New York, being impressed with the importance of Life Insurance, has recently taken out a policy in this Company for $5000, on the life of his son, a lad of 14 years of age. He purposes to pay the small annual premium of $76.50 in cash, and to allow the profits to accumulate for a series of years. On his son's marriage he will assign the policy to his son's wife—the annual interest on the profits can then be used in part payment of the premium.
>
> No young man should marry until he has obtained insurance on his life in favor of her who is to be his wife. But how seldom this is done. At that period of life, death appears distant, and attention

is not seriously drawn to the subject, until he has a young family about him. Then he begins to reflect upon the subject; and upon application, it may prove that he already has the seeds of disease in his system, and cannot obtain a policy, or the increased rate of premium may render it inconvenient. How much better it is, then, to insure in early life, when it requires but a small annual payment, and that, as it is believed, even if the life should prove a long one, would, as an investment, yield an interest of 5 to 6 per cent. This view of the importance of Life Insurance should claim the attention of all parents who have the ability to insure their children at an early age, as it may be the means of providing for their grandchildren a comfortable subsistence, instead of the children becoming a burthen to *them*—in the decline of life, when they, perhaps, have met with reverses, and thus be rendered unable to make provision for their support.

How differently, but still well, young Edward Anthony's policy served can be imagined from the melancholy end of the story. The boy, showing his father's enterprise, went to California in the Gold Rush, and died of fever at San Francisco when only 19 years old.

Just what program of agency development the Company had in 1845 is not entirely clear. The normal personal contacts of directors, the New York agents and other interested people were surely the basis for much of the good progress experienced. Advertisements in Newark and New York newspapers also attracted inquiries, as illustrated by the following letter addressed to Mr. Patterson from Petersburg, Virginia.

In looking over the columns of the *Journal of Commerce* I find an advertisement of the Mutual Benefit Life Insurance Company, of which you are president . . . I have but a short time since been much interested on the subject of life insurance, believing if properly managed and generally patronized that the community at large would be vastly benefited by it. The people, however, in this section of country from an almost entire ignorance of the subject do not seem much disposed to patronize it or to go into it in any way—some looking on such societies or corporations as entirely to benefit the few persons named as Directors and others, from the failure of a life insurance company in Baltimore some two or three years since look on them as unsafe, while very many particularly those of the Christian portion of the community look on it as immoral, or sinful. Had I had the talent and conversational tact commensurate with my zeal on the subject, I would meet such objections with some weight and influence. I look on a mutual life insurance office as an institution more beneficial to the community than an ordinary savings institution. While it has all the advantages of the latter during the

Lewis C. Grover

WALL STREET, *New York City*

continuance of a long life, it certainly has a much greater one in the event of premature death of any one insuring . . . In my opinion it can not when properly investigated be viewed in any other light than that of a charitable institution. . . .

The Mutual Benefit Life is the fourth oldest life insurance company now doing business in the United States. The New England Mutual was chartered in 1835 and began business in December 1843. In February 1843 the Mutual Life of New York issued its first policy. The New York Life, organized as a marine insurance company in 1841 and authorized to write life insurance in 1845, preceded the Mutual Benefit Life in the issuing of life business by only a few days.

The policy contracts of the first companies were all very simple agreements compared with what we know today. The Mutual Benefit Life's was short—just one page and mostly limitations. Benjamin C. Miller's, for instance, provided that the policy would become null and void:

1. Because of travel, without the consent of the Company, upon the high seas or beyond the settled limits of the United States (excepting into the settled limits of Nova Scotia and New Brunswick); or south of the southern boundaries of Virginia and Kentucky or west of the Mississippi River between June and November.
2. Because of military or naval service without Company consent.
3. Because of death "by his own hand, in, or in consequence of a duel or by the hands of justice or in the known violation of law."*

There was no provision for days of grace, change of beneficiary or plan, loans or nonforfeiture values of any kind, or settlement otherwise than in a lump sum.

The policy did, however, provide for deducting from death claim proceeds "all Notes taken for premiums on this Policy unpaid at that time." This provision reflected a basic feature of early days, i.e. the partial payment of premiums by note. This privilege was written into the Company's charter. In later years President Amzi Dodd pointed out that it was a recognition that the policy reserve belonged to the policyholder. Vice President Harry W. Jones recently emphasized further the logic that since the founders, right

* Another limitation added the next year in new policies and appearing in the contract for over thirty-five years was "or by reason of intemperance from the use of intoxicating liquors."

from the start, had granted that the insured had some claim to the policy reserve, it was natural that they should see it as not wholly forfeitable to the Company.

The first prospectus also stated: "Should it at any time be desirable for a person to sell his policy, where it is for life, the Company will purchase the same at an equitable rate." Such an attitude was the foundation for the Company's subsequent history of liberal treatment of withdrawing policyholders.

In 1845 neither the Mutual Benefit Life nor any other American company had a special actuarial officer (see page 29). The Company prospectus the next year reported, "The table of figures, and the rules, are made and calculated with accuracy, after the experience and practice of old English companies." President Patterson who sold and issued policies, who recruited salesmen, also was the man best informed about the British actuarial experience.

One phase of the life insurance business which today requires a great deal of attention was no problem in 1845. That was the investment of Company funds. The first Company by-laws set forth the basic principles of investment:

> It shall be the duty of the Finance Committee to invest the funds of the Company, to sell, transfer, change the same and reinvest them in Bonds and Mortgages on unincumbered real estate in the States of New Jersey and New York, the real value of which shall in every case be twice the amount loaned thereon, or in stocks* or other securities of the United States or of the State of New Jersey, or of the City of Newark in the State of New Jersey, or the State or City of New York, or the State of Massachusetts, but no loan shall be made by them to any Director.

* The word "stocks" in this connection is synonymous to "bonds."

But in the first year there were no funds for the directors to invest. Since the Company had no capital stock the only receipts were premium payments. With the note system described, the amount of cash collections did not seem more than a reasonable reserve bank account, as the first claim demonstrated.

On the other hand the note system provided an automatic investment as a Company circular explained:

> As the three-fourth part of the premiums are earning interest from the date of the policies, there is no time lost seeking investments, or paying expenses attendant on making them, or liability to suffer losses from decline in stocks, or fluctuations in dividends, or losses on bonds and mortgages, in the political excitement acting on the one, or calamity of conflagration, or dread of war, on the other, with expenses and delays of foreclosures, or difficulties in litigated titles to property.

The first claim occurred in December 1845. It was paid promptly without delaying the possible ninety days allowed by the policy. The insured was John H. Preston, a 35-year-old New Yorker. The story of his Policy 277, issued on the seven-year plan for the Company's then limit amount was reported anonymously in the Company's prospectus the next year:

> Mr. J.H.P., a merchant in Pine-street, insured with this Company in September, 1845, and died in December following, of remittent fever, and ulceration of the bowels. He had settled his premium by paying one-fourth in cash, and giving a note for three-fourths, amounting in all to only $76.50. By this arrangement he secured to his wife and two children $5,000, (less the amount of his note,) upon which they are now living independently. Had it not been for this insurance, they would have been a burden upon their friends.

A letter written by President Patterson the day after the payment of the Preston claim gives another interesting contemporary appraisal of the value of that insurance. It also sheds light on other practical questions. The letter, hand-written of course, was returned to the Company a hundred years later. The text of the letter with some punctuation and paragraphing added follows:

> Your most esteemed communication of the 15th inst. written at the desire of some of your Citizens is very acceptable, and I am proud to answer your queries, and make such explanations as required. Herewith we send you our prospectus. It sets forth our System and its advantages, clearly and simply, by which you find it purely republican, each policyholder being a member, and all mutually bound for the other and themselves.

We hold the Doctrine that our members have a better right to hold and use their own money, on loans to them, than to risk it on any other securities. Whatever premium they pay is returned to them in profits, and these profits with ¼ of the premium paid in cash, together with a secured note at 6 per cent interest, is a guarantee for payment of losses and expenses. The only other Mutual Company depending on its premiums for funds, but not paying the profits until the death of parties, has been in business 2½ years, and its exhibit shows that 25 per cent is full enough to meet losses and expenses. Consequently, though we hold the notes subject to assessments to be called for on notice of 60 days, there is little probability of such requirement. We start then requiring 25 per cent of the premium in cash, and a secured note at 12 months for 3/4th at 6 per cent interest and subject to assessments at termination of the year; if the Directors find no necessity for more, the interest on this 3/4 is to be paid in cash, and 1/4th part of the premium for the incoming year, with a similar note for 3/4th as at first given, and so in continuance.

Thus you see our operation, and the security of it, with the true Mutual System. The expenses of management are moderate, the attention of its officers devoted, and thus far now nearly 8 months in operation, the loss has been but $5,000 paid promptly yesterday to the great relief of a widow and her children, preserved from chilling poverty and distress, for her husband had not enough to leave to pay the expenses of his sickness and funeral, and was comforted in his dying moments that he had the policy on his life to secure his weeping widow and children from want.

Our success is unprecedented, having within 8 months from our commencement issued over 600 policies and the premiums amount towards or all of $60,000—and but the above loss; the sums insured rather exceed $3,500 to a policy, this well scattered, and none of an amount to permit immediate payment, though by the terms of the policy we have three months to pay in.

In return for this handsome application of yours and your fellow-citizens, I have entered into the above explanation, which I hope may lead to a connection with them. Though your town is small for an agency at present, it may grow with our growth, and being in a thickly settled and wealthy neighborhood much may be done when the Inhabitants enquire into the subject and wake up to its great benefits. We have appointed agents in Cleveland and Cincinnati.

The results of the Mutual Benefit Life's first nine months of actual operation were summarized at the end of January 1846. The directors proudly reported 936 policies issued for which premiums amounted to $88,636.30. They remarked:

This very unprecedented business for so short a time, shows the greatly increased attention the subject of Life Insurance has obtained, and presenting in an extraordinary degree the preference for the purely Mutual system.

The summary analyzed also the kind of people who had become insured. The largest group was "merchants and traders," 412. This classification is illuminated by comments already made. Another group is twenty clergymen,* interesting in view of the religious prejudice against life insurance in many places.

The earliest of these was Policy 5 on the life of Dr. James Scott, pastor of the First Dutch Reformed Church of Newark where Benjamin C. Miller (Company secretary) was president of the Consistory. The policy was for $2,000 on the seven-year term plan but the next year Dr. Scott made this application to the Company, "I, James Scott, propose to the Mutual Benefit Life Ins. Co. to change this to a Life Policy for the sum of Three Thousand five hundred Dollars and agree that the declarations herein contained shall be binding, same as the original declarations for the Two thousand Dollars for seven years." So far as known this was the first conversion of a term policy in the Company's history. It was a fortunate change for Dr. Scott's family for when he died twelve years later he was fully insured under the changed policy. Dr. Scott was the great-grandfather of the Company's present associate medical director.

Thirteen of the 1845 policyholders were designated as "servants." These were slaves, both male and female. In the case of slaves usually no surname was shown in the application. The insured was shown simply as "Jonas" or "Mary." In these cases sometimes, but not always, there is added explanatory word, "a slave" or "servant." These cases are a striking illustration of what is known today as the life value principle in life insurance ownership. A slave owner who paid $2,000, say, for a competent servant or skilled mechanic was very conscious of the risk of money loss through death. One of the early slave insureds was a carpenter whose owner marketed his services and collected his wages as a substantial profit on his investment.

* However, it should be recalled too, that the oldest continuously existing American life insurance organization is what we now know as the Presbyterian Ministers Fund. That was organized in 1759 under the name "The Corporation for the Relief of Poor and Distressed Presbyterian Ministers, and of the Poor and Distressed Widows and Children of Presbyterian Ministers."

These slave owners saw clearly the truth of old Benjamin Franklin's comment about life insurance: "It is a strange anomaly that men should be careful to insure their houses, their ships, their merchandise, and yet neglect to insure their lives, surely the most important of all to their families, and more subject to loss."

Thirty-nine "ladies" also were insured. That was unusual, for until a much later date many companies did not accept female risks. The first lady was Elizabeth Holbrook, age 21, wife of a young Newark lawyer, also insured. They owned Policies 18 and 19. Each was for $3,000 on the seven-year term plan. For Mrs. Holbrook there was a $15 extra premium. Policies on women issued later in the year apparently did not carry an extra premium.

The second policy issued for a woman was numbered 72. It was on the 19-year-old wife of a New York merchant, for $5,000 on the ordinary life plan.

Young John Lord of the New York City agency bought the third woman's policy on the life of his wife. The first single premium policy issued was Policy 206 for $852 with $400 premium. It was on the life of Mary Ann Patterson, wife of the Company's founder and president, Robert L. Patterson. Mr. Patterson was "the applicant."

During the first year also, another agent of the Company, John Neal of Portland, Maine, insured his wife, his daughter and his sister each for $5,000. His own action reflected conviction which showed in successful sales to other men, for sixteen of the thirty-nine women's cases in these first nine months after organization were written through his agency. Most were for $5,000, then the Company's limit.

Only one other agency outside of Newark and New York was active in insuring women. This was Washington, D.C. The agent there wrote five cases, three of which were on slaves.

A woman policyholder was part of a most unusual transaction

which appears in the first year's record. Policies 184 and 185 were applied for by a merchant, John M. Hood, "now at New York, of Ravenna, Ohio" on the lives of Robert Hood and of Ellen Curtis Hood, his wife. He was 27 years old, she was 32. The applications state that they sailed in the bark *Arab* on November 17, 1844 for "Manilla." Robert Hood's application says further that he resided in South America, 1837 and 1838, since then "in Manilla mostly."

On the doctor's report for Mrs. Hood following the question, "Is she sober and temperate?", the doctor replied, "Certainly."

In the applications for each of the Robert Hoods is a statement like the following:

> On the life of Robert Hood, gone to reside at Manilla.
> The regular rates for five years on $2,000 is $24.00 per annum, or for the twenty months from November 17, 1844, which insures him till July 17, 1846, $40.00.
> The sea risk insuring him from the 17th of November, 1844 to arrival at Manilla is 1½% on $2,000 added to the regular rate, or $30.00.
> The rate for one year after arrival at Manilla is 1½% on $2,000, added to the regular rate which insures him to the 17th of July, 1846 (allowing the eight months for the voyage out) $30.00.
> The rate for the remainder of time of his residence at Manilla (after the lapse of one year) is to be ½% on $2,000 per annum added to the regular rate.
> The sea risk for returning to this country will be 1½% on $2,000 added to the regular rate.

This itemized statement of the premiums is dated July 23, 1845. It will be noted that the insurance for these cases began before the Company was organized, dating back to November 17, 1844. Obviously, in the days of sailing vessels, there would not in the summer of 1845 have yet been any news of the voyage of the bark *Arab* on which Mr. and Mrs. Hood had sailed in November.

The extra premium charged for the Hoods' insurance was common practice apparently in the early days for a variety of factors. As noted, the policy limited travel or residence but policyholders were accepted quite readily with the extra charge. Apparently all applicants from beyond the policy limitations were not, however, charged the extra premiums.

Another interesting husband and wife combination was Policies 428 and 433 issued in November 1845 on the lives of Cornelia Barnes, "lady," and her husband, Daniel Barnes, bookkeeper of the

Pelican Life Insurance Company. The Pelican office in those days was at 65 Wall Street and the Mutual Benefit office was at 11 Wall. Mr. Barnes and his lady lived out in the country at 134 Christopher Street in the pleasant area of Greenwich Village. There is no evidence as to why Mr. and Mrs. Barnes bought their protection in the Mutual Benefit Life instead of in their own company except perhaps that the Pelican Life may not have insured women.

Of the thirty-nine women's cases, two became claims in 1846, two in 1847 and two not until years later. All the others went off the books, either by expiration of the term insurance or through lapsation. For instance, Mrs. Holbrook, the first woman insured, became a widow (her husband was also a policyholder) and dropped her insurance.

The causes of death shown for these early cases are interesting. One of the women died in childbirth, another after a ten weeks' illness due to female troubles. The third had been pregnant when she was insured, but bore her child safely and subsequently died of tuberculosis.

Loss 8 for the Company was not one of the first year's issues but became a claim during 1846 being only a few months in force. This policy was on the life of a young woman married to a Portland, Maine farmer. The doctor's report in the claim papers stated:

> She had the measles slightly and had got out, and was then attacked with cholera morbus, brought on by eating beans, and died within three days.

Several comments in these cases described in recent pages reflect the kind of application procedure at the beginning. The basic application was a statement of personal information, twenty-two questions signed by the applicant covering the proposed insured's date and place of birth, occupation, personal and family health, and amount and kind of insurance applied for. In addition, there was a simple statement from a doctor reporting a personal examination of the applicant, and a statement by "the Friend of the Party" answering questions on health and habits.

As noted, medical examiners had been appointed in Newark and New York. The prospectus announced:

> The Medical gentlemen will attend at the offices of the Company, in Newark, and No. 11 Wall Street, New York, daily, from the hour of 2 to 3 o'clock, P.M., and their fees be paid by the Company.

Dr. James Stewart, the "medical gentleman" in New York became a policyholder in July 1845 under Policies 177 and 178. The friend who made the required statements in connection with his application answering the question, "Do you think his life safely insurable?" facetiously replied, "No! For he will surely die at some time hence."

Dr. Stewart and Dr. Jackson at Newark apparently served somewhat as a medical board, assisting with underwriting cases from other areas. In connection with one of the women's applications from Maine, the local examiner, Dr. John Merrill (also a policyholder) wrote Dr. Stewart:

> Mrs. Martha M. Read has slender constitution. She is not capable of doing heavy or laborious work, but she has always been able since she was married to superintend her household affairs & her house is always in excellent order. . . .
>
> A large proportion of our oldest women never had robust constitutions, but have generally been feeble & dilicate [*sic*].
>
> I have reexamined Mrs. Read & see no reason for changing my opinion given in her first examination.
>
> I hope soon to be able to visit New York when I shall be able to get your views & those of the Board of Directors on this very interesting & important subject in the meantime I will endeavor to stand as an impartial umpire between the office & the applicant for insurance.
>
> In regard to George W. Sewall, I would merely say that I heard him answer the questions proposed by the agent amongst them the question respecting the health of his relatives. The question in Schedule B No. 3 which refers to insanity, I suppose from delicacy you had referred to the family Physician & I have never put it to an applicant.

Mrs. Read was insured and died the next year of tuberculosis.

"Consumption" as it was then called was a major cause of death in those days. There was of course a very limited understanding of the disease, its cause and effects. The tubercule bacillus had not been discovered and few people believed tuberculosis to be contagious. An interesting sidelight on this situation was the application made in September 1845 by an innkeeper in Bloomfield, New Jersey, Beers Hard. He stated that two brothers and two sisters had died of consumption. However, the examiner, asked whether he observed any circumstances tending to shorten the applicant's life, said no, and recommended him for the policy. Mr. Hard died of tuberculosis in 1854.

CHAPTER TWO

Progress to 1850

WITH THE PROGRESS OF BUSINESS,
funds accumulated so well that the Company was able to make its
first investment on March 21, 1846. The directors bought short-term
6% bonds (referred to then as "stocks") of the city of Newark for
$6,320. So the profitable and useful history of Mutual Benefit Life
investments in municipal securities was begun.

The Company's first real estate loan was made in May 1846 for
$1,500 secured by property in the city of Newark. A few days later
another real estate loan for $3,500 was made on property located
on Staten Island. Mortgage loans continued to be a very important
investment for the Company, mostly in city properties and suburban
homes and chiefly in New York State and New Jersey.

In 1847 during the war with Mexico, which had begun in May
1846, the Company made its first investment in Government bonds.
This first purchase was $20,000, 6%, United States Treasury Bonds.

In June 1847 the minutes of the directors show a purchase of
two 6% mortgage bonds of $500 each of the Morris and Essex
Railroad. This apparently was a temporary investment, since these
bonds do not appear in the annual statement at the end of the year.
The Morris and Essex Railroad was a local New Jersey line started
in 1835 which now is a part of the Delaware, Lackawanna and
Western Railroad system. Apparently railroad securities were looked
upon with caution, for a second investment of this type was not
made until twenty-two years later. This was $100,000 put into first

mortgage 7% bonds issued by the Newark and New York Railroad, now a part of the Central Railroad of New Jersey.

In 1846 the Company began a more aggressive program of agency building. Mr. Joseph Lord of the New York agency apparently undertook to locate representatives throughout New York State. Although Mr. Lord was not called a general agent at this period, apparently he acted in the capacity which would earn him that title today. The Company shared expenses and earnings with him in a way that was not usual with other representatives at that time. He went also to Maine, visiting Bangor and Portland, and to Boston. The following year he extended his activities to Virginia.

Mr. Seth Low of the executive committee of the board of directors also traveled on behalf of the Company in establishing agency centers chiefly in New England.

A letter addressed to President Patterson in January 1847 from a new agent in Whitfield, New Hampshire, reflects some of the difficulties of the day. He was still listed with the Company agents shown in the 1848 prospectus, in spite of his offer to resign.

> As no application has been made to me for insurance I of course have made no communication to you since my acceptance of the agency. Immediately after receiving your documents I stuck up notices of my agency accompanied each with a prospectus of the Institution in the Post Offices of Lancaster, Littleton, Bath, Haverhill and Oxford. I prepared the first number of a series which I intended to publish in papers of the vicinity and sent it to the Editors. But they all refused to publish without the same compensation as for advertisements. This I could not venture without stronger evidence that I should obtain patronage. The Editors all spoke in terms of discouragement in regard to the Institution. They said it would do for the cities, but not for the country. I thought when I accepted the agency I should probably close my ministerial labours here last fall. In that case I intend to travel thru the region in pursuance of my agency. But the people have provided for my staying with them another year. My ministerial labours prevent my going abroad much. Indeed I feel but little inducement to do so. . . .
>
> Should you wish to have an agent in this region who can devote more time and hazard more money in making the experiment of obtaining insurance I will transfer my agency to such a one.

The extension of the Mutual Benefit Life during these early years was really remarkable. The prospectus of 1846 gives a list of seventy-three agents located in sixty-nine towns and cities in sixteen states from Maine to Louisiana. The prospectus for 1848 names 138 agents in twenty-one states and the District of Columbia, Wisconsin Territory, and Toronto and Lloydstown in Canada. There is no record of activity of the agents in Canada. This list of agents included two west of the Mississippi: Stewart Newall at Galveston, Texas, and George D. Little at St. Louis, Missouri.

Many of the first agents were part-time representatives of the Company; for instance, the merchants who became interested in extending the advantages of life insurance to others. After a few years it became apparent that full-time representatives at important centers would be advantageous for the Company's business. Apparently these men were allowed to have sub-agents.

The wide response to the idea of mutual life insurance as offered by the Mutual Benefit Life and the continued progress of the Company encouraged the directors so that on May 27, 1847, they appointed a committee instructed "to make the necessary inquiry, and report at the next meeting of the Board as to the propriety of purchasing a lot and erecting a building thereon suitable for the transaction of the business of the Company."

While the new headquarters was a-building for the future, the Company won an important seal of approval on its activities. The original Company charter of incorporation was limited to twenty years. In January 1848 the New Jersey Legislature repealed that section and granted a charter of unlimited duration. The directors announced this fact with the proud supplement that "at the present time it [the Mutual Benefit Life] is issuing more policies, and transacting a heavier business, than any other Life Insurance Company."

The new building was located on the north side of Market Street only a couple of hundred feet from the first rented quarters on the southeast corner of Broad and Market. The lot cost $6,000.* It was forty-five feet wide on Market Street and one hundred feet

---

* The current assessed value of the land is $161,300.

deep. The building was three stories high, with floors of narrow Georgia pine plank, blinds on the second floor windows, gas lighting, furnace heat and a ventilator "on the most approved plan" on the roof. The total cost of construction was nearly $17,000. Director Charles S. Macknet was apparently the chief overseer of the work and the board voted him $150 "in consideration of the laborious and efficient services . . . extending over a period of nearly nine months."

The Company moved into the new building in July 1848, with an office force of three in addition to President Patterson and Secretary Miller. A resolution of the executive committee at that time ordered "that the officers and clerks be required to be at the office at 8:00 A.M. and that the office be kept open until 7:00 P.M." (Those were the good old days!)

A master mason who worked on the building's foundation was involved also in another important foundation in Mutual Benefit Life history. In January 1846 W. S. B. Clark bought a $2,500 policy on the whole life plan. Of course this contract had no nonforfeiture provisions of any kind, but in the Company's first prospectus the promise had been made:

> Should it at any time be desirable for a person to sell his policy, when it is for life, the Company will purchase the same at an equitable rate.

After only a year of ownership Mr. Clark decided to "sell his policy." The Company's old cash book under date of February 20, 1847, shows: "Returned W. S. B. Clark, on Policy No. 745, Canceled, $16.38." This was the first instance in the Mutual Benefit Life of the payment of a cash surrender value. In succeeding years the Company continued to deal liberally with withdrawing policyholders. For 1850, for example, the first year the record was shown separately in the printed annual statement, appeared the item: "Paid for purchased policies . . . $11,229.36." Thirty years later, when forfeiture was rampant in life insurance practice generally, President Amzi Dodd was able to say:

> No life insurance company has been more liberal towards its policyholders in protecting against loss from forfeiture by non-payment of premiums than the Mutual Benefit. The truth is, I think, that no company has treated its policyholders with a nearly equal degree of liberality.

In contemporary times the Company is still able to say:

Few, if any, companies match the Mutual Benefit Life in its level of first year cash values, and none shows a scale for early non-forfeiture protection for all of its policies comparable to the Mutual Benefit Life.

Another promise in the first prospectus concerned dividends. The statement read:

All persons insured become members, and are not liable beyond the amount of the premium to be paid by them. . . . The nett profits, at fixed periods are divided among them.

The 1846 prospectus more specifically stated:

Dividends of estimated profits will be declared upon the amount of premium paid upon each policy. The same will be made in January of each year, commencing in January, 1847.

A dividend of 35% of the premium was declared in January 1847 on policies issued in 1845 and scrip was issued for it. Similar action was taken in 1848 and 1849 on issues of 1846 and 1847.

A qualifying statement included in the report of the directors, recommending the third dividend, is interesting.

Your committee would not be understood as affirming that this Company can always make yearly dividends of thirty-five per cent, as in their opinion the only safe method to be pursued is to let the amount of dividends to be declared depend upon the position of the Company as presented at the close of each year, being careful at each annual statement to keep the Reserve Fund good, which they consider the safety valve of all life insurance companies.

A straight percentage of premium was returned as a dividend for more than twenty years, varying in amount according to Company experience. The dividend scrip was accepted in payment of premium notes or later was redeemable in cash.

Prepayments are an important protection for people buying life insurance today because of the promptness of "getting the Company on the risk" according to the present practice. It is surprising to find that similar practice was approved in the very early days. Resolutions of the executive committee in May 1848, with additions in July of the same year, provided:

Whenever a party applies for Insurance to an Agent if the Physician reports him sound, upon payment of the premium he shall be considered insured from that date provided the application is approved by the Company. If the premium is not paid at the time of application it shall be the duty of the Agent to ascertain that the party has continued in like good health as when examined and if the party has been sick require a re-examination at the expense of the party before delivering the policy.

The growing size and complexity of Company operations pointed to the need for skilled mathematical help. The Company had been following carefully the pattern of British companies. Now the directors felt that mortality in this country was probably better than in England, investment opportunities were brighter. Therefore independent study of rates and refunds would be desirable. On April 16, 1849 the directors moved:

> Resolved, that it is expedient for the company to employ a competent person as mathematician of the company, and that having great confidence in the testimonials and other information received as to the character and ability of Charles Gill, it is further
>
> Resolved, he be appointed a mathematician of the company, and to discharge such other duties as may be assigned to him, at a salary of $1,000 per annum.

Dr. Ward gave us an interesting review of Mr. Gill's life up to the time of his coming to the Company, and quoted the testimonials which impressed the directors in 1849:

> Mr. Gill was then forty-five years of age and was widely known among the mathematicians of both this country and Europe . . . At thirteen he went to sea and for three years was a sailor. During this experience the captain and other officers were stricken with yellow fever and succumbed to this disease. Young Gill's mathematical attainments were such that he was able to navigate the ship and bring it safely to port. Returning to his native village [in Yorkshire, England] he became a teacher during the day, devoting his evenings to the continuation of his studies in mathematics and literature. By articles contributed to mathematical journals he be-

came well-known to men of science throughout England. Coming to this country when twenty-five years of age, he found employment as a professor of mathematics and natural philosophy, and established a publication known as *Mathematical Miscellany*. This periodical gave special prominence to the presentation of mathematical problems, and invited from its readers the submission of answers. From this resulted contact with the most learned mathematicians of the country. Just when or how Mr. Gill became interested in the mathematics of life insurance we do not know, but his reputation as an actuary became so firmly established that the distinguished Actuary of the Mutual Life, the late Emory McClintock, referred to him in an article read before the Actuarial Society of America as "America's first actuary." At the time of Mr. Gill's appointment as Mathematician of the Mutual Benefit, T. S. Davies, a noted mathematician of England, said, "In England he (Mr. Gill) is considered to be the first of the mathematicians of America"; and Professor Pierce of Harvard wrote to him, "You have not your superior as a mathematician in the United States, either in powers of analysis or in elegance of solution."

Mr. McClintock's article quoted by Dr. Ward throws light on the traditional Mutual Benefit Life title "Mathematician." He explained that the term actuary was first used in England, and there indicated a manager of a life insurance company, or as Americans would say, the president. The name was also used for a dignified clerk. Several officers in American life insurance companies were named actuaries before the appointment of Mr. Gill but they did not have mathematical responsibilities. Therefore, Mr. McClintock concluded that Mr. Charles Gill of the Mutual Benefit Life was the first actuary in America as actuaries are now known.

Mr. Gill continued with the Company for only about two years. He apparently was dissatisfied with his salary even though it was soon raised to $1,500 a year. Subsequently he became actuary for the Mutual Life of New York.

During these very early years, Company officers and directors were laying more than the scientific foundation for Mutual Benefit Life operations. They were also establishing the Company's character. An important fact in Company history which appears again and again from the very beginning is the disposition of the executives to deal fairly with members, to do what is right, regardless of the terms of the contract or the loopholes of the letter of the law.

A dramatic illustration of this occurred very early in the Company's existence. In 1846 one Captain Simon H. Drum, an army officer, was insured by the Company when he was about to be sent to Mexico on active duty. He was charged, and paid, an extra premium of $137 on a $2,000 policy with a regular premium of $62.20. At the end of the first year his wife, who was living in Ohio, went to the Company's Cincinnati agent to pay the next premium.

The agent had just received a notice from the Company that no more insurance was to be carried on an extra-premium basis. He, according to his lights, dutifully refused to accept Mrs. Drum's money. He subsequently wrote the Company about this careful observance of their rules. Naturally in those slow-post days it took a long while for his letter to get to the home office, a long while for him to receive a Company reply. When the reply did reach him it said he had misunderstood the rule: the Company of course would renew *old* extra-premium insurance, only *new* was to be refused. The agent was instructed to look up Mrs. Drum and get her premium.

When he attempted to do that, shocking news awaited him. Captain Drum had been killed in the battle storming the gates of the City of Mexico. In response to that report, the Company wrote him to forward all facts of the case in careful order and promised that "principles of equity will govern . . . instead of strict legal rights." As one of the Company officers wrote a little later: "We should pay without delay. I should be ashamed to quibble. The effect would be, *as it ought to be,* to kill us at once." The claim was paid.

Consider what that meant, especially in those days, for the Company to take such action. At a time when corporations had little heart and few morals, the Mutual Benefit Life was doing what was right, was protecting beneficiaries according to equitable standards. With this attitude from the very beginning of its history, it is no wonder that the Mutual Benefit has left a shining record of service through the century that is gone. The performance of the past is reassuring strength for those who look to the Company in the future.

Another army officer who took part in the march on the City of Mexico was also a Mutual Benefit Life policyholder. This was Franklin Pierce of Concord, New Hampshire, who had volunteered as a private in a local regiment in 1846, soon was commissioned a colonel, and in 1847 was made a brigadier general. General Pierce purchased $5,000 of term insurance at Concord, in April 1847.

The Mutual Benefit application describes General Pierce: "height, five feet ten inches, good figure, well made." In answer to the question, "Is he sober and temperate?", the doctor answered, "Perfectly so." The doctor's appraisal of the risk was: "Risk good (under ordinary circumstances)." He lived to become fourteenth President of the United States.

Surprising as well as expected items of historical interest are found in the records of early policyholders. One of these is the application made on the first of May 1847 by a young newspaper editor of Brooklyn, who signed himself "Walter Whitman, junior." He applied for a $2,500 policy. In his application he stated in answer to the Company questions that he never had smallpox, gout, insanity, rupture, fits, asthma or spitting of blood. The statement by his friend, then required by the Company, testified that the applicant's habits were "temperate—exceedingly so." The doctor reported that the applicant was "about six feet, full, healthy, sedantary [*sic*] as an editor" and summarized the risk as "healthy, risk good."

This editor the world later came to know as Walt Whitman, the good grey poet. He once described his editorial job in Brooklyn as "one of the pleasantest sits of my life."

History and literary history tell us that almost every afternoon Whitman crossed from Brooklyn to Manhattan on the Brooklyn ferry boat. This trip he undoubtedly shared sometimes with the Mutual Benefit's agents, Joseph and John Lord, or the directors, Edward Anthony and Seth Low, and many Mutual Benefit policyholders, including the master of the Brooklyn ferry.

How many policyholders of the Company must have read with personal interest the now famous Whitman lines:

Others will enter the gates of the ferry
　　and cross from shore to shore,
Others will watch the run of the flood-tide,
Others will see the shipping of Manhattan north and west,
　　and the heights of Brooklyn to the south and east,
Others will see the islands large and small;
Fifty years hence, others will see them as they cross,
　　the sun half an hour high,
A hundred years hence, or ever so many hundred years hence,
　　others will see them,
Will enjoy the sunset, the pouring-in of the flood-tide,
　　the falling-back to the sea of the ebb-tide.

Perhaps too much cannot be claimed in the association with Walt Whitman because he paid only one annual premium of $56 plus $1 for writing the policy, and his policy lapsed at the end of the first year.

Another surprise in this early period is what looks like a kind of group insurance. There were two interesting cases on whalemen. The importance of the whaling industry will be better understood in remembering how much whalebone was needed in those days for corsets, hoop skirts, umbrellas and buggy whips. Whale oil was widely used for lighting. One of the important whaling ports was Sag Harbor at the eastern end of Long Island. Policy 3,125 was issued in October 1845. The following statement was a part of the application:

> We the firm of Gardiner & Sealey of Sag Harbor in the County of Suffolk & State of New York do hereby make application to the Mutual Benefit Life Insurance Company for Insurance upon the lives of the following named persons, the ages of whom is specified in the accompanying schedule marked A, and the amount upon each life is stated against each name. The condition of this insurance is, that each and every of the Said persons whose life is proposed to be insured is in sound health at the date of this application and if it should prove otherwise, then the insurance upon such individual shall not be valid against the said company. The parties whose lives are to be insured are employed on board the Ship *Marcus* engaged in the Whaling business and expected to return to the United States. . . . The whole Amount of insurance asked for in this application as shown by the Schedule A is Fifteen hundred and twenty dollars.

The Schedule A referred to showed:

1. Enoch H. Ryder aged 33 $1,000 One thousand dollars
2. Charles Cleveland aged 21 200 Two hundred dollars
3. George Ross   aged 23 200 Two hundred dollars
4. Henry Oakes   aged 37 120 One hundred twenty dollars

           ——————
          $1,520

The premium for this protection included an extra 2% of the face amount of the insurance, reflecting the hazards of that nineteenth century occupation. That the dangers were very real is demonstrated by the fact that in August 1847 the Company paid the claim on the life of Henry Oakes after certification by Enoch H. Ryder, who signed himself as "master" of the *Marcus*, that Henry was "drowned by the upsetting of a whaleboat while attempting to capture a whale on the northwest coast on June 2, 1846. Lat. 44° 37′ north long. 164° 20″ east." The delay in settling this case is explained by the agent who wrote to Mr. Patterson that Mr. Gardiner, who was the applicant for the insurance, had to wait for the return of Captain Ryder before he could submit the affidavit. The agent hoped that the affidavit as furnished would be adequate because it would be difficult to get statements from other members of the crew. "Nearly all or more than half of the crew were blacks, and they had either gone to sea or left the Harbor."

The other case was written on the lives of two other whalemen on the ship *Gem* also sailing from Sag Harbor. The policy for this case shows the names of the two insured men simply written in the margin of the policy. They were Elymas Case and Manuel Frank Oliver, each insured for $200. The policy was dated in October 1847.

The record of the voyage is reported in a most interesting letter written by the captain in the next year. The document is so faded that it is impossible to make out many of the words, but it gives a vivid story nevertheless.

> Honolulu
> November 28, 1848
> Honored Sir:
> With pleasure I inform you of my good health, sincerely hoping this may find you and your much respected family enjoying the same which certainly is one of God's greatest blessings.
> I left the Sandwich Islands April 6th for the Japan Sea, and took one sperm whale on my passage which made sixty-five barrels, and took my first right whale on the 28th of May. I took six whales in five days, they very good ones. Then I found no whales until the 19th of June. I came nearly leaving for the ———— Sea, but I thought I would go over to the ———— Coast. I did so and cut thirty whales there and I found whaling until the 10th of September. Then I cruised some and watered and came through ———— Straits the 3rd of October and took two more whales. The weather being bad, I left for the Sandwich Islands the 17th of October and arrived November 18th. I have experienced some terrible weather, one typhoon and many hard gales and received some damage, but the worst of all two of the lowest rudder spindles broke and the ————— one tore the brace from the stern post and it became adrift except hanging by the tiller. It happened just after a hard gale about three o'clock in the morning. There was a bad sea at the time and the ship was greatly endangered. However at daylight I had tackle to hook it to and after a long time got them hooked but it was far

from being secure. Then I had a mind to get it clear from the ship for I was afraid it would sink her, but I hit upon a plan which secured it beyond all expectations and most probably saved many lives for the whole crew were complaining and seven of them were down with the scurvy at the time. We all are in very good health considering the long time at sea. Elymas Case died 36 hours after I arrived. He was too far gone to recover. August 6th Manuel F. Oliver was taken out of the boat and drowned by getting foul in the line which was attached to the whale.

There was no ship's ship that stayed so late as I did in the whale ground. I have cut 36 whales. Thirty-two right and four sperm which have made 2300 barrels of oil, 150 of sperm. I shall lay about one month, I think, and then start for home. I shall cruise for sperm awhile. The damages will not amount to an ———— but I will try to make it if I can. I lost our ———— of sails nearly, head sails and some bulworks. The rudder head is badly ———— but I think it will do by ———— off. There is not a stick on the island to make one. I have just put the upper ———— on myself and got two old spindles for the rudder. They are the only ones to be had, and I think to hang the rudder in ————.

It is fine time in ———— and the gold fever rages much. No doubt it will be nearly deserted in February, for they all go to Californy about that time gold digging. Pork is only worth $90 per barrel at the mines and a great many articles at the same rate. Please give my respect to inquiring friends and you will confer a favor on your most obedient servant.

James M. Worth

Captain Worth's letter was notice of claim to the Company. There is a notation which indicates that the letter arrived on Long Island late in the spring of 1849. This was long after Captain Worth and his ship had been lost at sea. Claim payment was delayed until the fall, waiting testimony from a survivor of the ill-fated *Gem*. Isaac Talmage, the ship's carpenter, finally arrived home at Sag Harbor. It is not known whether he survived the shipwreck or whether he merely had laid over at Honolulu and did not sail with the ship on its last voyage.

Mr. Talmage's interesting statement follows:

Isaac Talmage of Sag Harbor in the county and state aforesaid being duly sworn deposeth and saith: that he sailed from Sag Harbor in the ship *Gem* of which James M. Worth was master upon a whaling voyage; that he was the carpenter of said ship; that he knew Elymas Case and Manuel F. Oliver who were mariners on board said ship; that in the month of August, 1848 the said Manuel Frank Oliver was killed by being drawn out of the boat by a line attached to a whale, and drowned; that this deponent was in another boat nearby that from which he was drawn and deponent saw him when he was drawn overboard and never saw him afterwards; that so far as this deponent remembers it was on the 6th of August, 1848; that Elymas Case died of the Scurvey [*sic*] a day or two after the ship arrived at the Sandwich Islands in the month of November 1848; that the deponent does not remember the precise day of the month but it was a day or two after the ship arrived and about the 20th of November; that after the said ship left the island and on her passage home she was wreaked on a sunken reef in the Pacific Ocean and the [ship or crew?] and cargo were entirely lost.

Captain Worth's reference to "Californy" and the "gold digging" is interesting. It was only about ten months previously, in January 1848, that James Wilson Marshall had found the first nugget in the tail race of Sutter's Saw Mill in El Dorado County, California. The news had spread like wildfire down the coast of South America and up to the Atlantic states and even to Europe. The stream of eager gold-seekers from every civilized country in the world was already beginning, which came to a flood with the famous forty-niners. In 1850 the gold output of the California fields was as much as the average production for the whole world in the preceding decade. Some joined the gold rush going by boat around Cape Horn. Thousands went overland, braving deserts and mountains and hostile Indians. Of course Mutual Benefit policyholders were well represented, and claim papers give vivid pictures of their experiences. The Company decided to have no sales agency at that time in California and to write no new insurance on forty-niners but did issue travel permits at extra premiums to old policyholders. In April 1849 the Company appointed a California representative, George Lewis Cooke, Esq., "to transact such business (except taking risks) as shall be committed to him by the Company." It was Mr. Cooke who the next year wrote Mr. Anthony the sad news of the death of his young son. He helped settle local claims and reported matters of interest, such as "those arriving by Cape Horn are more liable to sickness than those arriving by other routes."

The extra premium charged for travel to California varied from time to time. In June 1849 it was 10%, 3½% to be paid in cash and 6½% as a note, with the provision that if the policyholder returned from California in good health after his trip, the note need not be paid. The text of the permit given to Seth Russell of New Bedford, owner of Policy 1,111 for $5,000, read as follows:

> In consideration of the extra premium of 3½% (One hundred & Seventy-Five Dollars) the insured has permission to make a passage by any of the usual routes in any good Steam Sailing vessel to any port in California and reside at any port in California for one year from date. (If the party goes or returns via The Isthmus of Panama he is not to sleep on shore at Chagres.) The party has permission to touch at any ports on the Pacific Ocean. Should the party return to the United States previous to the expiration of this permit, then no extra beyond the amount now paid will be charged for such return passage. It is further understood that the annual premium of 3½% is to be paid so long as the party shall reside at the ports in California, but if he goes to the Mines, he is to be charged 6½% additional and he agrees to report the same by letter through the house of Waide & Co. of San Francisco, California. The 6½% (for which a note is given) is to be refunded if the party returns in sound health, to be decided by the Medical Examiner of the Co.

Many Mutual Benefit policies apparently were pledged as security when men borrowed money to finance their travel and grub stakes. One of these was on the life of Dyer J. Bottom of Orwell, Vermont, 6,491 issued in January 1849, "in favour of" Gustavus A. Austin. On October 31, 1850, the following letter was written from San Francisco to the policyholder's father:

> Friend Bottom: It becomes my painful duty to inform you of the death of your beloved son Dyer. He died at my house at Beal's Bar on the North Fork of the American River on Monday, October 28 of Cholera, after the illness of five hours. He was attacked at three o'clock in the morning, expired at eight o'clock. Medical aid was properly called. There was no help for him. It was a severe case of Asiatic Cholera. Dyer was in fine health up to the time he was taken. I met Dyer in Sacrimento [*sic*] on the 15th. He had just returned from the mines. I was pleased to see him. He told me he wished to get a situation in a store this winter as the rainy season was approaching and he did not like to remain in the mines. I have a store and public house at the Bar. I was in want of a clerk. I have to be absent a great portion of the time in Sacrimento and San Francisco to purchase goods. As I returned to my place, I invited

Dyer to go with me. He done so. Seemed to be pleased with the place and anxious to stay and made arrangements to do so. On the 25th I started for San Francisco. Dyer went to Sacrimento with me to take the team back. He returned on the 25th. During the time he was perfectly well. Ate his meals regularly, Mr. Davis, my partner, says and he didn't hear him complain in the least previous to the time of the attack. I had been with him for four or five days previous to my leaving. We eat together and I sleep with him, do not think he was any way imprudent in his eating, no more so than I was. I often cautioned him to be careful when he ate as the Cholera was raging to some extent in Sacrimento. The first of the month it broke out there and was fast assuming an epidemic state. Hundreds here fell victims and the prospect is now that it will continue to rage here during the winter. There is a great deal of excitement throughout the county. I regret exceedingly that I could not have been with Dyer in his last moments. . . . He was sensible of his situation and remained so until the last. He told Mr. Davis soon after he was attacked that all the doctors and medicine in the world could not save him. He was buried in a pleasant place near my house. As soon as I return I will see that something is erected for the memory and his grave properly secured. I have had his death published in two papers in this city which I will send you one.

This letter was forwarded to the Company by Mr. Austin with this message:

I furnished Dyer J. Bottom money to go to California. I took life risk in your Company. C. C. Mason is a man who was born and brought up in Orwell, Addison County, Vermont and was acquainted with Dyer before they left for California. There will be doubtless in the next steamer letters from those who went with Dyer to their friends here giving news on account of his death. I do not know how to proceed to get my insurance money. I write this for information.

After considerable correspondence, with the submitting of various kinds of affidavits from doctor, nurse, justice of the peace, character witnesses and so on, the Company was satisfied that the man who had died in California was indeed the policyholder insured in Vermont and recognized the claim of the debtor. The proceeds of the policy were paid in May 1851.

The interesting story of another policyholder appears in statements made under oath for the Company's records. They read in part as shown below. The first was by Nathaniel Cushing.

I reside on Horse Shoe Bar in Placer County on the North Fork of the American River, about 35 miles above Sacramento City. I came from Boston in the State of Massachusetts and have resided on Horse Shoe Bar for the last year and a half. I was acquainted with Philip Fiske. I first became acquainted with him about the middle of April A.D. 1850 on Horse Shoe Bar above described. He was apparently about 50 years of age, above middle height, stooped a little and hair inclining to gray. He informed deponent that he came from Rockport in the State of Massachusetts. He had a circular tent with "Rockport, Mass." painted on it. His business at the time I knew him was that of Ferryman, from Horse Shoe Bar to the opposite shore of the North Fork. On or about the Tenth day of May 1850 said Fiske was drowned whilst ferrying a passenger across the River. I was present at the time and was waiting for an opportunity to be taken across. The drowning was accidental, caused by the upsetting of the boat. It was a scow boat attached by a bow and stern line to a rope stretched across the River. Deponent thinks the boat filled, which parted the main rope and the boat sank with Fiske in it. He appeared once above water about two rods below the rope and was not seen afterwards, nor was his body ever recovered to the knowledge of this deponent. Deponent had been talking with Fiske just before he pushed off and was watching them at the time. And this deponent further says that a committee was appointed to take charge of the effects of Fiske. The committee was composed of three persons, Robert Robertson of Johnstown, Fulton County and State of New York, George Griffin of Portland, Maine and one other whose name this deponent does not now recollect. Robert Robertson above described took charge of his effects and realized what he could from them. What amount deponent cannot say. Said Robertson left for home sometime in the fall of 1850. Robertson was troubled with a cancer which covered nearly the whole of one side of his face.

A statement by George D. Hale gave additional details.

I left Rockport in the State of Massachusetts and sailed from Boston January 26, 1849 in the schooner *Boston* in company with Philip Fiske and others. Our company was called the Rockport Company. We arrived out in San Francisco on the 6th day of July 1849. On our arrival we went to Horse Shoe Bar on the North Fork of the American River together for the purpose of mining. I worked on said Bar as partner with Philip Fiske from July 20th, 1849 until about November 1st, 1849. We then removed together to Hangtown and worked together there until about the last of March 1850. Fiske then returned to Horse Shoe Bar for the purpose of establishing a ferry. I helped him manufacture his lumber for making his boat and I then left for another part of the mines. I returned to Horse Shoe Bar July 5th, 1850 and was then informed of the death of Mr. Fiske by drowning in May 1850. I saw Mr. Robert Robertson there, who told me that on the death of Mr. Fiske the miners on the Bar appointed committee of three to settle the estate of Fiske of which committee he, Robertson, was chairman. Robertson told me that he was selling the goods and effects himself but progressed slowly. In October following I was there again. Mr. Robertson had in his possession a pocket Bible belonging to Mr. Fiske with his (Fiske's) name written on one of the front pages, presented by someone (in Providence, I think) and a miniature of his wife and child and some other little keepsakes which Mr. Robertson told me he was going to take to New York himself and send to his (Fiske's) son in Providence by express on his arrival in New York. He told me at this time that nearly all the things were sold and that he realized some Two hundred and twenty-five dollars ($225) from the sale of Philip Fiske's effects.

Mr. Robertson, who was the chairman of the "Trusty Committee" to take charge of Mr. Fiske's belongings, was robbed in San Francisco on his way back to New York State. This complicated the presentation to the Company of facts about the claim and resulted in a great deal of interesting correspondence. There was further difficulty because of the fact also that as soon as he arrived in Albany, New York, Mr. Robertson had an operation for his cancer and died. A friend writing about that said:

Perhaps you may have seen an account of Mr. Robertson's surgical operation in the papers of the day. I can assure you it was a most frightful operation. The entire right side of his upper jaw back as far as the palate, including his cheekbones together with the floor of the orbit of the eye was entirely removed, leaving a horrid vacuum. He passed through this terrible ordeal without muttering a complaint. Dr. March of Albany who performed the operation said that he never saw a man endure so much pain with such remarkable fortitude. Mr. Robertson finally bled to death from a new fungus matter which grew out of the remaining half of the upper jaw.

The claim was finally paid to Mr. Fiske's family in October 1851.

The claim files and other Company records bring back very vividly many kinds of contemporary pictures. Slavery and all that system involved can hardly be appreciated in this day. Yet the sad story of Jacob, insured under Policy 5,213, stated as a matter of course that he was the property of a Charleston, South Carolina lady who received payment for his work. This policyholder is identified in the records only as "Jacob (slave)." He did not even own a name. The lady's brother, a Mr. Brown, who took charge of the slave for her when he was used by other people, made an official statement:

> Jacob complained to him on Friday afternoon the 10th of November 1848 of soreness and unpleasant feeling about the throat and neck and that more on account of the negro's being insured than of any apprehension of Jacob's being dangerously sick, sent Jacob immediately to Dr. Bellinger from whom Jacob returned in less than thirty minutes with medicine and directions for nursing. That Dr. Bellinger on Saturday morning (at which time the doctor pronounced Jacob very ill) and also on the succeeding day, Sunday, visited the negro. That every exertion was made to preserve Jacob's life and that every possible attention was bestowed. That on Monday morning, the thirteenth of November at 7 o'clock Jacob died. That two or three hours after Jacob's death, Edward Candler, the agent of the Mutual Benefit Life Insurance Company in Charleston was informed of his death and was requested (after the circumstances were stated to him) to make any investigation which the Company might require. That he, C. P. Brown, was ignorant of Jacob's ever having met with a puncture of a nail's running into his foot until the manifestation of disease (spasm) induced Dr. Bellinger to put questions which recalled to the negro's mind the circumstances of his having met with such puncture some eight or ten days before. That Jacob stated to him, C. P. Brown, that in removing some boxes in the capacity of drayman from the store of Messrs. Carter and Allen, a nail ran through his shoe into his foot and that he took it out immediately and had some turpentine put on the wound and continued at his business without apprehension until Dr. Bellinger told him that the accident was the cause of his sickness. That the above named negro man, Jacob, is the same whom he (C. P. Brown) insured in M.B.L.I. Co. in February 1848.

This $500 claim was paid in February 1849.

Many of the slave cases were on female lives, known in the records as "Maria (a slave)," or "Sally (slave of Mr. Waters)." This insurance was a kind of property insurance as mentioned previously, or possibly it might be called business insurance. Other than these cases, the first identified business insurance on the life of a woman was written in April 1846. In that year, a Mr. Charles Andrews of Boston, Massachusetts, applied for insurance on a couple who were building a hotel business in St. Louis, Missouri. The husband, William Munroe, is identified in the Company records as an innkeeper of Quincy, Illinois. He was then 55 years old and was insured for $1,000. His wife, Rebecca, was listed as a "lady." She was insured for $1,200. These were Policies 1,529 and 1,530. In May 1850 Mrs. Munroe died at St. Louis and Mr. Andrews presented his claim to the Company with the following statement:

> Mr. William Munroe and his late wife Rebecca Munroe are indebted to me to an amount exceeding Twenty-five Hundred dollars for monies advanced them to carry on the business of Hotel Keeping, that I obtained the policies of Insurance upon the lives of Mr. and Mrs. Munroe (to protect me for my advances) in the Mutual Benefit Life Insurance Company and so stated at the time of making the Insurance to Joseph L. Lord agent of the Company of whom I obtained the policies.

Mr. Lord, it will be remembered, was the enterprising agent in New York City. The claim was duly approved and paid in July 1850.

At the end of the first five years of operation the directors of the Company reported with considerable satisfaction concerning the prosperous condition of Mutual Benefit Life affairs. The following quotations from the fifth annual report to policyholders give an excellent summary of progress.

> The past has been a year of much apprehension on account of the epidemic which has scourged the land, and the general mortality has been greater than any year since the existence of the Company. We have, notwithstanding, promptly met all our liabilities for losses, without drawing on our permanent or invested funds, both of which

have been largely increased during the year. Much time and attention have been given to perfect our system of business—the whole Company has been more thoroughly organized, and we can recommend it with increased confidence to the members and the community at large. When the Company was organized, Life Insurance was comparatively a new subject in this country. The Mutual principle had not been thoroughly tried or its merits developed. When we issued our proposals and stated our plan of operation, many doubted its success, and others openly opposed it. For nearly five years, including the last cholera year, we have steadily pursued our course without encountering those disasters which interested opponents so confidently predicted, and the Company now stands before the public acknowledged to be one of the safest, and most equitable institutions of the kind in the country.

The secret of this success is to be found in the fact that those who have managed the business have been so industrious in protecting the interests of the Company, so prompt to correct errors that might occur, so thoroughly imbued with the mutuality of our system and their accountability to the members, that they have avoided threatened dangers and protected themselves from errors into which others less cautious have fallen.

During the past year our system has been carefully examined, and a rigid scrutiny instituted into all our business, under the direction of the best mathematical talent that could be procured in the country. Every transaction of the Company from its organization to the present time has been examined and accurately calculated. The result has been to prove that the business has been so conducted, and our calculations so made, as to secure the Company against every possible contingency. We have the satisfaction of knowing that we have the means of meeting every obligation in the payment of losses as they occur, and of dividends declared to the members.

As an earnest of this, the Directors, having paid the losses that have occurred and defrayed all expenses of the Company, have declared a dividend of thirty per cent, on the business of the year ending January 1st, 1849, payable with interest; and having calculated the value of every policy existing in the Company and laid aside the aggregate amount thereof as a reserve fund; having also reserved the sum of $200,000 of declared profits, as required by our By-laws; they commence the present year by ordering the payment of the *First* and *Second* dividends, being those declared in 1847 and 1848. Those members holding scrip are to be paid on and after March 1st, 1850, the interest ceasing at that date. Those whose dividends have been placed to their credit are to receive the amount with the interest by a credit on their notes as they mature, on and after Jan'y 1st, 1850, or if the notes are paid in full they receive the dividends in cash. In adopting this measure the Directors have proceeded with great caution. It has been with the assurance that we

have fully provided for the future wants of the Company by the
ample reserve fund we have created, that we have come to this
conclusion. We have been anxious to do what is right rather than
what would be popular. . . .

The Directors have had constantly in view, the fact that much of
our future success would depend on a rigid economy in every
department of the Company. They feel in reviewing the business
of the year, the greatest satisfaction in stating, that while other
Companies, whose affairs are considered as carefully managed, have
allowed their expenses to amount to from *twelve* to *twenty-five*
per cent on their receipts, our business has been so conducted,
that notwithstanding some extraordinary items of expense during
the last year, the whole of our expenditures of every kind, including
salaries, rent, commissions, taxes on agencies, physicians' fees, etc,
have amounted to but a fraction over *nine per cent*, an amount far
below that provided for by our calculations, and unprecedented in
the history of Life Insurance Companies. . . .

It must be gratifying to the members, to know that the success
which has attended us hitherto, has not been accidental, but has
been the legitimate result of the faithful working out of our own
system—a careful attention to our business—an increasing knowledge
of the subject of Life Insurance—well digested plans for conducting
the business—the most conservative rules in selecting risks—a rigid
adherence to every principle which would protect us against danger
and loss—added to all this, the thoroughness with which the *mutual
principle* is incorporated in our whole system—the fairness with
which every member's interest is protected—our carefully provided
reserve fund, and our profits annually declared to the members—
these are the things which have placed our Company beyond the
reach of suspicion or the fear of competition, and by the *past*, furnished the members with the best guarantee for the future.

CHAPTER THREE

Testing for Survival

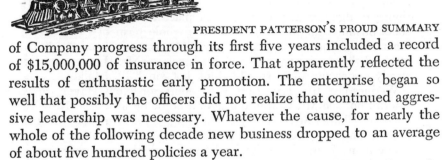

PRESIDENT PATTERSON'S PROUD SUMMARY
of Company progress through its first five years included a record
of $15,000,000 of insurance in force. That apparently reflected the
results of enthusiastic early promotion. The enterprise began so
well that possibly the officers did not realize that continued aggressive leadership was necessary. Whatever the cause, for nearly the
whole of the following decade new business dropped to an average
of about five hundred policies a year.

The influence of the Company had spread rapidly in the early
years but the far-flung agency representatives after making a brave
start, selling a few easy cases perhaps, became inactive. In 1851
there were only about sixty agents who handled premiums of as
much as $500 a year as is learned from a list of those to be bonded.

In September 1855, the executive committee ordered that:

> Measures be taken to revise the agencies by procuring a written
> statement of the location, character and qualifications of the agents
> of the Company and a statement as to whether the Company is as
> efficiently served in each location as is practicable. . . .
> That in order to accomplish this object at as early a period as
> possible, the executive officers be requested to visit the more promi-
> nent agencies in company with a director of the Company, so that
> the information obtained can be in the possession of the Board
> through some of its members, and that the subject of appointing
> a traveling agent be referred to the Board for its action. . . .
> That an examination of the census reports be made for the purpose

of establishing new agencies at points where the population and business will warrant it.

The sorry situation is reflected in a report of the special committee appointed a month later to visit *the most important agencies* in the New England States. Upon their return the committee "begged leave to present to the Board the detail of their doings from their daily journal." The original manuscript of this one-hundred-year-old report is in the Company's files. It gives a most interesting picture of agency operations a century ago as the fragmentary quotations show:

Tuesday, October 9th, 1855. Left Newark at 3 o'clock P.M., and New York at 4 P.M. Stopped at Bridgeport, called upon Messrs. Hawley and Sherman, made an appointment for a meeting after tea. Their office is well located over the Pequonac Bank, Corner of Main and State Streets. Mr. Sherman is an active talking man, says cannot induce parties to insure and pay money unless they can borrow, thinks Bridgeport at present a poor place for insuring lives—thinks some business might be done on the whole term of Life, one payment in advance, or on table paying at age of 50 or 60, if party attained those ages or sooner if death occurs. Mr. Hawley is a large, steady appearing man, should think not much of a talker. . . .

Wednesday, 6½ P.M. Left Bridgeport for New Haven, arrived 7½ did not see Mr. Galpin our agent, he being absent at New York. Office in Chapel Street in Lyon Building, is Secretary of Fire Insurance Company—well located. Had some conversation with his young man (Benj. E. Belcher) who said he had some spare time and would be willing to undertake the soliciting of policies and promised to consult Mr. Galpin on his return—thinks but little life insurance is done in New Haven. . . .

Thursday 7 A.M. Left Hartford for Providence arrived there at 11 A.M. Called upon Mr. Blodget, our agent—says he has plenty of time and endeavors to get insurers but the ground has been so completely worked over that for the past year or two nothing could be done—and he knows it has been the same with agents of other companies. . . .

On Monday, the 15th left Boston for Portland, Maine at 7½ o'clock A.M. Arrived at 12 o'clock noon, found our agent, John Neal, Esq. in the office of the agency which is favorably located in the midst of the banks and insurance offices, stated to him the object of our mission and the authority under which we acted, he seemed much pleased and coincided with our views and plans for increasing the business of the Company, says that the company stands well with all our members, as well as with the public generally, and expressed his clear conviction that the time had fully arrived for increased efforts, and as an evidence of his convictions placed before us one of the daily papers of the city of Portland in which he had advertised the substance of our recent publications. After spending with him most of the afternoon and part of the evening, at 10 o'clock took the steamer, *Daniel Webster* for Bangor where we arrived at 10 o'clock the next day, Tuesday, the 16th. Called at once at the agency and were much disappointed on finding that our agent, B. Plummer was absent and would not return during the week. His son, however, who appeared to be an intelligent young man was in the office and seemed to understand his father's business and the business of the agency, said his father was rather a modest man and had omitted advertising and personal efforts by talking with the people, upon urging him to take an interest in the matter as well as for his own sake as that of his Father he said he would do so, and would on the return of his Father, take hold in good faith not doubting the result of doubling the policies in that place. We left him cards which he will have distributed to our members and in business places of the city. He was authorized to expend in advertising not exceeding twenty-five dollars, will forward the papers and bills for advertising. At 4½ o'clock P.M. same day took the train to Waterville on the Portland Rail Road where we remained until 5 o'clock A.M. Wednesday, the 17th, arriving at Portland at 8¼ o'clock and changing cars there for Portsmouth, New Hampshire, arriving at the latter place at about 12 o'clock noon, found our agent Mr. Wendell engaged as Bookkeeper or confidential clerk in an extensive importing house, he is undoubtedly an honest, but somewhat inefficient man in the business of life insurance. After stating to him, however, the object of our call and handing him cards, he promised to make a strong effort to obtain new applications. . . .

Friday, the 19th, left Boston at 7¼ o'clock A.M. for New Bedford via Taunton, stopping at the latter place for three hours, had an interview with our agent Mr. Sproat, found him in the County Clerks Office, and a very intelligent and gentlemanly, but somewhat inefficient man. He complains of competition, says there are some six or eight agencies there and that the people have not taken the interest in life insurance that they ought to, he promised to exert himself. . . .

The directors naturally were open to a proposal a few years later made by Sears M. Loveridge of Ypsilanti, Michigan, that he be appointed "general agent" for "the Northwestern States." In 1858 the Company made a one-year agreement with him which was subsequently renewed when it proved satisfactory. It was Mr. Loveridge's duty to nominate agents and physicians to be appointed by the Company and to solicit applications. His salary was $3,000 a year plus 10% commission on all new policies secured. The territory assigned to Mr. Loveridge is not definitely known, but records of his activities indicate that Michigan, Indiana, Illinois and Iowa were among the "Northwestern States" where he worked.

In 1859 Mr. Loveridge also was appointed "general agent" for Philadelphia and vicinity. Later he developed the Pittsburgh area and eventually operated for a while in Boston. His obituary in 1878 gives an interesting picture of this man who brought energetic action to the Mutual Benefit Life at a critical time. Mr. Loveridge began his Company activity when about 35 years old. At the time of his death in Pittsburgh the reporter wrote:

> He was a fine looking, robust man, fifty-four years of age. He was long and prominently connected in this city with the life insurance business, and was one of the most successful men of that calling in this or any other city while engaged in it. He was a man of great activity, energy and will force, to which could be attributed his remarkable success.

Mr. Loveridge apparently had an iron constitution (which also is helpful in life insurance activity) for the reporter also wrote of "a circumstance in the life of Mr. Loveridge worthy of recalling and not beyond the memory of many." Mr. Loveridge was confronted one day in his office by a distant relative demanding financial support which he refused, and without warning the disappointed cousin drew a gun and shot him. The story continued:

> The ball entered Mr. Loveridge's stomach. His life was utterly dispaired of by his physicians, as the ball could not be probed for. He was confined several months to bed and strange to say the wound healed, the ball by some miraculous process ate its way through his bowels and was passed from his body in the regular manner, a case, his physician stated, that would not happen once in a century of shooting cases.

The Company did not at the early Loveridge period adopt the general agency system universally, but during the next few years references are found to the "General Agent of Massachusetts" and to a "General Agent for the Eastern Cities."

The general agent for the Eastern cities may have been Joseph L. Lord of New York City. From the earliest days he did traveling for the Company through New England and New York State, as was mentioned earlier.

A little handbook for agents entitled *The Mutual Benefit Offering* gives us an interesting impression of Mr. Lord and his sales techniques.

None who ever saw Joseph L. Lord, the much cherished Agent of this Company in New York . . . can ever forget his genial face, and the marvelous manner he had of relating the thrilling incidents which took place during his agency. Among them, no one was told with more vigor and general satisfaction than the following:

A friend of his, an old sea-captain, attached to an old line of vessels, running between New York and Liverpool, had long been desirous of insuring his life for $10,000; but his wife, feeling the need of saving all the family could to discharge a mortgage on their property in Brooklyn, objected so strongly that he desisted from his intention. He had a happy family, and while he was tossing upon the waves of the ocean, pacing the deck at night, watching the stars, or directing his ship when the storm-clouds gathered about the mastheads, or the waves rolled high and boomed against his vessel, with a power that no one can understand who has not breasted the waves during some of the great storms on the Atlantic, he often thought of his home and the dear ones, and what might become of them should he go down with his noble ship, and his family be left without better provision for their future. During one of these storms, in thinking this matter over, he made up his mind that, notwithstanding the objections of his wife, it was his duty to act. And just here let us invite the reader's attention to his conclusion.

The husband and father is the responsible head of the family, and, in such cases, he has a duty to perform from which the objections of even his life-partner cannot absolve him—an objection that arises from misapprehension, and which, under the enlightened facts of the last few years, is rapidly being removed, and has now almost entirely disappeared.

Upon his arrival in this city, he called upon Mr. Lord, and effected an insurance for $5,000, stating the facts above named, and that otherwise he would make it $10,000. The fact of his insurance was, however, kept from his family. In due time, the vessel went to sea, the captain, as usual, in command. The day was fair; happy passengers crowded the vessel's decks; some, having made money, going to Europe to visit the gay capitals, or to gaze upon its ancient walls, and meditate by its fallen columns and broken fountains; others to

wander about the pyramids of old Egypt, to sail leisurely upon the
waters of its sacred Nile, or to tread with devoted feet the Olivet of
our hopes, and the other sacred places hallowed by the feet of the
Redeemer. She sailed, and that is all that is known. She was never
heard of more. Not a spar or thread was ever wafted to the shore to
tell the story. The ocean closed over the sinking ship, the guardian
spirits hovered around; the rest we shall know when we have passed
over the silent river, or the blue waves of the darker ocean.

In due time, Mr. Lord, being an old friend of the family, was
sent for by the widow to talk over the affairs of her husband's
estate. " 'Let me know all,' said Mr. Lord leisurely, as if in medita-
tion, emphasizing peculiarly the word ALL."

The subsequent dialogue is reported in detail—the widow's
recital of "all," Mr. Lord's challenge about an important item
hidden, her bafflement, his disclosure, and the happy conclusion.

"Why, the Life Insurance Policy," replied Mr. Lord.
"What Life Insurance Policy? I would not let him take it. I would
never take the money, even if he had insured."
"But, my dear madam," said Mr. Lord, "I know you would not
let him take it; but for that, he would have taken $10,000, instead
of which he only took $5,000, and here is the policy. The money will
be due from the Company in a few weeks and I do not think you
will refuse it; for it is a precious legacy from your husband; and,
no doubt, as his proud vessel went down upon the sea, his last
thoughts were of you and his last minutes cheered with the reflection
that, though he was removed, the blaze upon the hearth would not
die out, nor his loved ones be driven from their cheerful home. The
policy—the policy—this policy, was perhaps, the last earthly thing
that gave him peace."
It is needless to say the money was paid and cheerfully taken.
It was the last voyage; but one premium had been paid. In a quiet
street in Brooklyn the family is still residing. One of the daughters
has grown up and is married. The cheerful fireside is still there.
The policy saved everything; and no Life Insurance Company has
a better friend than the captain's widow.
It is precisely here that Life Insurance is better than charity. It
preserves self-respect; does not merely keep families from poverty,
but continues the household the same as if the head had not been
removed, and leaves the future not suddenly to be changed, but to
be continued, and often with increased happiness, comfort and
means of refined culture.

In 1858 the Company published an interesting little book apparently as a sales promotion document or possibly as an aid for agents.

The title page showed it was intended to present "a plain exposition of the principles of life insurance, its nature, origin and progress"; and included "reasons why preference should be given to the Mutual Benefit Life Insurance Company by persons intending to insure." The rates in this book are given on the basis of $1,000 compared with the $100 basis used at the beginning. The limit of protection for a single life had been raised to $10,000. The purely mutual principle of operation and annual dividends are emphasized, for the latter set the Company apart from others at that time.

One section of the book presented "arguments in favor of life insurance," "answers to excuses for not insuring" and similar helpful material. A number of the comments are quaintly interesting.

> Surely such an institution deserves the consideration and the support of all prudent and reflecting men, and is double recommended, when it is considered how very small a sacrifice of some personal comfort or gratification will secure, by its means, the independence and happiness of a poor man's family. In this view of the subject, an unnecessary journey, an idle amusement, a few wasted days in each year, is a sacrifice of the education and clothing and food of objects the nearest and dearest to us all, should it please our Maker to take us from them. The tobacco chewer will readily consume his 2¢ a day, which will secure to his family in case of his death, and if he is 25, $385. What shall we say to the tippler of 25, who, if he drinks one shilling a day, sacrifices $2,240; a sum sufficient to make a poor family rich, at a moment when independence at least, is so important to them.

The various personal and printed efforts in sales promotion brought gratifying results. The year before the Civil War, 1,435 policies were issued and insurance in force had grown to over $25,000,000. The increasing new business and business in force represented activity mostly in New England, the Middle Atlantic and East North Central states. About one-third of the Company's current business was coming from New York State, followed by Massachusetts and Michigan. Considerable activity was being shown also in Washington, D.C., Maryland and Virginia where a substantial amount of old business was in force. Ohio, Indiana and Illinois accounted for a large proportion of the insurance in force and for a respectable share of the new business. In that year over one hundred new policyholders had become insured in Missouri. No new business at all had been reported from the South Atlantic states.

Although new business was low through most of the 1850's, until

vigorous sales promotion reversed the trend as has just been re-
viewed, the Company's insurance position was sound. The following
quotation from the prospectus shows the paramount objectives of
the directors during those years:

> The most natural inquiries which a person will make, who contem-
> plates procuring an interest in any Insurance Company, are, first,
> Is it a safe company? in other words, Is it founded on a proper basis,
> so as to be able to pay its losses when they occur? Secondly, Is it
> a cheap company? Will it give me the fair worth of my money, or
> are its charges exorbitant? Thirdly, Is it a well conducted company?
>   The Directors flatter themselves that these questions, so far as
> regards this company, may be safely answered in the affirmative.

An important new personality came into the Company at this
time, Joseph P. Bradley. As an undergraduate at Rutgers University
he excelled in mathematics as well as in Latin and Greek. After
graduating with high honors he entered a law office in Newark and
qualified as a lawyer. He served as the Company's mathematician
from 1851 to 1863. Some years after his Mutual Benefit Life connection his law career was crowned by appointment by President
Grant to the United States Supreme Court.

During this decade dividends paid by the Company increased
from the 35% level of the early years to 40% and then to 45%.
Announcing the 45% dividend in January 1860 to be paid on policies issued through 1858, the directors commented:

> Some, perhaps, would suggest a reduction in the rates of insurance
> But it must be remembered that a company that insures lives has a
> long future to provide for, and that society has, from time to time, in
> all ages, climates and conditions, been subjected to destructive epi-
> demics and plagues. It must also be remembered, that the value of
> money is liable to great fluctuations, and although the capitalist
> now realizes six per cent per annum, he may not do it forever.
> Hence, to the Directors of this Company, it has not yet seemed wise
> to reduce the present rates. It is true those rates now produce a sur-
> plus, but they may not always do so; and the Company should have
> it in its *power* always to provide for any exigencies that may occur.
> *The first object of a Life Insurance Company is safety.*

The reference to epidemics and plagues in the foregoing quotation stemmed from frightening current experience. The horror and
panic of cholera epidemics a hundred years ago are something
hard to visualize today. Vivid pictures of experiences that must
have been quite common are found in Company claim records.

For example, concerning a claim that was paid in 1854, there is a letter from a Milwaukee lawyer concerning the death of a 40-year-old man, Henry D. Garrison. The letter reads in part:

> No coroner's inquest was held . . . The cause of his death seemed very manifest to those who saw him die and who saw him immediately after the moment of death—to wit: a disease of the bowels like cholera or some kindred disease . . . It was not thought necessary or proper to hold an inquest under the circumstances, and the panic was so great at that time about the approach of cholera that he was buried only three hours after death.

An affidavit from one of the witnesses of the man's death read in part:

> That on the morning of Sunday, the thirtieth day of July last, his attention was attracted at an early hour—say six or seven o'clock, to a man apparently suffering much bodily pain on the sidewalk near his residence on Main Street near the corner of Division Street . . . That when he had dressed himself he went immediately out to the place where the sick man was, that when he reached the spot he did not seem able to speak but was sitting and leaning against some boards which were piled there; that he made a moaning noise as though suffering great pain and seemed extremely feeble and nearly to die; that in a few minutes a physician was sent for but that before the physician arrived, the eyes of the sick man became fixed, his body gradually slid down and he died quietly.

Spectacular as the cholera deaths were, tuberculosis was far more costly to the Company. In the years through 1857 for which there is an old tabulated record, nearly a fifth of all claims were for tuberculosis deaths. The great majority of these losses were on young people and in many cases only a few premiums had been paid. This led to extreme caution in judging underweight applicants. In 1858 weight became a question in the application.

In the 1850's, although the insurance in force grew slowly only from $15,000,000 to $25,000,000, the Company's assets tripled. The annual statement presented in the advertising itemized about $150,000 in city bonds earning 6% or 7%. About half the total assets was reported under the heading "Bonds and Mortgages on Real Estate, worth double the amount loaned." About a third of the assets was invested in premium notes drawing 6%.

In spite of the conservative standards for lending on real estate the Company granted a $20,000 loan in 1852 under a mortgage that was foreclosed ten years later. The property involved was 3,000 acres in the North Jersey mining area, including the famous Ring-wood Manor. The Jersey iron mines were in operation long before the American Revolution. The Ringwood mines produced iron for George Washington's cannon and for the huge chain that was strung across the Hudson at West Point to keep the British from going up the river.

The mines were still flourishing in early Mutual Benefit days and a number of the directors then were active in various kinds of iron industry. Their acquaintance with the Ringwood owners is easy to imagine. Part of this historic property is now the Ringwood Manor State Park, a gift of the Hewitt family who bought the 3,000 acres after the Mutual Benefit foreclosure.

Sometime in the very early years the Company began allowing for days of grace in the payment of premiums although they were not provided in the contract for more than half a century. The prospectus implied that grace would be allowed before the specific statement was made. The comment in the 1849 prospectus includes motivation as well as information:

> If the premium is paid within 30 days after it is due, (the party taking the risk of death, and of being in sound health during the said 30 days) the policy will be renewed without extra charge.

The Company in 1850 went beyond the contract in another way and issued a paid-up policy for a lapsed contract. This was first promised in print in the prospectus for 1850.

> Should it be desirable at any time for a person to sell his policy when it is for the duration of life, the Company will purchase the same at its equitable value, or they will grant a new policy whose present worth is the same as the one surrendered, securing the party without any further payment of premium an equitable sum at death.

The annual statements through these years also showed regularly an impressive figure "for purchased policies."

The first endowment contract was Policy 13,240, issued in April 1859. The document was the same as an ordinary life policy with inappropriate words ruled out and the statement added:

> Payable upon his arriving at the age of fifty, to wit on the 13th day of July 1884, or sooner, should the said party assured die prior to said date.

Of course the problem of a policy form for the new type of insurance was simplified because no contract showed any kind of non-forfeiture values at that time.

By the late 1850's President Patterson's salary had doubled his original $1,500 a year. But he was growing feeble after more than eighty years of strenuous activity in the Mutual Benefit Life and previous ventures. The leadership of the Company of necessity was being taken over by younger men. In 1860 Lewis C. Grover, who from the beginning had been Company counsel with a top salary of $2,000 a year, became vice president at $4,000. This is convincing evidence of his place in Mutual Benefit Life affairs at the end of its first fifteen years of operation.

The annual report of 1860 was a simple little four-page folder but through its figures and comments one can get an inspiring picture of devotion to purpose and satisfaction in the results being achieved. The assets of the Company are shown as $3,419,483. The total amount of insurance in force is not given, though other records show it was $22,203,437. The report emphasizes the number of Company members and the essential cooperative principle of Company operation, with some interpretation of the figures.

It possesses more Assets, as compared with its Liabilities, than any other Life Insurance Company doing business in the United States. (See report of Comptroller of New-York.) . . .

This Company has now the large number of 6,649 policies in force; yet an increase in the number of persons insured renders more certain the operation of the *Principle of Average,* upon which all *Life* premiums are based. All friends of the Institution must therefore perceive it to be important that those connected with it should call the attention of their acquaintances to the *Advantages* offered . . .

The Company was organized in 1845, on the purely mutual principle, without any subscribed capital. The members, in reality, insure one another, and the accumulated fund is entirely the result of the premiums paid by the insured, and is held by the Company in trust to meet its obligations to them. . . .

The *new* business of the Company for the year 1859 shows *an increase of sixty per cent over that of any of the past ten years.* The premiums received are one hundred thousand dollars ($100,000) *more* than those of 1858, while the losses are thirty-eight thousand three hundred and fifty dollars ($38,350) *less.*

This remarkable falling off in the mortality among the insured, is attributable to the fact that no epidemic diseases have prevailed during the past year.

The great increase of business, the Directors believe, is evidence of a growing appreciation by the public of the equitable plan of business pursued by this Company.

CHAPTER FOUR

The Civil War Era

FOR ALL AMERICANS THE DECADE OF the 1860's means the tragedy of the War Between the States. With the present day associations of "total war" it seems strange to find the Mutual Benefit Life completing a new building in the Civil War days. Of course plans were in the making for more than a year before the directors in June 1859 approved the design and specifications, and empowered the building committee to get bids and complete contracts. The action was taken with the proviso that "land, building, and furniture together with architects' fees do not exceed $100,000." The lot at the corner of Broad and Clinton Streets in the heart of Newark, a few blocks from the first home office building, had already been purchased at the cost of $20,000.

The new building was built of native brownstone quarried just a few miles north of Newark. There was a quaint record that the committee of directors went "in a hack to Belleville" to select the stone personally. From the Jersey quarries came also the stone that made mid-town Manhattan's famous "brownstone fronts." The directors also interested themselves in every detail of the furniture for the new building. It was made to order by Newark's foremost cabinetmaker, John Jelliff, and cost $3,000. The record said that the directors deliberated for some time about the hand-carved decorations on the solid walnut furniture for the directors' room. Should it be a flower or fruit design? The decision was a formalized flower, which is admired even today on the beautiful sofa which, with two chairs, the Company still owns and proudly displays.

The Company moved into the building, still known to Mutual Benefit people as "the brownstone building," in October 1862. The style of architecture was defined as "castellated Norman." The building was the pride of the city and the talk of the insurance industry. A reporter for a life insurance magazine visited the building and gave the following description of it:

> Imposing spectacle of substantial massive grandeur and refined architectural beauty; reflecting alike honor upon the taste and mechanical skill of the architect who planned and the mechanics who executed the work, as well as upon the enterprizing spirit of the Directors of the wealthy corporation who owns and now occupies the premises. In fact the Mutual Benefit Life Insurance Company's new office takes down and leaves in the shade all the other Life Insurance Corporation buildings that have gone before it.

Several years later a Newark literary magazine published an article describing the editor's observations of local structures and featuring the Company's home office as follows:

> Across the street is the handsomest building in Newark—that of the Mutual Benefit Life Insurance Company. The walls are of Newark brown-stone, seven feet thick. There are three stories and a capacious basement. The third story is devoted to a Masonic Hall—a most elegant apartment. . . . There is nothing in Newark at all comparing with this interior.—The walls and ceiling are of the beautiful white stone of Caen (on which we never look without remembering Charlotte Corday), and the ceiling exhibits a handsome frame-work of bronzed iron. Such a combination of solidity and beauty is most rare. The panelwork overhead is beautifully cut and wrought, and strong iron pillars, bronzed and gilt, support it. The floor is of the handsomest encaustic tiles. The fireplaces are of the Nova Scotia stone like that of which grindstones are made. The furniture, as well as the railings and other wood-work, are of solid black walnut, all strictly corresponding, and all made expressly to fit the apartment, as is common in the palaces of kings. The bronze gas lamps also correspond exactly with the other features of the place.

Mr. Grover, the President, knowing our literary tastes, conducts us into a delicious little snuggery of a library, filled with volumes all elegantly bound with Russia leather, so that the snuggery is odorous with the sweet perfume that Russia leather sheds on the air. But the books in this library are dull reading to be sure. They are all of the same sort—a sort of huge encyclopedia of men's names, ages, physical conditions, etc., duly indexed and alphabeted, to a number of volumes such as few encyclopedias will ever attain, let us hope.

We are going disgustedly out when Mr. Grover detains us with the quiet statement that there are in this snuggery twelve million dollars in securities. *Twelve million dollars!* Can it be possible that within reach of our fingers there are twelve million dollars' worth of papers? Let us go at once, literary *confrere!* An event has happened in our lives.

Suppose the ghost of that Civil War time reporter could visit the vaults of the Company today. He would see still in the archives some of the great old leather-bound policy registers. But what would he think to hold in his hand a single piece of paper representing $8,000,000 invested in a certain public utility, or a package about the size of an ordinary library book which is $100,000,000 worth of Government bonds?

Perhaps it was the elegance of the new building which inspired the directors to the further luxury reflected in the resolution adopted in 1862:

Resolved that the officers be empowered to provide refreshments for the Committees and Board meetings, it being understood that they shall be of a plain and simple character and that wines and liquors shall only be provided by express instruction from the Board.

The beginning of the war caused a sharp drop in new business in 1861, but business multiplied greatly in succeeding years. In July 1864 the Company's ten clerks submitted the following petition:

The undersigned, clerks in the office of the Company, respectfully represent, that, in consequence of the depreciation of the currency, the large increase in the cost of the necessaries of life, (amounting to from 60 to 300 per cent), the increased burden of taxation, direct and indirect,—their salaries are far less in value than was intended by the Board in fixing them, and than was expected by themselves, and are inadequate, with the utmost economy, to meet the unavoidable demands upon them, especially in the cases of those who have families:—

And in view of these facts, and of the increased business of the Company, involving additional labor and responsibility on their

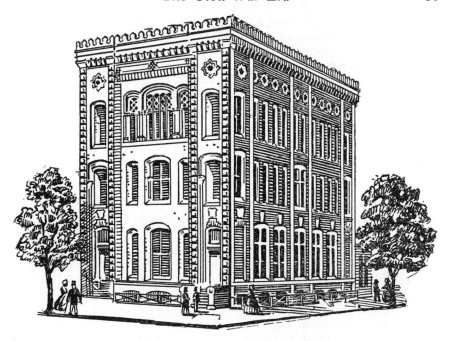

part,—they respectfully request, that the Board would make to each of them a suitable monthly allowance, in addition to their salaries, to be continued while the above-stated condition of things shall exist.

The board gave prompt and sympathetic attention to this petition granting a 25% increase in salaries effective from the beginning of the year. A few months later the current inflation was reflected further by action to increase the president's salary to $7,500 a year and the Company limit of insurance to $20,000.

By 1869 there were eighteen young men (the majority much bewhiskered, as seen in a faded photograph), and seven officers making up the home office staff. The office hours were then 8 A.M. to 7 P.M. These long working days, or possibly another offset to the high cost of living, may have been part of the reason why the officers were led to consider serving lunch to the staff. A committee of directors appointed in October 1869 to study the matter, reported:

> That they have made inquiry in New York of various banking and other Corporations who have adopted such a plan, and your Committee find that all of the Institutions of whom they made inquiry feel that the cost is well applied, that by the arrangement they keep their employees with them during business hours, and keep them

from many temptations that are presented in numerous ways, to those clerks who are obliged to seek refreshments in such places as offer them—particulars of which your Committee do not consider it necessary to enumerate.

The practice of serving meals, begun at the recommendation of this committee, has continued until this day. The first lunches were served in a basement room and were brought in from a neighborhood restaurant.

Going back to the beginnings of this decade one feels the burdens and the conflicts of the war. As mentioned, business fell off sharply in 1861. The contemporary report as presented in January 1862 by the executive committee gives a vivid picture of the problems.

The year just closed has been more disastrous to the business of the country than any that has preceded it. The memory of the oldest inhabitant cannot find its parallel since the foundation of the government. The rebellion movement which opened with the secession of South Carolina in December 1860 was followed by other states in rapid succession until it culminated in the fall of Sumpter [sic] in April last. From this time chaos reigned in the business relations of the country. Postal communications closed between the different sections, confiscation acts were passed by the Southern Confederacy and corporations as well as individuals felt the blow struck at our political and business associations. Strong indeed must be the political or business structure which could stand the shock. Staunch must be the vessel which could weather such a storm as has been pouring over us.

In looking over the history of the past year, the **Executive Committee** feel we have cause for gratitude that our beloved institution has thus far escaped so well from the dangers and trials we are passing through. In our last annual report we looked back over a year of greater prosperity than we had ever experienced, the signs of coming disaster were rising on the horizon and the mutterings of the coming storm were heard indeed but sensed in time we endeavored to prepare for it. The troubles in our Southern business we have guarded with all imaginable care. We early determined strictly to fulfill our contracts with the members and to require a strict compliance from them in regard to the payment of premiums. When it became impracticable for us to receive from our agents the premiums on which our contracts were based, we determined to discontinue the agencies in the seceded states and notify as far as possible all parties that unless their premiums were paid here, their policies would be forfeited. This was an act of absolute security as the confederate government undertook to confiscate and seize all the monies paid to the credit of the Company in the hands of agents.

The notice to agents and parties was given to the extent of our ability. Since August last, no communications have passed between the Company and its agents in the seceded states. . . . When the political difficulties of the country shall be settled, we shall undoubtedly have to consider and reinstate much of the business above referred to as we learn that many loyal citizens, members of the Company, have provided for payment of their premiums but could not get them to us. . . .

As the Board are aware, the Company agreed as the result of a conference with other life insurance companies to assume some risk in aiding the government in supressing the rebellion by advising our members to serve in the national defense on their paying an extra premium of 5% of the amount insured. The result has been that 168 permits have been granted on which an extra premium of $29,065 was charged, putting at risk $606,800 on 168 lives, 40 members have returned, leaving the present number 128—extra premium $23,465, amount at risk $455,500. One has died in service insured for $5,000.

Unfortunately no one now can locate that first Civil War claim, since more records for middle years of Company history were discarded than for the earlier period. Possibly the most noteworthy war claim, however, was on the life of General Joseph K. F. Mansfield. The General was insured at age 42 in August 1845 under Policy 225. He was then an engineer in the U.S. Army and paid $100 annual premium for his $1,000 policy. In August 1848 (after the War with Mexico) his premium was reduced to $34. In 1862 he was in command of the Twelfth Corps of the Army of the Potomac defending Washington in the Civil War. Early that fall General Lee led the Confederates in their first attempt to invade the North. They crossed the Potomac above Washington and thrust through Maryland. On this march, at Frederick, Maryland, occurred the incident reported in Whittier's famous poem. Barbara Frietchie, defending the Stars and Stripes, challenged the invaders:

> *"Shoot, if you must, this old grey head,*
> *But spare your country's flag," she said.*

And "Stonewall" Jackson answered:

> *"Who touches a hair of yon grey head*
> *Dies like a dog! March on!" he said.*

General Jackson and his men were part of Lee's army that on September 17 engaged the Union forces, including General Mansfield, in the "east woods," the "west woods," the "corn fields" and the "Bloody Lane" with the frightful carnage that became known as the Battle of Antietam. Nearly one hundred thousand men fought in the battle. Casualties numbered forty thousand, including more than four thousand killed, one of whom was General Mansfield. Historians count this one of the decisive battles of the Civil War.

News of the battle, its horrors and its losses, were on every lip. It is easy to understand why a representative of the Mansfield family wrote the Company: "Will it be necessary to furnish the Physician's certificate in proof of the death of Genl. Mansfield? He was shot at Antietam and died a few hours after."

During the war years death came suddenly to great numbers of policyholders through disease as well as from enemy fire. The horrors of the epidemics are hard to imagine in these days of medical progress. One interesting case was on a miller of New York who died of yellow fever at Wilmington, North Carolina, in October 1862. The necessary papers attesting the death were signed by the captain and adjutant general for the district since, as a note said, "the minister died and the undertaker, all of yellow fever, before they could give affidavit." Another statement affirms that the insured "was not engaged in any military or naval service or connected in any way with the war." What was a miller doing in army territory? Was he seeking war profits and paid too dearly for his commercial ambitions?

A typical war claim was on the life of a young druggist who in 1859 bought a $3,000 policy for which he named his three sisters as beneficiaries. When war came he paid an extra premium on his policy to continue its effectiveness in spite of his service in the army. He was killed in battle by a shell about three miles below Fredericksburg, Virginia.

In October 1862 President Patterson died. Lewis C. Grover had already assumed leadership of the Company, as has been noted, and was immediately elected president. A few months later another personality came upon the Company scene. In July 1863 Amzi Dodd was appointed mathematician, beginning an association of major importance to the Mutual Benefit Life. Mr. Dodd as a mathematician was largely self-taught, but as a contemporary said, "One of the chief delights of his life was the law of averages, and he never failed to impress the lesson that it was the basis of life insurance in all its relations."

The figure of Amzi Dodd in the height of his manhood, tall and lean with stovepipe hat and shawl about his shoulders (Abraham Lincoln dressed so, too), looms large in the picture of Company activities. For the next half century this man was the dominating influence in Mutual Benefit Life affairs.

Many retired members of the home office staff remember Mr. Dodd from their office boy days. They tell that one of their duties was to take new policies to him for signature. They found him awe-inspiring in spite of his habit of sitting comfortably at his desk, shoeless, in hand-knit white wool socks.

Dr. Ward tells, better than any of us today could do, the personal story of Amzi Dodd:

> We can the better understand Amzi Dodd when we acquaint ourselves with the ancestors from whom he came. Daniel Dodd, an English Puritan, emigrated to the New World about 1646, only a few years after the landing of the Pilgrim Fathers. He assisted in establishing a colony on Massachusetts Bay. After a time, in company with others, he migrated southward to Branford, Connecticut, a settlement on Long Island Sound, and there he became a member of the Colony of New Haven. These New Haven Puritans were distinguished from other Puritans by the strictness of their principles. To them their religion was the very center of their existence, and in matters of conscience they were unyielding and immovable. So imbedded in their character was this trait that it overshadowed all thought of safety and of ease. When by a royal decree of Charles II, the King of England, they were forcibly annexed to the Colony of Connecticut, they found themselves greatly out-numbered by those who held to views that were far more liberal. To them there came the choice of easing their conscience and submitting to this new condition, or of seeking a new home. One of the most picturesque incidents of the Colonial period is the migration of this band of sixty-four New Haven colonists* with their wives and children. We can well appreciate their feelings as they stood upon the decks of the little vessels that were to bear them away, and cast a last wistful look at their former surroundings. There were the cabins they had built

* Led by Robert Treat.

by the strength of their own hands. There were the gardens they had planted, and the fields they had tilled. There was the meeting house in which they had worshipped, and beside it the half acre in which their beloved ones were at rest. There, too, were the friends and neighbors with whom they had shared the joys and the hardships of frontier life. To all of these scenes they bade adieu as they set their sails and sought a new abode. After sailing through Long Island Sound, they passed the Dutch Colony of New Amsterdam, which had recently been acquired by the English and named New York. Then they crossed the Hudson River; and entering a smaller stream named "Passayek," they disembarked. Thus, in May, 1666, Newark had its birth.

In this group of sturdy pioneers was a young man Daniel Dodd, the son of the Daniel Dodd who emigrated from England. This young man was a mathematician and a surveyor. The services of such a person were of great value in the planning of a future city; and young Daniel, although still under age, was doubtless of great assistance to his fellow colonists. We can only surmise as to how much Newark is indebted to his vision for its Broad Street, which was then laid out, several miles in length and eight rods (132 feet) in width, and which has ever since been the pride of the city.

Daniel Dodd's son John, his grandson John, and his great-grandson John were a direct line of ancestors to Dr. Joseph Smith Dodd, the father of Amzi. All of these men were of high repute in their day and generation. Dr. Joseph Smith Dodd was for more than thirty years a practicing physician in Bloomfield, his native place, where he died "rich in the love and esteem of his fellow citizens." Amzi Dodd was born in Bloomfield, New Jersey, on March 2, 1823. At that time Bloomfield was a village of comfortable homes, about six miles from the center of Newark. Amzi's mother was Maria Grover, the daughter of the Reverend Stephen Grover, who was the grandfather of Lewis C. Grover, our second President. Amzi was carefully educated at home and in the Bloomfield Academy. He progressed so rapidly with his studies that when sixteen years of age he found no difficulty in entering the sophomore class of Princeton College, his father's Alma Mater.

Two and a half years later, in 1841, he was graduated with the highest honors; and because of his excellence in scholarship, he was chosen to deliver the Latin salutatory at the commencement exercises in September. In choosing a profession Amzi's first inclinations were for teaching. For the next four years we find him pursuing this vocation principally in Virginia, and enjoying intimate contact with the southern people. He had a hatred of slavery, but he had a high esteem and a deep affection for many of the families of the Old Dominion State, whose boys and girls were his pupils. The writer can well recall a conversation of many years ago in which Mr. Dodd referred to those Virginia school days, and especially to his visit after the Civil War to those scenes of his young manhood. The old Plantations were then sadly neglected; and the southern homes, formerly the centers of mirth and happiness and hospitality, were in ruins. Many of the people whom he had formerly known when in their affluence were now in dire distress, broken in spirit, and unprepared for the days of reconstruction that were to follow.

Throughout these few short years of teaching there was developing within the soul of Amzi Dodd a yearning for law. During the teaching periods he read law diligently and in his vacations he acquired a practical knowledge of law by serving in the law office of Miller and Whelpley, a prominent law firm in Morristown, New Jersey. In January 1848, he was admitted to the New Jersey bar as an attorney, and in 1851 as a counsellor-at-law. Soon after this event he became associated with the Honorable Frederick T. Frelinghuysen of Newark. A more favorable environment for a young man of Amzi Dodd's intellect and aspirations could not have been procured. Frederick T. Frelinghuysen* was one of New Jersey's most eminent attorneys, but he was far more than that. He had a great love for his fellow men and gave himself unstintingly to their service. His name was inscribed in large letters upon the roster of many religious, philanthropic and patriotic organizations. It was in this atmosphere of high intellect and broad human vision that Amzi Dodd began his career as a lawyer.

Mr. Dodd developed a great interest in public affairs. He served as clerk of the Newark Common Council and in the New Jersey State Legislature. He was Vice-Chancellor of New Jersey and a Judge of the Court of Errors and Appeals, the highest judicial tribunal in the state. After he became president of the Mutual Benefit Life he resigned public office but continued to be active and useful in public affairs.

Dr. Ward's further comments about Mr. Dodd's character and personality will give an understanding of his influence on the Company. Dr. Ward wrote:

In 1905, when I first entered the service of the Mutual Benefit, Mr. Dodd had retired as its President, but he still served the Company as its Counsel. He was daily at the office and it was my good fortune to have a seat beside him in the dining room. During these lunch hours, I learned to know and appreciate his true greatness. He was not loquacious, but when once his attention was directed to any subject, he would converse upon it with a knowledge that was truly remarkable.

Mention has been made of his greatness as a mathematician. He loved mathematics. Upon one occasion I heard him remark, "Did

* A statue of Mr. Frelinghuysen stands in Military Park in Newark, opposite the Robert Treat Hotel.

you ever realize the beauty of mathematics?" His mathematical mind could comprehend the movement of the planets and the laws governing them. This quality of mind enabled him to meet the problems connected with life insurance with great ability and with fine precision. Because he was a great mathematician, he could discern the true from the false, the sound from the unsound.

He was a great lawyer. He loved justice, and because he loved justice, he loved the profession of law, for he recognized law as the handmaiden of justice. His discriminating mind could detect the right from the wrong, and his adherence to the right was absolute and immovable. Upon one occasion I heard him say, "It is not difficult to do right, but it is very difficult to do almost right."

As a lawyer he was a great Vice-Chancellor and a great Jurist, and as a lawyer he inculcated into the very warp and woof of the Mutual Benefit those principles of justice which gave to every member of our organization full and equal rights. This sense of justice found expression in the principles of non-forfeiture, of mutuality, and of retroaction.

Mr. Dodd was also a great scholar. He loved literature and he was familiar with the best in literature. He had a great admiration for Shakespeare, but his favorite poets seem to have been Milton and Whittier. Possibly his Puritan ancestry gave to him a sense of kinship to Milton, who was one of the greatest Puritans. Not only was he familiar with his works, but he could quote his poems line by line and verse by verse. His fondness for Whittier may have been due to the fact that they both were abolitionists, and they both had a hatred of human wrongs and a desire to correct those evils; but I think that the greatest bond of fellowship was because of the simplicity of their faith. One was a Quaker and the other a Presbyterian, but both of them found a joy and a deep satisfaction in their religious beliefs. I once heard Mr. Dodd remark, "Is it not strange that men will converse so freely with one another concerning their business, but are so reticent conerning religion, which is of far greater importance."

Amzi Dodd was a sincere Christian. He held true to the faith of his fathers. That faith sustained him throughout his life; and when in old age he met the sorrows and the trials that are common to humanity, he faltered not, for his faith held firm. Upon one occasion, when he was in a meditative mood, I can well recall his recital of those familiar lines of Whittier:

> And so beside the silent sea
> I wait the muffled oar.
> No harm from Him can come to me
> On ocean or on shore.
> I know not where His islands lift
> Their fronded palms in air,
> I only know I cannot drift
> Beyond His love and care.

In that faith he lived, enjoying life's blessings, bearing with fortitude life's burdens, enduring without complaint life's sorrows. In that faith he died, leaving to us the memory of a life well lived, a service well rendered, a faith well kept.

Such were the character and the personality of the man who was to guide the Company through a generation of challenge and testing. Following the sound course laid by the conscientious and conservative stewardship of Mr. Patterson and Mr. Grover, Mr. Dodd expanded the Company's service, gave contractual substance to principles and practices that made the Mutual Benefit Life unique then and for generations to come.

The Company having been conservative in the assumption of war risks came out of the war without serious loss. In January 1866 President Grover reported:

> With the close of the war the risks incident thereto have been gradually ceasing. With from five hundred to seven hundred such risks, our losses exceeded the extra premium about $20,000, but including the regular premium, they fell below the amount received. Being mostly war risks, they have now nearly all ceased.

Another group of cases known in the Company's records as "Southern policies" presented quite different problems. Of them President Grover wrote also in the 1866 report:

> On the sudden collapse of the Rebellion, in the spring, when intercourse with the South was opened, large numbers of the eight hundred or one thousand members who resided there when the war broke out, came on; others corresponded with the Company; the friends of others who had died presented their claims, and the

urgent pertinacity with which all were pressed by women and men, clergymen, lawyers, business men, and parties of all descriptions, greatly increased the labor of the year. It was decided that one person should take entire charge of the whole subject, and see that the rules which were adopted should be carried out, so that there should be uniformity, kindness, and care in all the business of reconstruction. This business was sufficient to occupy the whole time of one person; and, added to other labors which were not diminished, have made the past a busy year. The large amount which appears in the settlement of $97,795.13, as paid for purchased policies, contrasted with that of the previous year ($35,000), showing between $60,000 and $70,000 difference, will give an idea of this part of the business. If we add to this the $50,000 or more paid by the Company for deaths occurring on that class of business, it will be seen that something over $100,000 has been disbursed on that account.

The "one person" taking charge of these cases was Amzi Dodd. His sense of justice and his kindly nature, as well as his personal ties of sympathy with the South, made him an ideal man for this responsibility. He surely carried out his work in the spirit of Lincoln's historic words in his second Inaugural: "With malice toward none, with charity for all, with firmness in the right as God gives us to see the right, let us strive on to finish the work we are in; to build up the nation's wounds, to care for him who shall have borne the battle, and for his widow and his orphan—to do all which may achieve and cherish a just and lasting peace among ourselves, and with all nations."

The service to Southern policyholders covered not only the cases of those represented by visitors to Newark. Mr. Dodd eventually went to Richmond and from headquarters there sought out policyholders who had not approached the Company. The greater number of these Southern cases were settled in the years 1865–1867, but the last were not reported for another ten years. The Company paid the "equitable value" of policies lapsed for nonpayment of premium, or death claims if the terms of the contract had not been violated. Also policies were reinstated if the policyholder so wished and was insurable. Settlements were made on 337 surrendered policies, involving an outlay of $88,000 in cash and a cancellation of $110,000 of indebtedness, a total of $198,000. This represented about a million dollars of business, out of a total outstanding at the beginning of the war of about twenty-two millions. In addition death claims of $148,000 were also paid on thirty-four "Southern policies."

It is interesting that one of the reinstated Southern policies was the first case written in Richmond. This was in June 1847 and on the life of Henry Exall, a 35-year-old architect.

The medical examination gives an interesting personal description of him as "five feet, ten inches high, dark hair, black full beard, medium sized man, active habits of life." He was born in England, but came to this country when he was about five years old. With the papers on this case is a little slip dated Richmond, Virginia, December 4, 1865, a statement signed by Henry Exall, "This certifies that I have not been engaged in the military or naval service or otherwise violated the conditions of my policy except by failure to pay the premiums when due." There is also a doctor's statement dated July 27, 1866: "I have this day re-examined Mr. Henry Exall (the papers in whose case were sometime ago sent on) and find him in perfect health and recommend the renewal of his policy." After the reinstatement Mr. Exall continued to have the protection of his policy and the claim was paid when he died in 1891.

In the Civil War days, as in subsequent war times, the Company did an important patriotic service in the purchase of Government bonds. When the war started, the Company owned no United States bonds; and by the end of 1861 held only $35,300 of such securities. The next year the sum had increased to $293,700; and by January 1, 1864, to $1,026,200 which was 19% of the Company's gross assets. For several years subsequently the total amount of Government bonds increased but their percentage of Company assets diminished, because of the greater rate of growth of the Company as a whole.

In spite of the losses and various increased expenses of war years, the Company's stewardship for policyholders was marked by successful economy. In 1860 and 1861 annual dividends of 45% were declared, and beginning in 1862 the rate was increased to 50%. In the prospectus of 1866 Amzi Dodd explained the Company's dividend procedure and principles.

> By the present practice of the Company, no dividend is declared on the operations of any particular year until a full year has elapsed thereafter; and no dividends are made payable until after the expiration of two years from the time of their being declared. Thus a dividend was declared in January, 1866, on the premiums paid during the year 1864, but such dividend will not be payable until the year 1868. It is then made payable throughout the year as the annual premiums become due. The dividends of this Company made in the foregoing manner have for several years past been fifty per cent of the premiums. It is sometimes asked whether dividends of the same amount will be made continuously in the future. No promise, expressed or implied, ought to be made by any life insurance company in regard to the magnitude of its future dividends, for it is obvious that if grounds existed on which such a promise could be safely made, the premiums themselves should be reduced and the unnecessary operation of taking money from the policyholders and returning it at the end of the year, or at any other time, should be dispensed with. It is precisely because the future is unknown and uncertain that premiums are raised to a height greater than probable contingencies will require. The very reason for such excess or redundancy shows the impropriety of promising what definite portion of that excess will be returned.

The lag between time of declaring dividends and paying them had disadvantages for both policyholder and Company, particularly when death claims occurred. Therefore, the Company paid a double dividend of about $2,000,000 in 1868 to help close the gap. (When another double dividend of nearly $3,000,000 was paid in 1875 the delay was completely eliminated, and thereafter dividends distributed each year represented the surplus from the year just before.)

In February, 1870, the board took another very important action in regard to dividends:

> A dividend of return premiums will be made in January, 1871, on a plan equitably adjusted to the ages and classes of policies.

So was begun the practice still followed today, the contribution system of calculating dividends, so very different from paying a straight percentage of premium regardless of age or class.

The premiums for life insurance are calculated on the basis of mortality tables, compound interest tables and expense estimates. The actual current cost of life insurance depends upon the actual death rates, interest rates and expense, including necessary contingency funds. In the contribution system of calculating dividends, savings or earnings from each factor (which differ for different kinds of policies, for policyholders of different ages and with different time of being insured) are determined, and the sum is the dividend.

The Mutual Benefit from the beginning was committed to the plan of dividends payable annually. The officers constantly have been very conscious of their responsibilities as stewards for the members, their obligation to manage the Company's business with safety but also with equity. Equity, in their thoughts, involved the return of premium overpayments to policyholders as promptly as possible, as well as in amounts carefully adjusted to the contributions of policyholders.

Company dividends have always been high compared to the business as a whole. But repeatedly Company officers through the years have voiced the standard: "The first object of a life insurance company is safety." In this period President Grover wrote:

> While dividends are important, and no pains will be spared to make them of the most favorable kind, it should not be forgotten that the main object of a policy is not to produce dividends, but to secure indemnity against the evils of premature death. This is the paramount end and value of Life Insurance.

The experiences of wartime surely emphasized to the Company the inevitability of adjustments in life insurance ownership over the years. No one at the time of purchase could know what his needs or desires might become in the future. To meet this need the Company in 1862 began issuing policies on the limited payment plan providing automatic paid-up insurance in case of lapse proportionate to the premiums paid. For example, one case that became a claim was a $2,000 policy on the ten-payment life plan. The insured paid only two premiums, two-tenths of the contract number. When he died some years later, the Company paid $400, two-tenths of the amount insured.

In 1868 a guaranteed cash value provision was made a part of the contract. The 1845 Company prospectus had promised cash values "in equitable amount," and the first was paid in 1847, as has been described. But now the 1868 edition of the contract guaranteed the cash surrender and paid-up privilege after payment of two full years' premiums. The directors voted to guarantee these rights also to owners of previously issued policies, beginning the practice of the principle of retroaction so important in Mutual Benefit Life history.

In an interesting review of Company history made in 1955, Vice President Harry W. Jones emphasized the great significance of the Company's innovations with these new policy forms and the public commitment to retroactive extension of the benefits to old policyholders. He said the Company "thus cut itself off from any possibility that these reserves might become available to be squandered on new business."

This action was the raising of an ensign in the battle for sound life insurance. It told policyholders and the world just where the Mutual Benefit Life stood in the wild days that were coming.

Mr. Jones further pointed out that this era was the first of successive cycles where the Mutual Benefit stood alone, or nearly alone, in the industry, against developments judged by the Company to be contrary to equity and mutuality and sound life insurance principles.

CHAPTER FIVE

The Shaking of the Companies

DURING THE WAR COMPANY BUSINESS increased spectacularly, from less than $5,000,000 annual sales in 1860 to more than double in 1863 and double again in 1864. With some fluctuations, business continued to increase to a peak of nearly $32,000,000 in 1868. For the next decade, however, the general trend was down, dropping to a $5,000,000 low again in 1878.

The war, as has been noted, cut off the Southern agencies completely. None of these was re-established for many years after the end of hostilities. In the middle sixties, however, the plan of sales promotion leadership in the field, begun by Mr. Loveridge in "the Northwest" was expanded. President Grover wrote in 1866:

> The system of Territorial Agencies, organized sometime since, by which, at a central point in a given state or territory, the Company has an able and efficient agent, who gives his whole time to the business and through whom it is transacted with local agents, and whose compensation depends on commissions from the business, has proved a favorable means of more thorough discipline and efficiency. . . . The claims of the Company have been fairly represented in the Eastern, Middle, Western, and Northwestern States.

This was a time of national expansion. The transcontinental railroad was completed with the driving of the golden spike in Utah on May 11, 1869. Union soldiers were getting land grants in the West, ambitious young homesteaders from all over the Eastern seaboard were finding freedom from tradition and family restrictions as they founded new communities beyond the Mississippi. One young Mutual Benefit policyholder from Virginia, writing home from Wisconsin, waxed eloquent about the wonderful new country where any man might try his own new ideas without criticism, and not be compelled to build every fence just the way his great-grandfather had done.

The Mutual Benefit Life was not slow to adopt modern improvements. Among interesting Company relics is the first used "business machine," patented in 1868. It is a sort of circular slide rule made of brass, called "The Adder."

Fortunately a page of advertising and directions for use have been carefully saved also. This "two wheeled velocipede of figures" was hailed as the "only practical adding machine in the world," "quick as lightning, sure as fate, compact, convenient, certain, cheap."

Dr. Henry Ward Beecher, most popular preacher of the day, wrote his testimonial:

> When I first saw the name, "Adder," I took it to be an animal, but finding it to be a machine, I have experimented with it, as have my children, until we are sure that no accountant need fear that he will be bit by buying it. To those as dull at figures as I am, it must be an invaluable relief. It is an ingenious and useful machine, and must be a valuable help to accountants.

The advertising copy goes on to ask: "Why wear out brains when brass wheels can be worn out instead? Why take up a valuable accountant's time when cheaper labor can be employed to do work which is purely mechanical?"

A few years later another modern invention was acquired when the directors ordered for the outer door of the vault "what is termed a chronometer lock."

At this period, for at least a decade, an edition of Company reports and prospectuses was printed in German. This evidences the floods of intelligent, thrifty German immigrants who were strengthening the life and business of our country. They responded to life insurance as part of the opportunity for self-reliance and self-betterment in the Land of Liberty.

The Company, both in home office and field, lived through most difficult days in this period after the Civil War. The war stimulated the life insurance business, and all business. With increasing public demand for life insurance, the business looked like a good place to make money. Many new companies were started. Keen competition developed. Unscrupulous and extravagant practices began to appear. The ideal of mutual life insurance as a *cooperative service* became overshadowed by life insurance as a *business,* offering big chances of profits for high-powered promoters.

The reports of President Grover give a vivid picture of contemporary events. In 1869 he wrote to policyholders:

> Several new Companies, some purely Stock, some Mutual have organized during the year. Capitalists seem to have supposed that the large returns made by some Mutual Companies to their members as the result of long years of economy and care, would warrant them in investing large sums, as in a Bank or Railroad enterprise, and that like returns could be realized. In other countries this might be so, and perhaps it will be here; but it would seem to be a characteristic of the American people to desire to manage their own business, to elect their own rulers, to control their own money, and to realize the profits for its use. There can of course be no serious danger to the business from the formation of well conducted Stock Companies, if the conditions required in a well conducted Mutual Company are complied with. Either may be well or badly conducted. Either may, by extravagant expenditure for rents, advertising, salaries, commissions to officers or agents, forfeit all claim to public confidence, and add to the wrecks of fortune and character which are yearly witnessed in our larger business centres. . . .
>
> With regard to the Agents, we have seen how faithfully they have stood by their principles, how hard it has been at times for them to maintain their position and their integrity to themselves, their employers, and the insuring public. The lavish offers of 30, 35 and 40 per cent commissions on premiums to be obtained, accompanied by seducing words and artful promises, would seem almost enough to corrupt any one whose integrity was assailable. It is true that a shrewd and intelligent mind could see in the extravagance of the offers made that they must be a sham or a counterfeit, a delusion or a snare, involving perhaps the loss of influence and a good name to promote some stupendous fraud. An intelligent, virtuous mind would not yield to such temptations; a weak or vicious one would. Judged by this rule, the Company has reason to be proud of its corps of active, intelligent Agents. Like Generals of Division, they have controlled their subordinates, kept up order and discipline, infused life and vigor among the troops, added largely to their numbers, and in every contest of which we have heard have come off victorious over their opponents.
>
> All honor to so noble a band; and occasion is here taken, while rendering them the praise which is their due, to say that the experience of the year has more than ever convinced us that the proper manner of conducting a well ordered Life Insurance Company, is to have as agents able men, of good character, trained as to a pro-

fession, fairly compensated as like services in other professions are, that both they, their families, and the Companies they represent, may be honored and respected. . . .

As we congratulate the members that we hold to the system which gives them a good medium of communication with the Company in the person of a moderately paid but well compensated agent, so at THIS TIME we felicitate ourselves that we have adhered to the mode of distributing surplus and returning premiums to the members which we have acted on from the beginning, nearly a quarter of a century ago; a system plain, simple, uniform, which all can understand, which compels economy and prudence, discloses any attempt at extravagance or fraud, and above all enables every intelligent member to understand the manner in which his business is conducted.

Our dividend system is not the result of ignorance or chance. It is as much the result of intelligent design as the adoption of our name of "Mutual Benefit," or the thoroughness with which every member on entering our association becomes one with us, and entitled from the first to a full and equal participation with the oldest member in all the rights, immunities, and privileges of the Company.

The men who organized this association understood their business well. They learned all that could be known on the subject in the Old World or the New. They applied the best principles of business with which they were familiar to the conduct of its affairs. They were not speculators or schemers; they had no idea of acquiring wealth or making fortunes for themselves or others from the business. They never proposed to grow rich from the money they professed to gather and take care of for the widow and the orphan. They were philanthropists and intelligent Christian gentlemen, with heads to plan, hearts to feel, and hands to execute.

Again in 1870 President Grover commented to policyholders about current events in the business:

Now there are sixty [companies] reporting to the Commissioner and about as many more who do not report at all, making one hundred and twenty companies scattered in every section of the country and under all kinds of influences, competing for business and offering all kinds of inducements for it. Aside from the lowering of rates of premium, and raising the commissions to a fabulous amount,* some waive all restrictions to occupation, travel, or residence. Some make all Policies incontestible from any cause (from date of issue). . . . These . . . show such a departure from fundamental ideas, inseparable from the business of life insurance, that it

---

* Mutual Benefit Life agents' contracts for 1871 showed 15% first year and 5% renewal commissions.

is to be expected the coming years will result in a terrible shaking among the companies.

With the purpose of conducting the Company's business on the soundest possible scientific basis, the directors in 1870 adopted a new mortality table. Heretofore only tables developed from English statistics had been available. The reserves had been calculated on the Actuaries' Table and the premium rates on the Carlisle Table. Now a new table, developed by Sheppard Homans of the Mutual Life of New York, had appeared and the Mutual Benefit Life was among the first to use it. This table became the standard for American life insurance companies and was used by the Mutual Benefit Life for seventy-five years. Interesting comments about the table's development were made by Mr. Homans at the organization meeting of the Actuarial Society of America:

> When I first entered life insurance, American companies were dependent on foreign tables entirely. We had no statistics of American mortality . .

He reported that he first investigated the experience of American life insurance companies, including the Mutual Benefit Life. He found that there was a manifest and marked difference in the rates of mortality among the holders of different kinds of policies.

> I reasoned with myself as to the causes, and I came to the conclusion that if men were left to their own judgment and inclinations they would by instinct, not necessarily by any process of reasoning, select that form of policy which was best suited to their own individual interests: that those who had some reason to believe that they would die sooner than the law of nature would indicate would naturally select the short term policy; that those who had no reason to believe they would die sooner or later than nature allowed, would naturally select a whole life; while those who had reason to believe they would live to enjoy the benefit, selected the endowment.
>
> I also found, very much to my gratification, in comparing the rates of mortality in this country with the rates of mortality in Great Britain, as shown by the Actuaries' Table, and still more by the Carlisle Table, that the rates at the middles ages, were far less in America than in Great Britain; although the rates at younger ages and older ages were greater; I accounted for those peculiarities on these grounds: we live faster; we burn the candle at both ends: young people are apt to die more rapidly here than in a more settled and conservative community, and the same would hold good with men in advanced years. Our energetic way of living would carry men in the middle period of life over periods when, in a more staid

community, they would succumb to influences prejudicial to health. I believe these peculiarities have been found to exist in all later experiences.

I also collated the experience with regard to geographical districts. I followed the plan laid down by Mr. Gill,* of dividing the United States into six territorial districts. The first was the New England and Middle States; the second, the Western States; the third, the Southern States on the Atlantic seaboard; the fourth, the Southern States on the Gulf; the fifth was California; and the sixth were those which could not properly be included in either one of the other divisions. I found a marked difference in respect to mortality in different localities; but I find from later experiences that those differences are fading away. In the West, in early days, through the want of proper sewerage, and want of water supply, the rate of mortality was greater. In the South, I think, there is a marked improvement. In California, of course, the differences are very marked.

The result was that after I had collated the experience of the Mutual Life, I drew a curve representing the approximate rates of mortality at different ages; and then found, by a simple method of adjustment, the rates of mortality now called "The American Experience Table"—a name, however, that was not given by me. The table has for its basis the experience of the Mutual Life; but it is not an accurate representation of the experience of that individual company. In other words, it is not intended to be, and never was claimed to be an accurate interpretation of the experience of the Mutual Life. I take it that no mortality table, however correct it may be as an exponent of the mortality of the past, will necessarily be a correct exponent of the mortality in the future; it may be a close approximation, and that is all we want. We want, in the first place, a table which will be safe. The American table is safe, because it is based on the mortality of lives where the experience in the first five years is eliminated; that is, the effect of recent medical selection is eliminated. It was more of a happy accident, or a happy thought, than anything else, that I made the termination of that table the age of ninety-six. In all the records of experience in different countries— Great Britain, France, Germany and this country—there is no record of any individual attaining the age of one hundred years being insured.

In 1871 the board of directors reaffirmed the Company's objectives in contrast to many competitors:

> The object of the Company is to offer the benefits of Life Insurance to all of sound health who desire to avail themselves thereof, and to afford insurance at the lowest cost consistent with perfect security, and adequate remuneration to those who are employed as agents.

* Mr. Gill had been mathematician of the Mutual Benefit Life.

This resolution was an implied criticism of the reckless underwriting practices and the extravagant expenditures of many other companies.

In the annual report of 1871 the Company again focused attention on its unique record with this simple statement:

> The distinguishing feature of this Company is economy in expenses. Its investments have always been made with such care that not one dollar has ever been lost.

The "shaking among the companies" foreseen by President Grover surely came. In the decade of the seventies, 83 of the 120 companies mentioned by him disappeared. Some were taken over by other companies, but many simply failed. Of 71 companies operating in New York State in 1871, 46 went out of business before 1880, 32 with complete loss to policyholders.

Many unusual factors contributed to economic instability in that decade, as Mr. Grover summarized in his 1873 report.

> The year 1872 has been an eventful one for Life Insurance. It opened on a business pressure at the West, caused by the Chicago fire,* which affected other sections also . . . and destructive conflagrations in the principal cities, culminating in the Boston fire, made unprecedented havoc of property and life.
>
> The State and general elections absorbed the attention and disturbed the minds of men, for a considerable portion of the year.
>
> These with other causes, tended to the decrease of new insurance, and also affected the renewals of former policies. Parties who were pressed for necessary means, were obliged to sell their policies to provide support for their families; the number of such cases was unprecedented. Casualties, deaths from violence, and suicides, materially increased. The great event of the year, however, has been the increased mortality in all sections of the country—beginning in the winter of 1871 and 1872, with typhoid pneumonia, which prevailed in many sections like an epidemic, together with acute diseases of the brain and other vital organs. The intense cold of the winter, and peculiar character of the atmosphere, exhausted life so rapidly that the mortality steadily increased and continued into the spring and up to summer, when the extreme heat did *its* part, and the ravages of death continued until the fall, when, as usual, large numbers of the aged and feeble fell under the influence of the changing season, and brought us to the close of what will probably be shown to be the most fatal year of a generation.

* No Mutual Benefit claims from the fire can be identified. Apparently there were none.

Such was the background for the great panic and subsequent depression beginning in 1873. These conditions all had their part in bringing on failures of life insurance companies. But scores of these companies had been built on the sands of ignorance, dishonesty and unsound practices. It was to be expected that they could not stand when the rains descended and the floods came.

The era knew catastrophies of many kinds. In June 1876 the country was stirred and horrified by the frightful Indian massacre at Custer's last stand against the Pawnees and Cheyennes in the West. A man who had been Government advisor on Indian affairs since the days of President Lincoln was Henry B. Whipple, a Mutual Benefit policyholder.

Bishop Whipple (the first Episcopal bishop for Minnesota) was well known as "the apostle to the Indians." They trusted him and called him "Straight Tongue." He had purchased his first Mutual Benefit Life policy in New York State in 1848 when he was a student, and others later through Chicago after he became Minnesota bishop. In August 1876 Bishop Whipple requested a travel permit since the Government had asked him to "go on a commission to the Sioux. Our route, I suppose, will be by the U. P. Rwy and thence to Red Cloud and Spotted Tail."

An interesting comment appears with the papers:

> I suppose that no man in the Country has so much influence personally with the Indians as he has, not only those half Civilized but also the wild Indians who recognize him as their friend. . . . As all of our companies have more or less interest in the lives of Soldiers and citizens exposed during the War, it is manifestly for our interest, aside from all motives of humanity, that it should be stopped as speedily as possible.

Bishop Whipple went safely on his mission and was able to secure a treaty with the Sioux opening up much of the best Dakota territory to white settlement. He died at the ripe old age of 80 from heart trouble and his Mutual Benefit insurance was paid to his children.

During the years of unwholesomely stimulated growth of other companies, the officers of the Mutual Benefit Life had constantly affirmed lack of interest in new business for the sake of size alone. This was in line with the basic concept of the Company as an association of members cooperating for mutual help. However, it was probably a reaction, too, against the extravagant ambitions and promotions of other companies. In 1866, at the close of the biggest year yet in Company history, President Grover had written:

> In regard to the business of the year on which we have entered, a few words may properly be said. It is clear that, if it is desired, our present large business may be greatly extended.
>
> It would seem that our main care should be to give our greatest efforts to keep the business in perfect order in all its departments, carefully guarding all the interests of the members; and in all that relates to character, see to it "that no man takes our crown," while in all that relates to "who shall be the greatest" we leave others to struggle in the race.

In 1874 the same attitude is expressed:

> It has not been thought proper heretofore, nor is it proposed hereafter, to enter into competition with others for business; nor is it considered justifiable for those intrusted with such important interests as are involved in a Life Association to hazard anything for the mere purpose of increasing the size of the Company.

The Mutual Benefit Life was not alone in standing against the evils developing in the life insurance industry at this time. There is an interesting pen-written letter dated December 9, 1875, from the president of the New England Mutual inviting Mr. Grover and Mr. Dodd to meet him and representatives of several other companies to discuss "a reform in Life Insurance." One of the proposed conferees was Elizur Wright of Massachusetts, a stalwart defender of sound life insurance. In fact one historian said of him: "To no one man in the history of life insurance in the United States do we owe such a debt of gratitude as we do to Elizur Wright."

As a young man Mr. Wright had undertaken a study of the English life insurance system on behalf of Massachusetts life insurance companies. The enthusiasm which his scholarly investigation was developing was rudely interrupted by an acquaintance who denounced the whole institution, declaring, "Life insurance! Life insurance, indeed! Why, sir, it is the greatest humbug in Christendom!" and who demonstrated his point by taking Wright to a Royal Exchange policy auction.

That London scene was routine in the early nineteenth century. In those days life insurance policies generally included no surrender values, yet they had a market value. Each Thursday afternoon old men, with resources exhausted, brought themselves and their policies to the auction block at the Royal Exchange. There speculators observed their age and weakness, appraised the possible profits to be made from taking over policies hopefully soon to become claims. Policies were sold to the highest bidder, and oftentimes mysterious deaths followed.

This sight inflamed Elizur Wright who already was a crusader on the subject of another kind of slavery in America. He returned to Boston to enter upon a new battle.

He began campaigning for the legal reserve system to make life insurance safe, and for nonforfeiture values in the contract to make life insurance fair. He became considered a lobbying crank about the Massachusetts State House. But in 1858 Massachusetts passed the bill for nonforfeiture rights and the legal reserve. Mr. Wright was appointed the first insurance commissioner for Massachusetts and did a monumental pioneering work in that state for eight years.

Naturally he was much interested in the practices established by the Mutual Benefit Life and there are evidences of his frequent contacts with officers of our Company.

Many years later Vice President E. E. Rhodes wrote of this relationship. He quoted a letter written in 1875 by Mr. Wright to Mr. Grover, a letter otherwise now lost:

> Practically, and at least so far as the solvency of the Company is concerned, the *note experiment,* which your Company was the first to try thoroughly, has proved a success. It has demonstrated the fact that the Company can recognize to a very important extent the right of the policyholder, subject to a proper charge for withdrawal, in the reserve as an individual trust fund.
>
> But such right, once conceded, ought to be more scientifically and rigidly defined. And the practice of life insurance must be more successful and satisfactory to all parties, when it conforms as nearly as practicable to such definition.
>
> There is a mystery about life insurance, arising out of the use of *commuted premiums,* which is too favorable to dishonest management. And now that such management is moving to retrace all steps

in the right direction, and ignore totally all recognition of the rights of the policyholder in the reserve, it seems to me it is the time for the companies that do recognize them to concert together, and see if they cannot be better defined to the satisfaction of all parties. Is there any reason why the policy, or contract, cannot be more thoroughly harmonized with the natural equities which pertain to the business? Is not the present time a crisis in American Life Insurance, beyond which it must either recede as rapidly as it has thus far advanced, or by some new departure commence a growth more adequate to the real demand for it among our people?

To the Mutual Benefit, which was the first to take a step partially recognizing the distinction between *insurance* and *self-insurance,* I look for this new departure. And if it takes the step, I am confident it will be supported by at least two or three other companies, each strong enough to make a success of the measure alone. In fact, nothing seems easier at the present moment than to carry public opinion overwhelmingly with you. If the great mismanagers of life insurance appeal to the wonder and imagination of the people at the Centennial with their piles of marble and money, let us appeal to their plain common sense with clear statement of the equities and lucid fidelity to the rule of them.

I hope to hear from you before long on the question whether something worth doing cannot be done.

Mr. Rhodes added a further comment:

When Mr. Wright's letter was received, Mr. Amzi Dodd, who was then the Company's Mathematician, was giving a good deal of thought to the question raised by Mr. Wright, the outcome of which was this Company's general non-forfeiture system adopted in 1879. While it cannot be said that Mr. Wright was the prime mover in the matter, I remember hearing Mr. Dodd say that Mr. Wright's attitude encouraged him to proceed.

The contrary industry climate under which the Mutual Benefit Life was operating during those years is reflected in President Grover's comments to policyholders early in 1879:

The strength of a life insurance company is not in the dimensions of its business, but in its capacity to give insurance with the utmost safety and economy to its members.

Nothing is gained, and much may be lost, by expansion of business, where expansion does not add to the security, or lessen the cost of its policies. . . . The coming in of new members is not essential to the advantageous fulfillment of all its obligations, by a company well established and solvent; without issuing a new policy, its existing policies could be carried without serious disadvantage to their holders, in respect to their annual cost, and could be paid with equal certainty when due. New members are obviously requisite for a company's permanence, but not at all requisite for its solvency, and much less important for the interests of the existing membership, than much of what is sometimes said on that subject would seem to imply.

The Company officers were sure of their convictions as to principle, but open-minded as to scientific information. When Mr. Dodd traveled to Europe in 1877 the board requested him "to collect such information and materials and to purchase such works on life insurance for the library of the Company as he may be able." This is the first mention of the Company reference library.

As further strengthening of the Mutual Benefit Life position in deed as well as in word, the Company adopted the Nonforfeiture System of 1879. This is a landmark in history for the life insurance business as well as for the Mutual Benefit Life. Previous nonforfeiture provisions had been generally available *at request,* if at all. Now the Company began issuing a policy which absolutely prevented forfeiture after two premiums had been paid. The same benefits were extended to old policyholders also. The new policy stated the term for which the policy protection would be continued if no further premiums were paid, and the policyholder had the extended insurance without asking for it. From the beginning the Company, and then Amzi Dodd in his turn, had stood strongly for an important principle. To quote Dr. Ward:

> . . . a principle which was not at that time generally accepted, namely that the reserves held by the life insurance companies were a great trust fund, not wealth belonging to the companies but a debt owed by the companies to their members. Mr. Dodd emphasized that to deprive the owner of a lapsed policy of his reserve might be legally right under the terms of the contract, but it was morally wrong.

Mr. Dodd's thinking leading up to this action is expressed in a report he made to the directors:

> Companies generally hold out, by their publications that they will purchase policies upon what they may deem equitable terms if purchases be applied for in due time. These equitable terms mean different things in different companies. I think there is no company in which it means so liberal dealing with the policyholders as in this Company, though I do not say that I am satisfied with our practice. . . .
>
> Its impolicy [referring to a current offer of another company to rebate 30% of the first and second years' premiums on new policies] consists further in the generally wrong and unwise notions it proceeds on as to the management of the business. It attaches an undue importance to the getting of new policies. It is a forcing process, which results not in a sound and healthy growth, nor in the maintenance of a sound and healthy state . . . The true test of success should be the pecuniary advantage derived by the assured from the company. The amount of the company's business is not a test of success. When new policies or a larger business does not tend to diminish the cost to the members of their policies, or add to the security that the policies will be paid at maturity, there is little or nothing to be gained by getting new policies. . . .
>
> The . . . Company is colossal in its magnitude. What its real inward strength and resources are it is difficult to affirm. But it is probably true that by the prevailing methods of competing for a life insurance business, that company can and will outstrip its competitors. Whether this be so or not, such competition is not in the interests of policyholders, and cannot, therefore, lead to true success. I think the time has come for *a new departure*. And that if any one of the largest and best companies should now take it, by turning its whole efforts to putting its agency system on the best possible basis, reducing its expenses to the lowest practicable point, and adopting in respect to the reserve values of all policies, surrendered or forfeited, a rule of action beyond controversy fair, the speedy success of such a company over others not doing the same things, would be as certain and as conspicuous as it would be deserved.

And so "the speculative period" of life insurance history with its "shaking of the companies" was coming to an end. Public confidence in life insurance generally was badly strained.

An imaginative reading of the following editorial in the *New York Daily Tribune* gives an impression of the contemporary life insurance climate. The article was quoted in an interesting little pamphlet entitled, *How to Become a Successful Life Insurance Agent.*

The confidence of the public in life insurance, properly—that is, honestly—administered, was never better deserved than now. . . . the weak, young, fraudulently managed companies have found their graves and their survivors have fully proved their right to live . . . Beyond controversy, life insurance, with all its admitted imperfections, and in spite of the barnacles of corruption which for a time attached themselves to it, has proved itself a vast public benefit.

The same leaflet quoted the *Insurance Times* for March 1878 in its appraisal of the Mutual Benefit Life and reported interesting details about the Company's investments in this period.

The inherent vitality of this company and the massive solidity of its strength and greatness have been brought out more clearly than ever by the "hard times" through which we have so long been passing. It was never so strong as now. . . . The officers, patrons and friends of the Mutual Benefit Life may well point with satisfaction and pride to the solid, safe and profitable nature of its assets of over thirty-three million dollars, about half of which consists of cash, United States 6 per cent and other government and municipal bonds of the most reliable and excellent quality. The great caution and foresight displayed by the company in its investments in bonds secured by first mortgages on real estate (a full schedule of which is on file in the Insurance Department of New York and that of New Jersey, and open to the inspection of all) have been rewarded with results especially happy in this period of decline in the value of such property, inasmuch as the company has thus been protected from loss, and its substance preserved substantial as ever, showing a clear surplus as regards policy-holders of $2,414,002, calculated on the highest actuaries' rate of mortality, and the exacting standard of interest at the rate of four per cent allowing the payment this year, 1878, of dividends to its fortunate policy-holders amounting to $1,512,799 and giving the company a special guarantee fund of $901,202, altogether unappropriated, and a safeguard against any unusual or possible contingency.

We have enumerated a few of the prominent facts in relation to the Mutual Benefit Life, because we think they ought to be known and pondered by the public. They show what a genuine life insurance company is and ought to be. They show that this company with its 42,796 policy-holders, with an insurance of $126,193,045, is now more than ever entitled to the confidence and favor of the people of America. They show that the animadversions and disgrace that have been provoked by the mismanagement of other life companies, have no relation to this one, and that, for security, trustworthiness, and the good it has wrought and is destined to effect, it compares favorably with any corporate institution in the world.

This same helpful little pamphlet of advice on successful life insurance selling gives a picture of contemporary sales philosophy:

> Why is it that a man will make up a party of friends, and spend $50 or $100 for a few days' shooting trip; a day up to the races at Jerome Park, Long Branch, or Saratoga; for a few boxes of cigars, or a few cases of wine, and do it all without compunction, when, if the necessity is urged upon him of securing a little life insurance for the wife and family against a rainy day, he will get mad and intimate something about people minding their own business? Only two trips a year such as we have hinted at will carry $5,000 to $10,000 of insurance! Which is the better way of spending the money?
>
> Wherein lies the difference between neglecting to provide for your household while living, and leaving them to certain starvation, as far as you are concerned, at your death? Yet how many a man lies down on his bed and dies, leaving his wife and children not only penniless, but absolutely entailing upon them the cost of his burial. Nothing can be more horrible to his survivors—nothing more dishonorable and ignominious to himself. Better would it be to train up your family in penury and want—better to inure them to the bitterness of poverty—better to treat them with uniform contumely, and thus prepare them for the insults and neglect and scorn of the world, than to surround them with all the appliances of wealth, to make luxury a necessity, to hang their happiness on the slender thread of your own existence, and, when it breaks, to cast them upon the world little better than beggars?

The Company came out of this troubled period of life insurance history as the third largest life insurance company in the country. The Mutual Life of New York was more than twice the size, and the Connecticut Mutual about one-third larger. The Company was proud of its record. To give Mutual Benefit Life policyholders and the public an official and unprejudiced expert judgment of its affairs, the officers in 1880 invited a searching examination by the supervising authorities of New Jersey, Massachusetts and Ohio. The following quotation from the investigators' official report after their five months' study is revealing.

> After nearly forty years of continued prosperity and growth, supplemented and sustained by integrity of management, strength of resource, and unquestioned reliability, the Mutual Benefit Life Insurance Company surprised its patrons and the country by voluntarily inviting an official and searching investigation of its business record and condition, now for the first time undertaken by State authority.
>
> Having successfully and without impairment of public confidence encountered the severe ordeals imposed in seasons of unusual depression and wide-spread calamity in the business world, while faithfully

and generously fulfilling the sacred trusts of a great and beneficent organization, it was not supposable that such examination was necessary or called for . . .

The unfortunate experiences which, through mismanagement or dishonesty, or both, have overtaken so many insurance enterprises, particularly Life, at home and abroad, during the last half century, provoking unfriendly criticism, prejudice and distrust, and injuriously affecting even the best and wisest administration, furnish in themselves emphatic approval of its decision.

In view of these significant facts, we can do no less than express our hearty appreciation of the high sense of duty and responsibility which prompted the desire for such thorough and authoritative examination as would confirm and vindicate the long and honorable record of this old Company. . . .

In reviewing the history of the Mutual Benefit Life Insurance Company, as developed during the progress of this long and searching investigation, many facts of special interest not previously cited would legitimately fall within the scope of an official report.

In their scrutiny of its general management, and particularly its accounts and other data connected with the adjustment and settlement of policy claims, the Examiners have been agreeably surprised at the very exceptional liberality of the Company, showing a manifest purpose to be generous as well as just in all its dealings, and to avoid as far as possible all unnecessary litigation, never in any case indulging in petty resort to escape obligation, or subject the policyholders to annoyance or loss.

We find, also, that while maintaining a conservative management, in which active vigilance and economic methods of administration have been so marked and effective, its adoption of a broad and liberal policy has been in many important particulars in advance of legislation or even public demand.

We have only to add, that in the equitable and honest exemplification of such a policy, the beneficent mission of life insurance finds its best and noblest fulfillment.

CHAPTER SIX

Two Decades of Expansion

LEWIS C. GROVER HAD BEEN PART
of the Company from the very beginning. He was one of the
organizers and as a young lawyer he had been instrumental in
getting the Company's charter. Through formative and difficult
years his aggressive leadership and sound understanding of mutual
life insurance contributed greatly to Company progress. In the late
fall of 1881, however, circumstances required that he relinquish the
presidency. Theodore Macknet, who had been a director for a
decade, was made president. Mr. Macknet is little known in Mutual
Benefit Life history. He was apparently a team-player and sought
the good of the Company rather than self-aggrandizement. His
unselfish spirit is expressed in the following letter dated January 16,
1882, which he addressed to the board of directors.

When in the emergency of the resignation of Mr. Grover I accepted
at your hands the Presidency of the Company, I continued as you
are aware to hold and to be responsible for my former positions of
Treasurer of the Company and Trustee of its Real Estate.

It was evidently impossible for me to continue to hold these
several positions, and attempt to carry their accumulating burdens,
hence it became a matter of serious consideration with me to deter-
mine what course the interest of the Company and my duty to
myself and my family required that I should take with reference
to them. My experience in the Financial Departments of the Company as Treasurer and Trustee have been especially pleasant and
agreeable to me, and they are sufficiently important and responsible

to tax the energy and command the entire attention of any man.

It has seemed to me therefore that the true interest of the Company would be promoted, if I could continue to devote my time, energy and attention to that Department alone. The way for me to do this became clear by the consent of Mr. Dodd to accept the Presidency of the Company and give up the high and honorable judicial positions he held in the Courts of the State.

I therefore cheerfully resign into your hands the position of President which you so kindly bestowed upon me because I believe that I can better serve the Company in the direct control of its Financial Departments and because Mr. Dodd's thorough mastery of the science of Life Insurance, his long and intimate connection with the Company and his familiarity with its past history and future needs especially fit him for the position of its President.

As Mr. Macknet's letter implies, Mr. Dodd's work as mathematician of the Company since 1863 had not been a full-time occupation. For some ten years he had been serving as Judge of New Jersey's highest judicial tribunal, the Court of Errors and Appeals, and as Vice-Chancellor, under appointment by successive Governors of political party different from his own. He resigned these positions when he became president of the Mutual Benefit Life on January 16, 1882.

Mr. Dodd's successor as mathematician was young Bloomfield J. Miller. Mr. Miller was a native of Newark, educated at Newark Academy and Rutgers University. Mr. Dodd had brought him into the mathematical department of the Company before college graduation, at a time when he was only 17 years old. In 1871 he had been appointed actuary. Those who worked with Mr. Miller over the years were united in characterizing him as a most unusually "lovable" man. They commented about his sweet disposition and unassuming manner. The memorial adopted by the Actuarial Society at his death said of him:

A marked feature of his professional career was the unflinching courage with which he maintained individual opinions, especially those relating to the equities of life insurance, and the justice of the claims of policyholders to liberality in the provisions of their policies, and the exclusion from them of restrictions, commonly included in the practice of an earlier period, and no doubt this manly independence influenced others to the adoption of similar views.

Mr. Miller was one of the actuaries who responded to the invitation of five leaders in the actuarial field to meet in New York in 1889 to form a professional organization. The meeting program combined fellowship, organization business and discussion of professional papers. The first evening's dinner menu showed some tempting and timely items: *Filet de boeuf à l'Actuaire, Ice Cream à la Tontine, Premium Cakes, Fruit Reserves* and *Coffee not on the Contribution Plan.*

The following day Mr. Miller was elected treasurer of the Actuarial Society of America organized at this gathering, later served as vice president, and became its president in 1897.

A few years after he became Company mathematician Mr. Miller employed a young Newark high school boy who was destined to succeed him and Mr. Dodd most honorably in actuarial leadership of the Company. That boy was Edward Everett Rhodes. Mr. Rhodes has published some of his memories of those early associations with Mr. Miller and Mr. Dodd:

> When I entered the service of the Mutual Benefit, the Mathematical Department consisted of seven clerks, one of whom was a woman, advanced in years, whose joy it was to render any little service required with needle and thread and to bring us jellies if we were ill. The department was then located on the third floor of the old brownstone building. Mr. Miller's office was on the second floor. I had not been with the Company very long when he came to me one morning and told me that he wanted to have the table on which I worked taken to his room and that I was to work there. I wondered what I had done that I could not be trusted to work with the other members of the department. I soon discovered the object of the move. From that time on, I underwent a course of actuarial training such as, I like to think, has not before or since been afforded anyone else. I must have tried Mr. Miller's patience sorely but he never showed it. Again and again he would say, "Are you sure it is clear to you? If not, we will go over it again." At times he would invite me to spend the night with him at his home in Perth Amboy, and there, as in the office, he would endeavor to inculcate in me the principles of actuarial science.
>
> Mr. Miller's kindness was universal. I never heard him order anyone in the office to do anything. It was always a request, and we who were associated with him endeavored to anticipate his wishes.
>
> When he was a child he lost one of his arms through an accident, but he could do many things with one hand better than others could do them with two hands. He was an expert billiard player and an expert swimmer. He could sail a boat.
>
> One day when Mr. Miller was absent from the office, a question arose involving the treatment of a policyholder. I saw that there were two ways of handling it, one to the advantage of the Company

and the other to the advantage of the policyholder. There was no rule governing the case and I thought I would better take it to Mr. Dodd. I did so and instead of telling me how to treat it, he asked me what I would do with it. I told him I would adopt that course which was to the advantage of the policyholder. He asked me why. I told him I thought it was the right way. He then looked at me very sternly, and said, "Young man, go back to your desk and never come to me again with a question regarding the treatment of a policyholder when there is a right and a wrong way."

The Company in those days was still quite a family affair, with a paternalistic flavor. A Christmas "offering" of $50 to each employee was continued through all this period (having begun in 1870), although the finance committee authorization for 1884 included the instruction to "say that this is a gratuity for this year and may be discontinued hereafter."

Office rules were published and each new employee accepted them by signing the statement:

I have received a copy of the within, and agree to comply with the rules named, and such other rules and regulations of the Company as shall be made known to me.

OFFICE RULES

—of—

THE MUTUAL BENEFIT LIFE INSURANCE COMPANY.
(Prepared by Request.)

1. Office hours commence at 8 A.M., when all are expected to be in their places at work, and, except when absent on leave, or at meals, to continue employed until the work of the office is completed for the day.
2. Each one is expected to be diligent in the business assigned him, and to be ready in cases of emergency, or when requested by an officer, to attend to any business in any department where his services are needed.
3. All will consider it their duty to obey the Rules, and directions of the Officers, to make known to the head of the Company anything affecting its interests that may come to their knowledge, and to abstain from communicating the Company's business to others, except as directed by the proper authority.
4. Knowledge of the business is important to those engaged in it. Earnest effort alone can secure success. It is expected that all will strive to understand and improve in each department of the business. Such course will always be observed and appreciated by the Officers and Directors.

5. The Company is in a measure affected by the reputation of those in its employ. Personal habits and reputation are therefore important, as none are employed who are known to be profane, intemperate, or to practice gaming or other like vices, so it is expected that none will indulge in extravagant or expensive habits, contract debts, or otherwise subject themselves to public comment and censure. All are requested to cultivate habits of order, neatness and cheerfulness; to take daily out-door exercise; to avoid every habit that is calculated to injure the health, and aim in every way to attain the character and acquire the reputation of a sincere Christian gentleman.

A retired officer of the Company reminisced about the Mutual Benefit as he found it when he became the newest boy in the book-keeping department in 1890.

Correspondence was almost altogether written with pen and ink. President Dodd wrote the bulk of his letters in his own hand, writing personally on every possible occasion letters of comfort to beneficiaries. Others in the Home Office, with the exception of the Mathematical Department, when they had letters to write, furnished a memorandum of the proposed contents of the letter to the Correspondence Department where the letter was composed in longhand and dispatched to the addressee.

One of this new boy's first tasks was writing premium notices, a job then done by hand.* Later he worked on recording of payments, which was also done by hand in huge ledgers.

As the size of the office staff increased various patterns of work became more formalized. In the 1880 office rules the beginning of office hours was stated definitely, the end was simply when the work was completed for the day. This flexible standard was continued apparently until 1899 when new rules were promulgated, giving the closing time as 4 P.M. The new rules also stated:

Reading of newspapers, and all other diversions from the work of the Company, are strictly forbidden during office hours.

* This became a typewritten operation in 1908 and then an Addressograph procedure in 1919.

The 1899 schedule continued, except for a change from 1:30 P.M. to 12 M. Saturday closing, for the next twenty-five years. At this time also the board of directors set Wednesday of each week as a regular meeting day, and that schedule has continued until now. Previously the board had met irregularly.

There are many retired home office veterans who recall their early days with the Company in this period. One who came to the Company in 1897 and retired in 1945 wrote some vivid reminiscences for the home office newspaper a few years ago:

> To begin with the difficulty of obtaining employment with The M.B.L.I. Co. was quite obvious in those days. You had to know somebody and if your written application for a job resulted in an interview, you were questioned as to what Sunday School or Church you attended, how you spent your spare time, (evenings and Sundays) and if you smoked or drank liquor. Your compensation started at $20.83 per month, payable monthly, with $50. for Christmas. Two weeks vacation without special consideration for length of service after the first year. Office hours were 8 A.M. to 4 P.M. Monday through Friday and 8 to 1:30 P.M. Saturday. However, we worked overtime if necessary without additional compensation, other than our supper, when necessary. Good lunches were served six days a week. Places were set for 10 at each table. Linen table cloths and napkins were provided once a week unless someone was unmannerly enough to spill something. We provided our own napkin rings. The lunch period was a time for relaxation and frivolity.
>
> We were one big family and 100% loyal. There was a saying at the time "that if you want to know what the President of a concern is like talk to the office boy." The first job assigned to a new clerk was to fill ink wells. They had to be washed out weekly and refilled with fresh ink and many a tray of ink wells crashed to the floors. Another duty was to take policies, after they had been written, to Mr. Amzi Dodd, President, and Mr. E. L. Dobbins, Secretary, for signatures. I recall being in Mr. Dodd's office on such a mission when Mr. B. J. Miller came in. Mr. Dodd, after greeting Mr. Miller, who had been to Paris on a vacation, introduced me to him and invited me to stay. A rooky being introduced to the Company's Mathematician? Morale building started at the top and I believe the present officers are just as thoughtful as in years gone by.

These reminiscences referred to the Christmas bonus and to the pleasure the staff members found in meals together. At this period the Christmas dinner, served home office members on December 24, was elaborate, as the following menu, printed on a gaily ornamented menu card shows.

GRAPE FRUIT
CELERY . . . RADISHES . . . OLIVES
OX TAIL SOUP
OYSTER PATTIES . . . POTATO CHIPS
ROAST RHODE ISLAND TURKEY
DRESSING . . . CRANBERRY SAUCE
PRIME RIBS ROAST BEEF
CAULIFLOWER, CREAM SAUCE . . . MASHED POTATOES
BOILED SWEET POTATOES
APPLE PIE . . . MINCE PIE
ENGLISH PLUM PUDDING, BRANDY SAUCE
VANILLA AND CHOCOLATE ICE CREAM . . . ASSORTED CAKES
NUTS . . . FIGS . . . FRUIT
ROQUEFORT, EDAM AND AMERICAN CHEESE
TEA . . . COFFEE

The growth of the Company's business during the 1880's and 1890's required increasing staff. The first stenographer-typists employed by the Company were boys. The pioneer was hired before 1890 but no one knows exactly when. The second employed was a lad of 16 who came to the Company on January 1, 1890,* in the finance department.

There was increasing departmentalizing of the work, improved procedures and expansion of operations in many ways. In the underwriting of risks, for instance, the medical board increased to three doctors. One was Dr. Edgar Holden who had come to the Company shortly after the close of the Civil War. He had been a United States Navy surgeon throughout the war and was an eyewitness of the historic battle between the *Monitor* and the *Merrimac*. He was for over forty years a medical director of the Company and was an exceptionally brilliant medical student. Dr. Ward commented that one of his most interesting scientific studies was about the contagion of tuberculosis, when that was not yet an accepted fact. Another

---

* New Year's Day was not then a holiday.

doctor, Dr. George Van Wagenen, served the Company for more than fifty years and as a frail visitor from his retirement home in Florida is well-remembered by many in the Company today. He was one of the founders of the Association of Life Insurance Medical Directors in 1889 and through that organization contributed to sound underwriting developments.

Although a doctor's examination was part of the earliest requirements for Mutual Benefit insurance, it was very elementary as will be recalled from previous comment. In 1874 the Company began requiring a chemical urinalysis report in connection with applications for more than $10,000. This was still a rather uncommon test for when the Company announced its requirement it sent all examiners a pamphlet of complete instructions as "a useful guide for those inexperienced in making such examinations."

In 1886 reports of chemical urinalyses were required as part of all medical examinations, as today. At the same time microscopical examinations were adopted for applications over $10,000. This again was ahead of the times for some examiners, for one wrote:

> I do not own a microscope and have had no experience in the use of the same but I will borrow one from my fellow practitioners and will report my findings.

From the beginning, information about vaccination for smallpox was a required part of the application. Apparently if the applicant had not been vaccinated or refused to have a vaccination the Company declined to issue insurance or limited the protection. This came to mind in an interesting way a few years ago when New Jersey had a smallpox scare. A local policyholder wrote:

> My policy (bought in 1895) carries a smallpox waiver on account of not being vaccinated. I was very foolish to do such a thing, but we do such things when we are young. I have been vaccinated twice now, both took. The first took well, leaving a large scar, the second was light, being only a small scar.
>
> I ask that you please advise me if the waiver can be annulled now, and what will be necessary for me to do to make it null and void. The policy is 52 years old and I would not like to have it as it is, if it can be changed.

The Company replied that rules in regard to smallpox vaccination had been liberalized in 1924 and the changes retroactively benefited all policyholders. He could rest easy that the Company now would pay the claim if he died of smallpox.

Two decades after 1880 saw developments too in Company investments. Experience in local city mortgages had been disappointing and new opportunities were sought. A special committee was appointed to "go West for the purpose of making enquiries and reporting upon the expediency of the Company making loans on Bond and Mortgage and Real Estate in the Western States." The report was favorable, and the first of multimillion dollar streams of capital began to flow from Newark to distant parts of the country.

The first four Western city mortgage loans were all made in 1882. Two were in St. Joseph, Missouri; and one each in Evansville, Indiana, and Chicago.

The first farm mortgage was for $500 on 159 acres in Buchanan County, Missouri, valued at $5,000. At the opening of the Company's National Farm Loan Office at Ames, Iowa, in 1954, the early farm loan activities were described as follows:

> As early as 1882, Mutual Benefit Life was sending funds into the great western farm region which later was to become known worldwide as the "Corn Belt." Money was needed to build this reputation and it was needed to construct farm buildings, to drain swamps, to lay tile, to clear cut-over timber lands in this magnificent country with its dark rich soil. A young and vigorous region was pushing ahead. It was doing it with Mutual Benefit dollars, and with funds supplied by others who had the courage and the foresight to see what hard-working, courageous young farmers were accomplishing.
>
> In those early days, farm loans were made through financial correspondents. These men were actually farm mortgage "circuit riders." A horse and buggy took them down dirt roads to secure loan applications, and to make appraisals. When their straw valises were filled, the mortgages were taken East to the money markets and there they were sold. It was through purchases of mortgages from such firms that Mutual Benefit Life started in the farm lending field.
>
> The Company's farm portfolio increased rapidly, and in 1900, only eighteen years after the first farm loan was made west of the Alleghanies, it exceeded $24,000,000.

The period of the 1880's and 1890's brought also an important development of the Company's policy contract. Mr. Dodd had been the leader in establishing the nonforfeiture system of 1879 as previously described. Mr. Miller had been associated with him in working out the new plan and naturally was imbued with the Mutual Benefit ideal of improving Company service to old policyholders and new members. Mr. Miller in turn, apparently became recognized in the life insurance industry as the exponent of contract liberality, as was reflected in the appraisal of him by his contemporaries at the time of his death. This is an interesting illustration of the continuity of idealism and standards of stewardship in the Company. Each generation, nurtured in the councils of its predecessor, coming to its own time of leadership, assays the values of what has been done. Each succeeding generation then discards the dross and builds into its own operations what has proved true.

In 1882 a new policy form was adopted which removed all restrictions as to residence and travel after three years. In 1886 the contract was again revised and tables were included showing specific figures for loan and extended insurance and paid-up values. In 1895 cash value figures were written into the contract. All these changes were made retroactive to old policyholders. Line upon line they built the Mutual Benefit defense against policyholder forfeitures.

In the 1892 contract had appeared for the first time the provision that "this policy while in force will participate annually in the Company's distribution of surplus." Dividends, of course, had been promised in the prospectus from the beginning.

In 1900 the Company made a major and complete revision of the contract. One very important change was the increase of the reserve basis from 4% to 3%. In his announcement Mr. Dodd stated:

> As is well-known by private investors and financial institutions, there has been a marked reduction during the last two or three years in the rates of interest obtainable on investments such as Bonds and Mortgages, and Railroad and Municipal Bonds.

The changed reserve basis meant that conservative management felt that it was no longer safe to assume that 4% could be earned on the Company's reserves. With only 3% assumed as the growth from interest earnings, reserves must henceforth be larger to guarantee the final results promised.

The 1900 contract also granted grace in the payment of premiums without interest and made the benefit retroactive.

Most important, from the service point of view, was the inclusion in this 1900 edition of the contract of a series of "Special Privileges." The first gave the policyholder the right to change the beneficiary. This, of course, had been allowed previously but had not been stated in the contract.

Special Privilege 2 gave the beneficiary the right, in case of a claim, to request the Company to hold the proceeds and pay an "annuity of three per cent." Provision was made to allow the withdrawal of the fund at the end of any year and ending the "annuity." This was, of course, a version of the present settlement option of proceeds held at interest.

Special Privilege 3 gave the beneficiary under a claim the right to have proceeds paid in annual instalments (up to thirty) rather than as a lump sum. Interest of 3% was guaranteed in calculating the instalments.

Such was the beginning of income settlements for life policies. The Company had previously offered special income policies of several sorts. First was in 1890, a form known as an optional endowment. In this contract the insured had the privilege at maturity of having the endowment proceeds held at 4% interest payable to him, with payment of the proceeds at his death. The maturing endowment was exchanged for a "paid-up life and annuity certificate" which provided for that arrangement. It is interesting that in the year this new endowment plan was put on the market, an old form endowment purchased in 1870 matured. For that policy also the insured was granted the settlement of the paid-up life and annuity certificate planned for maturities under the new policy form. Again old policyholders were getting benefits offered to new members.

Another experiment was the instalment bond which was issued beginning in 1893. This contract provided for the face amount of the policy to be payable at death in equal annual instalments for a limited number of years. It was the forerunner of the plan offered under Special Privilege 3.

A few handwritten individual income settlement agreements have been found in old policies, dating from before 1890. Very frequently in Company history new privileges were incorporated in the policy only after the benefit had been a matter of practice for some time.

A further illustration of this occurs in connection with income agreements. An advertisement of the Company in 1905 describes the Special Privileges 2 and 3 and adds another offer:

> When requested the Company will append to its Policies Supplemental Agreements providing for the payment of Continuous Instalments of an amount depending upon the age of the Beneficiary at the maturity of the Policy.

This plan of settlement was not incorporated in the policy contract until 1908. This also is the first use of the term "supplemental agreements" which were to become so important in Company service.

When the Special Privileges were incorporated in the new policies, the Company made them available also under old policies. Printed forms were furnished old policyholders for adding these benefits to their old contracts.

While the Company was growing steadily in size and service exciting things were happening nationally. Some of these events brought the need for decision on matters of principle.

The moral leadership of President Dodd in his own day and the importance of the precedents which he established for following generations appear in connection with the national presidential campaign of 1896. William Jennings Bryan of Nebraska was campaigning for free silver. Financial leaders in the East were much disturbed by what they considered the threat to sound money. Campaign funds to defeat Bryan were solicited vigorously.

Among the directors of the Mutual Benefit Life there was some disposition for the Company to contribute to this war chest. Mr. Dodd personally was strongly in favor of defeating free silver. However, he emphasized to the board the trust character of their responsibility to policyholders. He pointed out the undoubted difference of opinion on this issue among the members of the Company. He asserted that it would be a downright breach of trust to devote any part of policyholders' funds to a partisan political purpose. So strongly did he feel that he announced that he would be obliged to resign his office if any contribution were made from Company funds. No contribution was made, and again adherence to strict principles of trusteeship spared the Company from later criticism. Other large Eastern companies which did contribute faced serious charges on this issue.

In 1896 gold was discovered in the Yukon Territory of Alaska and the Klondike rush began the next year. "Walrusia" and "Seward's Icebox" as it had been called by political enemies in 1867 when Alaska was purchased for two cents an acre, was proving a national asset. Of course Company policyholders were among the gold rush adventurers, free to go with no hazard to their life insurance under policies owned for more than three years.

One interesting claim was on the life of William Miller who for many years was teller of the Citizens National Bank of Winchester, Kentucky. In the winter of 1897–1898 Mr. Miller went to Alaska and died there at the Seattle Hotel in the city of Skaguay on March 1, 1898. Claim was made under Mr. Miller's $2,000 Mutual Benefit Life policy, which incidentally had lapsed, and protection at the time was being continued under the nonforfeiture system.

Inadequate proof first was offered that the man who died and William Miller of Kentucky were the same person. Therefore a representative of the family who had known Mr. Miller for many years in Winchester, went to Skaguay the following summer and had the body exhumed. He testified that "he immediately recognized said body to be the body of William Miller," that he "caused a photograph of said body to be taken in the cemetery immediately after the corpse was taken from the grave." He also took from the body a pair of linen cuffs with identifying marks which he described. The cuffs and the photographs of the corpse in the coffin are now in the Company files. The claim was paid.

In the spring of 1898 American tongues were reciting the doggerel:

> *Dewy was the morning upon the first of May;*
> *Dewey was the Admiral, down in Manila Bay;*
> *Dewy were the regent's eyes, those royal orbs of blue.*
> *Do we feel discouraged? I do not think we do.*

The Spanish-American War was in progress. Admiral Dewey had just destroyed the Spanish fleet in the Battle of Manila. With

Admiral Dewey, commanding his flagship, the U.S.S. *Olympia,*[*]
was a Mutual Benefit Life policyholder, Captain C. V. Gridley. His
name has been famous for years since it was to him that Admiral
Dewey spoke his much quoted words, just before the battle opened:
"You may fire when ready, Gridley."

The Spanish War began and ended during the year. President
Dodd summarized Company experience in his report to policyholders the next year and reported the death of Captain Gridley.

> When the war with Spain was imminent the Company announced
> its readiness to give permits, upon applications therefor, to those
> insured by policies that had been previously issued, to engage in the
> naval and military service of the United States, without extra
> premium or charge. This offer did not extend to those applying for
> policies after the war was declared and proposing to engage in such
> service. To such applicants the amount of insurance was limited to
> $2,000 in each case and for it an extra charge was made of 5 per cent
> of the amount insured. . . . Three deaths were considered to be
> direct results of the war. . . . A fourth, and a notable death in the
> naval service, was that of Captain Charles V. Gridley, of Erie, Penn-
> sylvania, insured August 12th, 1873, for $5,000, then a naval officer
> 29 years of age. In March, 1897, he was ordered to the Asiatic
> squadron, and on July 28th, 1897, assigned to the U.S.S. "Olympia,"
> which at the naval battle before Manila, May 1st, 1898, was the
> flagship of Admiral Dewey. Captain Gridley, then in command, had
> been and then was sick, but wished to remain on the bridge with
> the Admiral during the fight. The Admiral would not risk losing all
> the senior officers by one shell, and sent him to the conningtower.
> These circumstances appear in the proofs of loss, from which it
> further appears that the roar of his own and the enemy's guns
> affected the sick commander, so far aggravating his disease that
> he was invalided soon after and ordered home. On the way
> from Hong Kong to Kobe, in Japan, June 5th, he died from cirrhosis
> of the liver, with extensive hemorrhage of the bowels. His death is
> stated by the attending Surgeon-General in his certificate accom-
> panying the proofs to have been much hastened by, if not due
> entirely to his exertions and excitement in the battle. His remains
> were buried at Erie, the place of his home. His age was 54.

In the fifty-fifth annual report to policyholders, distributed in
1900, President Dodd tabulated the record of the progress of the
Company during his presidency. From 1882 through to 1900

[*] It was the U.S.S. *Olympia* which brought the body of the Unknown Soldier home
from France to Washington in 1921. On the deck of the ship, outlined in brass tacks,
were the footprints of Admiral Dewey when he gave his famous order to Captain
Gridley.

the number of policies and the amount of insurance owned and the Company assets showed an increase each year in every item. Ownership more than doubled to 106,178 policies for $265,266,269 in 1900; and assets also increased from $34,000,000 to about $69,500,000.

During these years also he commented frequently about the advanced age attained by policyholders. He mentioned "Benjamin C. Miller, in his 98th year; and Caleb Baldwin, in his 101st year, both of Newark, New Jersey, . . . to be seen walking daily in our streets with steps indicative of years yet to come."

With the current interest in gerontology a further quotation from Mr. Dodd's message to policyholders is timely.

> The foregoing statistics of longevity may be noted in passing as more pleasantly suggestive to Americans approaching elderly years than the observations of our famous countryman, Mr. Hawthorne, while Consul in Liverpool. Of a visit to Stratford-on-Avon he writes: "Here, too (as so often impressed me in English towns), there appeared to be a greater abundance of aged people wearing small clothes and leaning on sticks than you could assemble on our side of the water by sounding a trumpet and proclaiming a reward for the most venerable. I tried to account for this phenomenon by several theories, as, for example, that our new towns are unwholesome for age, and kill it off unreasonably; or that our old men have a subtle sense of fitness, and die of their own accord rather than live in an unseemly contrast with youth and novelty; but the secret may be, after all, that hair dyes, false teeth, modern arts of dress, and contrivances of a skin-deep youthfulness have not crept into these antiquated English towns, and so people grow old without the weary necessity of seeming younger than they are."

CHAPTER SEVEN

The Tontine Battle

DURING THE LAST QUARTER OF THE nineteenth century a new cycle of competition and contrast developed between the Mutual Benefit Life and most of the rest of the life insurance business. The issue this time was tontine dividends. The scheme was inspired by a plan offered by Lorenzo Tonti, a Neapolitan banker, to mend the fortunes of Louis XIV. French investors were invited to buy into a fund that would pay no return currently but would yield very large profits to those still living after a certain period of years. The idea proved so popular with seventeenth-century speculators that the name and the device have continued to this day.

One life insurance company in New York conceived the idea of a tontine plan for life insurance dividends. Instead of making refunds of premiums currently to policyholders, the company proposed holding dividends through a period of years and then dividing the fund among those policyholders who had not died or lapsed. The idea caught popular imagination. Fires of speculation were fed by extravagant promises of probable results. Competition was unscrupulous and furious. Naturally the first tontine pressures were felt by Mutual Benefit Life representatives in the field. About the time these troubles began a committee reported to the board of directors about the field organization as follows:

> The Agency system commenced with the organization of the Company. Through the agencies nearly all applications have been

received, policies issued, premiums collected, losses and dividends paid, and members communicated with from all departments; new rules and regulations have been made from time to time intended to improve and perfect the system, and at the present time it seems that all branches of the Company are inseparably connected with the agencies. . . . The State and District Agencies number 39 and are located in all sections where the Company conducts business, connected with and subordinated to them are 235 local agents and solicitors commissioned by the Company and subject to their rules. . . .

Mr. Dodd reported to policyholders:

The localities in which the Company's appointed and active agencies are placed, are Maine, New Hampshire, Massachusetts, Rhode Island, Connecticut, New York, New Jersey, Pennsylvania, Ohio, Maryland, West Virginia, District of Columbia, Illinois, Michigan, Wisconsin, Iowa, Minnesota, Nebraska, Missouri, Colorado, California, Oregon, Nevada, Kentucky, and the central and eastern parts of Tennessee.

The indoctrination which these representatives, as well as policyholders, received is indicated by quotations from President Dodd's reports to policyholders.

The non-forfeiture character of the Company's contracts is a constant and complete satisfaction, and is found by experience to be in every way advantageous to the members and the Company. . . . It is at variance with the views on which what are called the Tontine methods of insurance proceed, which look more or less to the losses by forfeiture from some of the insured as a source of success to the Company, and of anticipated gains to some of its members at the sacrifice of other members.

These methods have not been adopted or approved by this Company and are in fact inconsistent with the general policy and purposes which it seeks to promote. With those who approve and practice the Tontine methods we have no controversy and no competition. The insurance which this Company offers and for which it finds a growing and satisfactory demand, is to those who desire indemnity against the evils of untimely death: who desire it at the least outlay of money compatible with the highest security: who wish to make use when they need it of the accumulated funds in the hands of the Company belonging to their policies, either by way of loan to keep up their premiums, or to meet some exigency in their affairs: and who when no longer desirous to keep up their policies, can avail themselves of their value without inconvenience or loss by a surrender or exchange. The Company's aim and its endeavor is to give to every one of its members a full equivalent for all that is paid to it: and in what form this equivalent shall be given, is left as largely as practicable to the option of the policy-holders themselves.

He who is blessed with long life contributes under the mutual association to pay the policy of the insured who fall by untimely death. This beneficent mutuality of interest and agreement, based on an observed natural law, applicable with mathematical certainty to the whole body of members, frees the contract from the vicious taint of betting on the side of an individual member, and makes it a matter of scientific certainty on the side of the associated members as a whole. A legitimate policy contract stands on the intent that the fortunate are to be the benefactors of the unfortunate. In mutual insurance there is no place for an inequality of benefits or payments which indemnity against death does not necessarily require. The immoral element of lottery gains, however alluring, is excluded. Holding this view of the true nature of life insurance, we have never regarded with approval the Tontine system, wherein this mutuality is impaired, and forfeitures by those who die early, or are disabled by adversities, become the gains of their more favored associates. Our methods are studiously adapted to an opposite result. Every year's experience adds to the satisfaction we have in conducting the business on these methods. Our members universally approve them. Twelve years of trial have proved, beyond dispute, that their operation is beneficial to the policy-holders and to the Company.

Yearly distributions of surplus enable our members to maintain their policies with the least requisite outlay of cash. Whatever moneys are not needed for the unquestionable security of the Company's contracts are surplus. Its retention by the Directors does not aid them in the fulfillment of their duties as trustees. Its retention is an unnecessary burden. Its distribution tends to promote careful, economical management. It furnishes to the policy-holders the criteria for judging the management. It is unfavorable to, and preventive of extravagant expenditures, of excessive salaries and excessive commissions. It does not keep the policy-holders in ignorance or doubt as to the actual cost of their policies, but enables them to know it clearly and definitely each year. As beneficiaries they are entitled to such yearly accountings from those who are charged with their interests, and are conducting their affairs. If they are dissatisfied, they can, under our system, surrender their policies and withdraw on just and equitable terms. This relation of the members to the Company is increasingly satisfactory to both, and while it exists tends naturally and strongly to the prosperity and growth of the business.

Burton J. Hendrick, the classic historian of this age of life insurance history, wrote:

Amzi Dodd

FREDERICK FRELINGHUYSEN

Only three companies kept themselves entirely free from Tontine: the Mutual Benefit of New Jersey, the Connecticut Mutual of Hartford, and the Provident Life and Trust of Philadelphia. . . . Dodd's great contribution to life insurance is the non-forfeiture plan adopted by the Mutual Benefit in 1879. . . . Naturally he abhorred the Tontine System. . . . He made non-forfeiture the prevailing idea of the Mutual Benefit. . . . He made no hysterical bids for new business; he did desire, however, a steady and healthy growth. He would not meet the high commissions paid in New York, but he did pay slightly more than Greene * and made more popular agents' contracts. His company thus acquired the reputation of being progressive without adopting the excesses of the time. Thus Amzi Dodd succeeded† where Greene had failed; he increased the size of his company. He also kept the Mutual Benefit free from scandal.

So the pressures increased. To strengthen home office leadership for the agencies, which for many years had been the responsibility of general executives of the Company, Mr. Dodd appointed a superintendent of agencies in 1896. He chose Lucius D. Drewry, who had been for a decade a successful Mutual Benefit Life salesman in Tennessee and North Carolina. Mr. Drewry remained at the home office only a year and then went back to the thick of the battle. He became general agent for Ohio, Tennessee, Alabama and Mississippi, with headquarters at Cincinnati and Chattanooga. He laid the foundation for a generation of strong representation of the Company in that area, and brought into the business his nephew, James Sutton Drewry, who became one of the greatest builders of creative salesmen the business has ever seen.

After nearly thirty-nine strenuous years of service President Dodd announced to the board his desire "to commit to younger hands" the executive leadership of the Company. Thus Frederick Frelinghuysen was elected president January 20, 1902.

The local newspapers of course made much of the noteworthy current event, and their comments are still heartwarming.

To almost every resident of Newark, the terms "Mutual Benefit Life

---

* President of the Connecticut Mutual.

† Mr. Dodd won for the Mutual Benefit Life the name of "The Policyholders' Company," which it was to feature proudly down the years of the future. The words were used in 1896 in a joint report by the supervising authorities of New York and New Jersey: "The Company's policy contracts are very liberal, and its treatment of policyholders is, if possible, even more so. It is, in the fullest sense of the word, a policyholders' company, and is administered solely in their interest."

Insurance Company, Amzi Dodd, President," have been synonyms of strength, success, probity and reliability

That a man of seventy-nine years old should desire to lay down the task of caring for $74,000,000 assets and running a business of $15,000,000 a year is not remarkable. . . . He is probably as well fitted for the duty as ever, for his health is excellent and his wonderful intellectual powers are unabated. . . . It was undoubtedly made easier for him by the fact that Frederick Frelinghuysen, his associate in the business and the son of his old friend and law partner, was to be his successor, and the wise and conservative policy which has marked the conduct of his great enterprise will be continued.

While he has planned his life with deliberate care, to get the best that life could give him and to make the most of his capacities, he has also been a very human, sympathetic and practical person. And none need ask a better friend or kindlier, more charitable and liberal adviser and helper in life's struggles.

Dr. Ward's comments about Mr. Frelinghuysen and his ancestors give us a good background for understanding the Company's new leader.

Frederick Frelinghuysen was of Dutch descent. Among the colonizers of the New World the Dutch occupied a foremost position. They were hardy mariners and they were also thrifty merchants. . . .

They brought with them from the old country the Dutch Reformed Church, and in the settlements which they established, the church was always a prominent feature. In 1719, there came from Holland to a church of one of these Dutch settlements in Raritan, New Jersey, a young divine lately ordained, Theodorus Jacobus Frelinghuysen, who was destined to be the founder of one of the most remarkable families in American history. It gave to the state and nation in six generations, besides many profound scholars and distinguished preachers, two soldiers of the rank of General in the Revolution and War of 1812, a member of the Continental Congress, two Attorneys-General of the State of New Jersey, a nominee for Vice-President of the United States, a Secretary of State of the United States, four United States Senators, three college presidents, an acting Governor, and a Mayor of the City of Newark. All of these soldiers and statesmen were also distinguished for their good works of religion and philanthropy.

The new president, Frederick Frelinghuysen, was son of Frederick T. Frelinghuysen, who had been United States Senator and Secretary of State, and from 1878 to 1885 had served as director of the Mutual Benefit Life.

Frederick Frelinghuysen was graduated from Rutgers University with high honors, studied law and became a banker. As president of Newark's Howard Savings Institution, then New Jersey's largest mutual savings bank, he was elected a Mutual Benefit Life director in 1891. So he came to the Company presidency with a rich background of experience and a specific acquaintance with Company ideals and operations.

Mr. Frelinghuysen announced promptly his intention

> . . . to administer the affairs of the Company upon the same general conservative lines that have in the past earned for the Company its high reputation for economy, prudence and regard for the individual equities and interests of its policyholders, avoiding all entangling alliances with other financial institutions, and all plans which do not legitimately appertain to the business of Life Insurance conducted on the principle of the greatest good to the greatest number of its policyholders.

Mr. Frelinghuysen came to the presidency near the end of a period which Historian Hendrick characterized as thirty-five years of "progressive degeneration" and "constant warfare between the good and the bad in life insurance."

Trading on the gambling instinct, leaders of several companies especially promoted their tontine schemes with wildest extravagance. The ferocity of the race for size and the brazen disregard of principle were incredible. To build their business they paid commissions beyond all actuarial justification, with increasing bonuses and prizes for larger sales which led to overwhelming sales pressures, rebating and many attendant evils. As the business increased, huge surpluses accumulated for which the day of accounting was in the far future. With these policyholder funds, unscrupulous officers paid enormous salaries to the favored, did lavish entertaining, bought pretentious real estate, influenced legislators, manipulated investments—until the stench of life insurance rottenness became an offense to the nation. One president publicly boasted that he cared not at all about the kind of life insurance he sold; his only object was to be the world's biggest company.

The fires of these years hardened the steel of the Mutual Benefit Life field organization. An army of crusaders developed. They presented the claims of the Company with the fervor of evangelism.

At this time, in 1903, the Company's magazine, *The Pelican,* came into being. The editor was Alfred A. Drew, a young man who had begun his life insurance career in 1895 in St. Louis, as an agent for the Company. Through *The Pelican* Mr. Drew provided ammunition for a militant field force. He made the magazine the mouthpiece of Mutual Benefit idealism and an aggressive sales philosophy. Each issue quoted policyholders and insurance authorities as to the superiority of the Company. Many said the Mutual Benefit Life was the best life insurance company. Others said the Mutual Benefit was the best after their own. Accompanying such a comment was a quotation from Jonathan Swift, "It is a maxim that those to whom everybody allows the second place have an undoubted title to first." Mr. Drew in *The Pelican* presented comparative figures showing the advantages of Mutual Benefit protection over other specifically named companies. He delighted to give case studies of results under tontine policy maturities. Many of these not only showed values far below the fabulous promises of twenty years before, but also poorer than the record of the Mutual Benefit which had paid annual dividends with no chance of forfeiture along the way.

Naturally everybody in the Mutual Benefit Life felt personally justified and avenged for the sufferings of a generation, when the sins of the offending companies caught up with them. This was the end of a second cycle of Mutual Benefit defense of sound life insurance operations. Judgment came in the New York State legislative

investigation which began in 1905. This was known variously as the Armstrong Investigation, because Senator William Armstrong headed the investigating committee; or the Hughes Investigation, because Charles Evans Hughes, later Chief Justice of the United States, was its counsel.

The committee held fifty-seven continuous hearings from September through December. In those days there was no television to bring the investigation into every home across the land. The newspapers and the weekly magazines, however, made the life insurance scandals household talk. The pointed pens of the cartoonist made the chief ideas of inquiry clear to those who needed pictures. The accompanying drawing shows how a contemporary cartoonist satirized the flagrant nepotism of the big companies then reaping justifiable criticism.

The companies were most searchingly questioned about their records and practices in four general areas.

First, as to the actual control of the business and the responsibility of directors and trustees as a check on management officers.

Second, as to investments, particularly in relation to real benefits for policyholders.

Third, as to expenses which had become both unjustifiably extravagant and including very dubious fees for lobbying.

Fourth, as to dividends.

Mr. Hughes and the committee had the task of analyzing the facts brought out in the investigation and formulating recommendations based upon them. Naturally in his study of life insurance affairs he became impressed with the Mutual Benefit Life experience and when the time came to work out basic legislation he asked for help from Mr. Edward E. Rhodes, then Company mathematician. At the time of Mr. Hughes' death in 1948 Mr. Rhodes reminisced about that experience. He said that he took up temporary residence at a hotel in New York City. The work of the committee was done at Mr. Hughes' home on West End Avenue. The group would meet at ten in the morning, adjourn for lunch and dinner and usually work until ten o'clock at night. Sometimes, however, it was two o'clock in the morning before the men finally put aside their labors, and then Mr. Hughes often would have some work he wanted done between adjournment that night and the meeting the next day.

When the new legislation was finally adopted, it altered the course of life insurance history. The State of New York henceforth applied the highest standards in life insurance company regulation and it has become one mark of sound operation to be a New York-licensed company.

Mr. Frelinghuysen's reports to policyholders naturally referred to these momentous events. In 1906 he wrote:

> It is gratifying to state that the year 1905 has been one of our most prosperous years, and though life insurance has been "on the rack" and the insuring public has never before been so competent and anxious to thoroughly know the business, we have prospered as seldom before, in the amount of new business written and the savings on death losses, and everything tending to make up success in the Company.
>
> Probably never have so many men understood what good business in life insurance is, as today.
>
> The recent legislative investigation in New York has brought to light many abuses which have crept into the business of life insurance.
>
> This Company has been called upon for and has furnished detailed statements of every phase of its business and expected to testify to the details.
>
> The inquiries submitted to us were as to our securities, of whom purchased, the date of purchase and the price; as to our loans, to whom made, when, and at what rate of interest; as to our agents' contracts, which were shown to be identical with every agent; as to our policy contracts, which were shown to be more liberal than those of any other company; as to our legal and legislative expenses, which were found to be entirely within the limits of propriety and to involve no suspicious or improper object; as to our salaries, which were shown to be most moderate. The returns of this Company were frequently used as a standard for purposes of comparison with other companies. We deeply regret we were not accorded a showing at the investigation, but with nothing to explain away, and with no rumors or suspicions to allay, we could not demand a hearing. . . .
>
> The confidence of the public in the Company is greater than ever, and our good name has prevailed through all the misgivings among the insuring public.
>
> The revelations of the investigation disturbed public confidence in life insurance, and we probably suffered somewhat from a general distrust in all companies, but it was more than made up by the discrimination of the more intelligent and discerning public. The principles of annual dividends, of small expenses, of isolation from other financial institutions, of an absolute and simple fiduciary administration of the Company have been more than endorsed, not only by the public, but by every committee which has sought thor-

oughly to reform the business of life insurance. We have always held to no partnership with trust funds, and it has saved not only our individual, but our Company's good name. . . .

The disturbed conditions in life insurance will doubtless soon subside, and good come of the disturbance. It may be safely said that life insurance, its theory and its honest administration have passed through the ordeal unscathed, and that men, rather than life insurance, have been found wanting. When fidelity and honesty and wisdom have been applied to the business, the policyholders have prospered.

WITH NEPOTISM RULING LIFE INSURANCE CONCERNS, HOW CAN A POLICY HOLDER ESCAPE WALKING PLANK?

The end of the story was summarized the next year:

> During the year 1906 we have written and revived $61,607,702 insurance, the largest business we have ever done, a very satisfactory result, and reached by no departure from our long-established conservatism in selection of risks,—moderate amount of insurance on any one life—and moderate commissions.
>
> Our policies have called for no change by reason of new demands made by recent or pending legislation, as they contain all of, and more than the privileges recently demanded. We have had to issue no policies changing the form for dissatisfied policyholders.
>
> There has been anxiety as to what would be required of the Company by legislation, but so far nothing has been required of it more than the Company has always given. Pending legislation calls for reduction of premiums, but not to so low a figure as we have. . . .
>
> The business of the Company for the year, the largest in its history, was done through the unusual zeal of our agents, who had to contend with the public's disturbed confidence in all life insurance, and with the extraordinary efforts of companies which appreciated that 1906 was the last year in which they could do business free from the stipulations of the Armstrong Law. . . .
>
> With the injection into the field of numerous small state companies appealing to state pride and local feeling, the business of the old and established companies has been subjected to extra competition. We have not changed our first year's commissions, and we must restrict ourselves, as we always have, to the interests of our present policyholders rather than reach out after new business at too great an expense to our present members. For years we have followed this conservative course . . .
>
> In considering proposed legislation, the New York Legislative Investigating Committee and other bodies made use of the plans and practices of this Company. The history of the Company and the propriety of the conduct of its business, its low expense rate and low premium rates, have been favorably commented upon by such bodies, and at their request the Company's Mathematician spent considerable time during the year conferring with them and advising them regarding proposed measures. It is pleasing to know that at this time the Company is so generally turned to as having the standard according to which other companies might with advantage to the public transact their business.

In the troubled years from 1880 through 1905, Company annual production increased from about $13,000,000 to $61,000,000. Insurance in force grew steadily, year by year, from $121,466,979 to $392,548,092. Little wonder that the Company now was prepared to enter upon a period of accelerated expansion and success.

CHAPTER EIGHT

Through World War I

WITH THE COMPANY'S STEADILY growing business at the turn of the century the elegant brownstone building, even with its several additions, became just too small. Therefore beginning in 1905 a new building was erected on the old site. The work was done in sections over a period of years, office operations being shifted with the demolitions and constructions. George B. Post of New York was the architect.

An old record book of the committee handling details of the building project gives a number of interesting items. In 1905 for temporary day's work for "maintaining communications by telephone and call bells and for temporary lighting during building operations," the foreman got $7 a day; the journeyman, $6; and the helper, $4. There was also correspondence with the "Water Board" of the city about the need for "high pressure water service" for the "high" building.

The finished seven-story white granite and marble edifice had a one-hundred-foot façade on Broad Street with four huge pillars running from the top of the first floor to the top of the fifth. The sixth floor was a "blind" vault room. The building was nearly two hundred feet deep along Clinton Street. The Company occupied the top six floors of the finished building in 1908 and remained there until 1927.

A part of one of the handsome marble columns of this building and its beautiful Corinthian capital, may still be seen standing on the campus of the School of Architecture at the University of Michigan at Ann Arbor. Colonel William Starrett, a University alumnus, was instrumental in sending these "fragments" to the architectural garden at Ann Arbor. He was a member of Starrett Brothers, contractors for the new home office which followed that marble building.

Beneath its granite and marble the building was of hollow tile construction. The architect reported that that had proved especially strong in the recent San Francisco testings of fire and earthquake.

A feature of the building was a broad marble entrance corridor from which ascended a massive bronze-railed stairway, placed, according to the directors' minutes, "to be as important and striking as practicable." The stairway continued, though with less elegance, to the seventh floor, and was for many years the scene of a cherished Company tradition. The day before Christmas a group of Company singers slowly descended the great stairway caroling the old hymns. "Adeste Fidelis," "Hark, the Herald Angels Sing" and other favorites for a little while stilled the typewriter and the adding machine.

Naturally the occupancy of this new building gave rise to news stories in the insurance press, one of which is interesting:

> The Mutual Benefit Life is now comfortably housed in its new building. This is an interesting fact, but it derives its interest from the vastly larger fact that the company is an interesting company. It is large. It is honorable. It is useful, and it has always been both honorable and useful. . . .
>
> Be thou chaste as snow and clear as light, thou shalt not escape calumny. In a world where no person can expect to avoid being somewhat misjudged, an insurance company cannot expect to please in every single instance; yet the Mutual Benefit is one which has never been publicly accused of any fault, and if there is a company

which has been less denounced or blamed in private we have not heard of that fortunate one. This has truly been a policyholder's company. Its name is so expressive, and its career has been so honorable, that no company in the field has been more often complimented by having some sham organization seek to have itself mistaken for the genuine by partly copying the title. The people—and they are many indeed—who maintain that this is really the one best life insurance company in the field doubtless cannot convince everybody else; but they are honestly of that belief, and they have very substantial reasons for asserting it.

The new building gave more commodious facilities for the addition to the staff of women employees. The first record of a woman employee was in 1862. Another was mentioned in 1863 and in 1868 Miss Cordelia O. Ross joined the Company and worked until retirement in 1910 at the age of 70. From time to time an occasional other woman appears in the list of clerks.

The Company adopted a general policy of hiring women workers in the spring of 1909. One of the Company's veteran women employees today recalls that when she came to the Company in January 1910 she was the sixteenth girl in the Company employ. She took the last place at the second of two dinner tables seating eight girls each. She recalls that the others were young people like herself, except three "old ladies" who had worked in the brownstone building.

Twenty-three officers were on the home office staff by the end of 1910, and 233 clerks, 49 of whom were women. At this time separate dining rooms were established for women, for male clerks and for officers. All had colored waiters until the manpower shortage of wartime when the first waitresses were brought in. Meals were served family style with a set menu, but anyone might substitute roast beef if he did not like the daily entree.

Having women workers in the office was not without its distractions. On one occasion in these early days the Mutual Benefit Life broke into print with a sensational news story. Agents from Chicago to Boston sent clippings to the home office wanting to know "What happened?"

A vice president's official answer was this:

We have not attempted, and do not propose to attempt, to lay down any rule other than that our young women shall dress modestly. With very few exceptions this rule has been complied with by the entire staff.

> We employ a woman who exercises a general supervision over the conduct in the office of the women employees. If one of the clerks affects a style of dress which is not suitable for a business office, she is spoken to by this supervisor. Generally this is sufficient; but we had one offender who did not listen to such admonition, and the writer, therefore, talked with the young woman. In some way unknown to us, knowledge of the incident was acquired by one of the Newark papers, which proceeded to embellish and publish it.

The famous Dorothy Dix mentioned the affair, approving the Company, in her nationally read column. Her description of offending girls she had observed in business offices makes us wonder how she would survive a visit to us today. She wrote:

> Everyone has seen that something should be done to curb the dress mania in girls . . . but no one has known what to do about it. Shocked old ladies have held up their hands in horror over skirts that climbed higher and higher toward the knee line and stockings that get thinner and thinner until they have almost reached the vanishing point.
> When you went into an office you couldn't tell whether the fluffy-headed maiden in gorgeous array that you beheld at the typewriter was the millionaire proprietor's daughter on her way to a party or a poor working girl trying to earn an honest living. . . .
> When she's rigged up in flimsy chiffons, with high heeled slippers on, and with beads rattling and bracelets clinking, she doesn't look like an intelligent human being who would understand her job.

In 1903 the Company had resumed the insuring of women, which had been discontinued after some early poor experience. The limit set was $5,000 ($50,000 was the limit for men at the time), and the female applicant must have her own income and propose to pay her own premiums. In each case the agent was required to send a "Preliminary Statement" to the Company and wait for approval before getting a signed application. Official advice indicated, "Teachers, Stenographers, Typewriters [*sic*], Clerks, Milliners, Dressmakers, Artists, etc., form the most eligible class." It was also promised that "policies on the lives of women will in all respects be similar to policies issued on the lives of men."

In these days of anti-discrimination laws, it is interesting to recall that the Mutual Benefit Life has always insured negroes although with special care in underwriting because of the recognized mortality hazards. As mentioned before, the first negro policyholders of the Mutual Benefit Life were slaves.

In 1906, the Company reported a special study of mortality

covering the years 1890 through 1904, which included 1,383 policies on negro lives. For the first five years in which the effect of selection would be expected to be apparent, the mortality for the negro group was 53.6%. The general experience for the same period was 55.1%.

However, for the sixth through the fifteenth year of the period under study, the negro mortality was 132.3% while the general mortality was 71.5%.

These studies indicated the need for especially careful underwriting of negro risks, but the Company never excluded them completely. Just a couple of years ago the Company paid an interesting claim on the life of a minister, born a slave on a Virginia plantation in 1858. He was educated at Hampton Institute in Virginia, where the son-in-law of Amzi Dodd was president, and in 1904 he bought an ordinary life policy. After years as a teacher and pastor in many parts of the country he was living, well and active, in Washington at age 96. He collected from the Company the proceeds of his own policy, ordinarily payable only at death.

The use of information about blood pressure as an aid to underwriting was begun in 1911. At first only the systolic reading was reported, and it was required only for applicants over age 40 and where more than $15,000 of insurance was involved. In 1915 the report was required for all cases, but diastolic readings were not included until five years later.

The promulgation of the first ruling about blood pressures in 1911 is amusing today:

> After careful investigation this Company will join the list of Life Companies which require a record of systolic Blood-Pressure as part of the regular medical examination, without extra charge.
>
> The sphygmomanometer is now so simple and cheap, its diagnostic and prognostic indications so valuable in medical practice, that its use has become general among progressive physicians, most of whom either own, or can have the use of, the instrument when needed.

As a suggestion to examiners, the circular added that the test should be made "*after* the physical examination is completed and the applicant has regained his composure."

The value of urinalysis had been increasingly recognized through its use for more than a generation. When preservatives were developed which made possible the mailing of specimens to the home office, that was required. At first these were examined by an outside specialist, Dr. Richard N. Connolly. In 1913 the Company established its own laboratory with Dr. Connolly supervising technicians on its own staff.

In 1908 a major labor-saving machine was acquired by the Home Office. This was a Rectigraph for photographing applications. Previously copies required as part of the policy had been written by hand.

During this period the proportion of business each year on the lives of old policyholders increased markedly. President Frelinghuysen referred to the figures with great pride in successive annual reports. The Company limit was raised to $75,000 in 1909 and to $100,000 in 1912.

Mr. Frelinghuysen also reported regularly the proportion of term insurance in the year's production. He wrote in 1909 of "the tendency in life insurance today to increase new business by writing Term insurance" and commented that it "has been discouraged among our agents by admonition from the Home Office from time to time." The admonitions brought excellent results and for the next decade term insurance averaged about half of its previous level.

A new contract form in 1908 again increased Mutual Benefit liberalities. It guaranteed nonforfeiture values whenever the reserve exceeded $10 per $1,000 of insurance. This meant in most cases cash values after the payment of only one annual premium, and in some after only a semi-annual or quarterly premium.

Concerning this change, Mr. Frelinghuysen wrote to the policyholders in his annual report:

> In accordance with the unwritten law which should govern a mutual company, the Board of Directors has by formal action extended to all outstanding policies the benefits secured to persons now insuring under the new policy forms, so far as practicable.

The stir this action caused in life insurance circles is easily imagined from the statement the president made to the policyholders the following year:

> The new values given to our policies this year have been claimed by some to be for the purpose of attracting business—a sordid view to take of the liberalizing of our policies. Such a view might be justified if we had withheld the privileges from millions of outstanding insurance. The effort of this Company has ever been, and in it it has always led, to give every value to each policyholder, which was consistent with conserving the interest and safety of the policy-

holders in general. The new values given properly and justly belong to the policyholders.

These years were proving very successful ones for the Company. The panics of the early 1900's caused no difficulties. Concerning 1903 Mr. Frelinghuysen wrote:

> The decrease in market values while large, in no way reflects on the management of the Company. This depression in the market has been largely in first-class securities, and has been called a rich man's panic, the financial situation requiring that prime securities had to be placed on the market in large numbers. The fundamental principle of our calculations being on a par value, our calculations were in no wise affected by this depreciation of market values, and the depreciation has enabled us to buy good bonds at a reduced price, and will really turn the apparent misfortune to a profit. While estimating our securities at present market values shows a depreciation, the fact that we sold no securities during the year shows that the depreciation caused us no real loss. We buy our securities for permanent investment, and are never compelled to sell at unfavorable times.

At the end of 1907, the president reported:

> The year which has passed has been one of general anxiety to the financial world. Probably no branch of that world has felt the anxiety so little as that of life insurance. In recent years, with all the carping against life insurance, the public might have supposed that it was the most vulnerable, but to-day they know that a life insurance policy is the most liquid asset in hand. We have seen market values of certain lines of investments decline, but we have not given the stability of the Company a moment's anxious thought.

These general financial difficulties contrasting with the stability of life insurance encouraged the growth of income service for life insurance proceeds. Settlement options having been made a part of the Mutual Benefit policy contract adopted in 1900, it is natural that *The Pelican* for the early part of the century included much material about the advantages of income arrangements for policy claims. In 1915, a persuasive article on this subject included the following reflection of economic conditions.

> It is generally admitted that $50. a month is the absolute minimum income on which the average American family can live normally if deprived by death of the husband and father. That means a total of only $600. a year, which may sound small to many men and which is small in that it is the minimum.

Frequently during these years President Frelinghuysen mentioned the service in his reports to policyholders, in 1917 commenting:

> Income insurance has become an important feature in our business, where the insured seek to have the principal of their insurance retained by the Company and with the interest and earnings thereon paid to the beneficiaries in annual or more frequent instalments. . . . During the year we have provided income insurance in the sum of about $20,000,000 about equally divided between new policies so placed originally and old ones changed to that plan.

Success was reflected in the dividend history of these years. The Company three times increased the dividend scale, in 1910, 1912 and 1915; and paid four special dividends, in 1910, 1913, 1914 and 1916. Favorable mortality especially contributed to this good situation.

Still another noteworthy action was the increase in reserves on policies issued before 1900. In 1912 these reserves were brought up to a 3½% basis from their original 4% basis, at an original cost to surplus of over $2,000,000. What all these actions meant in building Company morale and in contributing to Company reputation can be sensed from contemporary reports. The announcement about 1912 plans was made to the New York City agency at a special meeting the day before Thanksgiving in 1911. *The Pelican* reporter pictured that occasion:

> For some time past rumor has been rife that great things might be expected from the Home Office of the Mutual Benefit Life Insurance Company, to take effect on January 1st, 1912, and there has been much speculation as to just what could possibly be added to the plans already in force.
>
> When it was recalled that the Company recently raised its dividend scale and in addition thereto declared a special dividend in 1910 and gives first year values, and has granted extended insurance automatically since 1879, and that it has consistently and persistently practised retroaction, it seemed that there was little the Home Office could give for the new year.
>
> When, therefore, the New York Agency force, one hundred active men, assembled at the Hotel Martinique on Wednesday, November 29th at four o'clock, we little dreamed that Thanksgiving Day was to begin for us many hours earlier than the legal date.

Vice President E. E. Rhodes and others from the home office then announced another dividend increase and the increase of reserves for old policies. Dinner was served where

... the inner man was so well satisfied that we fear many a man had to postpone his Thanksgiving Dinner to the following Sunday. Music and song abounded, all joining in the choruses.

By no means the least enjoyable event of the evening was the summing up of the side lights, the inferences, and practical views of the whole subject, by our General Agent, Mr. Cerf.* He ably impressed the thought, firmly fixed in his own mind, and doubly impressed by the events of the day, that we should be men of conviction because our business is of the highest order; men of enthusiasm because our cause is just; and men of loyalty because our Company is the best.

An outsider's reaction to the Mutual Benefit in 1912 is expressed in an insurance journal of the day:

The Mutual Benefit has furnished one of the greatest sensations in life insurance in recent years. That it is able to increase its reserve and dividends at the same time shows that it has been managed in the past with the greatest wisdom. That it gives to old policyholders, as well as new, the full benefit of its increased gains shows that it senses the true meaning of mutuality, and no policyholder in the Mutual Benefit need fear that his interests will be sacrificed for any purpose whatever.

The mention of Mr. Rhodes as spokesman for the Company at this time is natural. When Mr. B. J. Miller died suddenly in 1905, Mr. Rhodes had been named mathematician. He was at that time quite young and (before his work with Mr. Hughes after the Armstrong Investigation) relatively unknown. Mr. Frelinghuysen announced to policyholders the succession of Mr. Rhodes and added that he was "not only thoroughly equipped with the science of the department, but also imbued with the principles and practices of the Company." Here again is seen that continuity of ideals of management that has proved so favorable for Mutual Benefit Life policyholders.

In 1909 the Actuarial Society of America, of which Mr. Rhodes was a member, and the Association of Life Insurance Medical Directors undertook a broad study of the effect of certain conditions, such as occupation; and of certain impairments, such as overweight, on length of life. Mr. Rhodes was a member of the committee

---

* Mr. Louis A. Cerf, general agent in New York from 1905 to 1927. Mr. Cerf was an orator of the old school, a powerful leader and salesman. Those who remember him can well picture the empassioned speech he must have made following the outline reported.

responsible for this work for some twenty years. The first report of this study, known as the Medico-Actuarial Investigation, was made in 1912 but supplementary research continued for many years. The conclusions of this investigation were of immeasurable value to life underwriting and useful also for life conservation efforts of various kinds.

The twentieth century saw important agency developments in the Mutual Benefit Life. From shortly before the turn of the century began the succession of special officers designated for sales promotion and agency building. *The Pelican* was making Mutual Benefit men, scattered from Maine to California and from Michigan to Texas,* aware of each other; and known to each other, at least by name. *The Pelican* for the first time in 1905 printed an honor roll of the Company's one hundred leading agents for the previous year.

Company officers began more extensive field traveling, agency meetings were held and reported in *The Pelican* in considerable detail. One of the most interesting of such reports was in 1903, concerning "a very enjoyable and equally successful meeting of the Mutual Benefit's Michigan agents . . . to extend a hearty welcome to State Agent A. S. Johnston . . . just returned from a four months' trip abroad, during which . . . he has taken in the Orient and all the principal European cities."

Mr. Johnston had left the agency to the leadership of his cashier, Donald Clark, who "soon after Mr. Johnston sailed from New York, called upon the Agency forces to bend their every energy, individually and collectively, to the end of maintaining the record of production, month by month, that had already been established, holding out no other inducement than that every agent who wrote and paid for a specified amount of new business would be invited to visit Detroit, at the agency's expense, soon after Mr. Johnston's return."

Mr. Clark's promotion was richly successful, and led an observer to predict a great future for the new leadership team.

This was indeed prophecy, for the Johnston and Clark agency became for a generation an outstanding organization. Raleigh R. Stotz, today a dean of Mutual Benefit general agents with an outstanding

---

* The Mutual Benefit had reestablished agencies in a number of southern states around 1890. Because of legislation which the Company considered unfavorable to policyholders generally, it withdrew from operation in Texas and in Wisconsin in 1907.

record of man-and-agency-building, grew up in the Johnston and Clark agency. H. Bruce Palmer, today the honored Company president, was brought into the business by Mr. Clark. Even in these recent heavily scheduled years Mr. Palmer at least once a year visited Mr. Clark in his South Carolina retirement home in tribute to Mr. Clark's part in his own business success.

Many things typical of this early twentieth century era of selling seem quaint today. *The Pelican* reprinted with commendation samples of advertisements run by an agent in New Hampshire. These were parodies of nursery rimes, for example:

BOBBY SHAFTOE'S GONE TO SEA,
well insured his life will be, for two M.B.'s has he, and they both run to me. When he comes back he'll take No. 3.—Bonny Bobby Shaftoe. M. stands for MUTUAL and B. is for BENEFIT. The Company your grandsire was insured in.

Another bit of advertising that became a Company legend was done by an agent in Blackfoot, Idaho. The local businessmen had been asked to participate in a big town parade. This agent had a boy lead a cow in the parade, placarded on each side: "The Accelerative Endowment policy* of the Mutual Benefit Life Insurance Company is the best policy in the world. This is no bull."

The sentimentality of the age seems almost incredible. For instance, *The Pelican* reprinted an advertising leaflet recommended for use at Christmas time. At the top was the photograph of a solemn little curly-haired girl with the following verses, "To My Daughter."

---

* The Accelerative Endowment plan for the use of dividends was unique with the Company. Introduced in 1875, it was popular for fifty years. Under this plan dividends currently were used to change the original policy to an endowment at a progressively early age. From year to year definite notice of a change as made was given the policyholder. An ordinary life policy in those days was actuarially an endowment at age 96. As each successive dividend became payable it was used to advance the maturity date. Thus the policyholder would see the date advance from age 96 to 90, . . . to 67 . . . to 63, etc. Results under the accelerative endowment plan were very favorable, and pleasing to those who lived to receive them. However, since the dividends were used as endowment premiums there was no extra dividend fund payable if the policyholder died before maturity. This created many misunderstandings and the plan was eventually discontinued. Several generations of Mutual Benefit representatives, however, promoted the contract very enthusiastically under the slogan "Endowments at life rates."

Thine eyes are springs, in whose serene
And silent waters heaven is seen;
The twilight of the trees and rocks
Is in the light-shade of thy locks.

Thy step is as the wind, that weaves
Its playful way among the leaves
And all the beauty of the sky
Is in thy heart and on thy face.

The forest depths, by foot unpressed
Are not more sinless than thy breast;
The holy peace that fills the air
Of those calm solitudes is there.

At the bottom was the punch-line:

A policy may be made to provide an annual income throughout the
life of a daughter (or son), and will always KEEP THE FATHER'S
MEMORY GREEN AT YULETIDE.

There was much solid meat presented to *Pelican* readers, though
served in slightly different form than is used today. For instance,
in 1905 appeared a little article entitled "Watson is a Fool," a dialog
between a life insurance man and a doctor. This develops the life
value idea which is associated with much effective selling in later
Mutual Benefit years.

Doctor Johnson.   Is it true that Watson's mills have been burned
    to the ground?
Agent Jones.   Yes.
Doctor.   How much insurance?
Agent.   None.
Doctor.   Oh! What a fool!
Agent.   By the way, doctor, are your buildings insured?
Doctor.   I don't own any building.
Agent.   How do you invest your money?
Doctor.   I do not invest any. I have a good income from my pro-
    fession, but my family expenses eat most of it up.
Agent.   Then if you die, your wife and daughters will carry on your
    business.
Doctor.   My dear Sir, I am a physician; how can I leave my practice
    with a parcel of women?
Agent.   Then your income ceases at your death?
Doctor.   Yes.

Agent.   How much assurance do you carry on your life?
Doctor.   None.
Agent.   Ahem!—Yes, you are right, Watson *is* a fool!

Through all these years *The Pelican* constantly ran stories of "unexpected legacies," case reports of claims paid under Mutual Benefit policies which were happy surprises to the beneficiaries. A few quotations from typical testimonials will be of interest.

To an agent in Leavenworth, Kansas:

> In 1867 I paid one of your predecessors a part of the first premium on a twenty payment life policy. After which, not knowing your Company as well as I do now, I decided to drop the insurance, but the rest of that premium was paid long ago, not by myself, but by the dividends earned by the policy. I destroyed the policy and the receipt for the partial premium as papers of no value. Imagine my surprise, after thirty-seven years, to be accosted by you, who had been born in the interval, with a check to my order for more than I had invested!
>
> It is not the payment, which is comparatively small, that commands my gratitude or admiration, but the underlying principle— the fact of the existence in the modern commercial world of an institution so anomalous, not to say unique, as to go so far out of its way to pay debts never demanded, or even dreamed of.

To an agent in Winston-Salem, North Carolina:

> My brother was sure that his policy had lapsed, as he had taken the loan value on the policy a year or two before he died and had not paid the last premium, which was past due, but I understand the policy was kept in force because of dividends which reduced the loan, leaving a value which was applied to purchase automatic extended insurance. And from what I can understand, if my brother's policy had been in any other company I would not have received one penny. I certainly want every good man in this county to take a policy in this grand old Company, as from what I have learned about insurance recently, the Mutual Benefit does more for its policyholders than any other company.

In 1907 Alfred A. Drew became superintendent of agencies. He was already well-known to the field forces as editor of *The Pelican*. He carried on an increasingly effective personal campaign in building conviction and confidence among Mutual Benefit Life representatives. Mr. Drew was a very positive character, a dynamic personality and a man who, by display of personal interest and an enormous correspondence, bound to himself a host of friends.

A typical *Pelican* report of an agency meeting gives some understanding of his agency building principles and practices.

> Mr. Drew was called upon to give the agents a little inspiration. He said that idealism is possible in the life insurance business. He also suggested that the Company was nearing the time when only active men, who devoted their whole time, thought and energy to the work of selling Mutual Benefit Life Insurance and to advancing the cause would be sought by the Company and its general agents. . . .
>
> Mr. Drew pointed out in a forceful manner the weapons which only Mutual Benefit men possess, to challenge attention and respect, and showed some of the best ways of overcoming possible competition.

Mr. Drew brought to the home office as his assistant superintendent of agencies a successful young agent from Michigan, William Winton. Mr. Winton, like Mr. Drew, traveled extensively up and down the country eloquently preaching the gospel of the Mutual Benefit Life. He was greatly beloved by the agents and not a few men of middle age today sign themselves "William W. ———" as namesakes of their fathers' friend.

It is little wonder that President Frelinghuysen could write to policyholders:

> The increase in our new business written attests the growth of the Company in public favor and the activity and attainments of our agency forces. Our men in the field have become imbued with the beneficent results of the Company and work with a zeal not alone for their own livelihood. They realize that while serving themselves and their families they are really securing a blessing to those they serve—probably no line of business has such a result of gain both to him who gives and him who receives.
>
> The faithful, efficient agent has to be educated and developed in mind and character—being masters of their own time their supervision calls for managerial ability of a high and tactful order—and love for the Company and for the beneficent results of the business are potent factors in the making of an agent—and such agents when thus developed are a valuable asset to the Company. Such men are sought by other Companies and are constantly offered alluring contracts; but with very few exceptions they prefer to retain their connection with this Company. (1910)
>
> Our agents are enthusiastic, appreciating more and more that the Mutual Benefit gives more to their clientele than would any other company, and that they have nothing to explain away as not in the interest of the policyholders—that to the bounds of safety the policyholder is given all that can be given. (1912)

In the first decade of the twentieth century the general sentiment was that the world was getting better, the achievements of man were unprecedented. One of the first rude shocks to this comfortable state of mind was the *Titanic* disaster. Hailed as "the largest, newest and fastest of ocean steamships" and "absolutely unsinkable," the *Titanic* sailed from Southampton on April 10, 1912. Four days later, on a clear starlight night, the ship struck an iceberg and sank in three hours. Some seven hundred survivors, mostly women and children, overcrowded the few life boats, and fifteen hundred passengers and crew were drowned. Eight victims of the disaster were Mutual Benefit Life policyholders. One man had owned his $50,000 policy less than a year and had paid only $608 in premiums.

World War I, beginning in 1914, was another shock, but the civilized world was not prepared for developments which followed. The next year as the great passenger liner, the *Lusitania,* was preparing to sail from New York to Liverpool the German embassy published warnings that vessels bound for Europe must pass through the war zone and passengers must travel at their own risk. People did not really believe that German submarine warfare would extend to passenger ships, and also there was great confidence that the *Lusitania's* high speed would overcome any danger from torpedo attack. Again confidence was misplaced. The *Lusitania* was torpedoed twice and sank in twenty minutes, with the loss of nearly twelve hundred lives. Over one hundred of these drowned passengers were American, two held Mutual Benefit policies. A young flour dealer of Indiana some five months previously had bought a ten-payment life policy on the accelerative endowment plan, in preparation for his old age. Traveling to Europe on business, he was one of the men drowned. The other was a missionary to India who had owned his policy for sixteen years. At the time of the disaster he was returning to his field after furlough.

Although the United States was not yet in the war, 1915 saw the beginning of claims from battle deaths. The first was on the life

of a Frenchman who had purchased his Mutual Benefit Life policy in 1913 when he was head waiter at the famous old Plaza Hotel in New York City. When war broke out the next year he returned to France, entered the army, was wounded in battle and died in October 1914. The proofs of loss (all written in French) were duly submitted and the Company paid the claim early in 1915.

There were three Company war claims in 1916, all for policyholders killed in battle in France. One of these was a soldier in the German army, one was a Michigan man enlisted with the Canadians, and the last was a man from Baltimore serving with a British regiment.

The new terror of infantile paralysis struck the country also in 1916. The Company at that time was not insuring children under age 14 and the mortality was heaviest for very young children. In fact a Company bulletin stated that "the danger of death was not very great over age 10."

There were, however, four deaths from "the dread disease." All were men—ages 22, 23, 38 and 40. The first claim was on a fifteen-payment life policy for which only nine months' premiums had been paid and which was running under automatic extended insurance—another case that would not have been a claim with other companies.

The United States declared war on Germany on April 6, 1917. The echoes of "Over There" and "Keep the Home Fires Burning" hang over the next years. The Mutual Benefit Life service flag—for home office and field representatives—showed 435 stars in the summer of 1918. The first gold star was for a young home office worker who died of influenza at Camp Dix in October 1918, soon before he was to go overseas.

Three days after war was declared the Company adopted a war clause for new insurance for those subject to the war hazard. It set a charge of 10% of the amount of insurance ($5,000 limit) as an extra premium for those "engaged in military service outside of the States of the United States and the District of Columbia, or in naval service."

Other companies adopted different clauses and the resulting confusion and competition were very unfortunate. Therefore when a uniform war clause was recommended by the Insurance Commissioners, the Mutual Benefit Life promptly adopted that. It applied to all applicants of military age with an extra premium of $37.50 per thousand.

One of the World War I draftees still remembered today is Sergeant Alvin C. York from the Cumberland Mountains of Tennessee. Marshal Foch, presenting him with the Croix de Guerre said: "What you did was the greatest single thing accomplished by any soldier of any of the armies of Europe." Singlehanded he had captured 132 Germans, killed 25 of the enemy and cleaned out 35 machine gun nests. Rookie York came into the army as a conscientious objector. His captain was Edward C. B. Danforth, Jr., in private life a representative of the Mutual Benefit Life in the Georgia agency. Captain Danforth recognized this tall, strong young mountaineer, a man of integrity and character, as a valuable prospect for the citizens' army. He spent many hours talking with the boy and finally satisfied him that he could with honor be a fighting soldier. Some have called this Salesman Danforth's largest sale.

The war was mercifully short. Casualties were much fewer than had been feared. One year after the United States entered the war there were a million men in France, but hostilities ended seven months later.

During 1918 the Company paid 361 war claims, and the next year 195, including both battle casualties and service deaths from disease. One of the policyholders who died was killed in action on November 11, 1918, less than five minutes before the cannonading along miles of battle front stopped and shouts of joy from millions of men began.

Immediately after the Armistice the Company resumed insuring young men without a war clause. (World War I was "the war to end wars.") It announced that extra war premiums that had been paid would be refunded. In addition, cases which had already been settled on the basis of return of premiums only, for men insured in wartime without the war clause, were reopened. Beneficiaries were paid the balance of the face of the policy. This was deemed justifiable because the impact of war deaths had been so light.

Although casualties from the war were no strain to the Company, death stalked the land in another form. President Frelinghuysen referred to it as "the most disastrous pestilence this country has ever known and one which tested the stability of the Company." This was the influenza epidemic which began in Spain and spread rapidly over all the civilized world. It reached its peak in the United States in 1918, though continuing with considerable violence into early 1919. It was particularly shocking to the country and hit the life insurance business heavily, because young people especially were smitten. For the country as a whole the average age at death for the 1918 influenza epidemic was 33 years. In the last three and a half months of 1918 the Company had 874 influenza death claims for nearly $3,000,000. Over four-fifths of these policyholders were under age 40 and had been insured for only a short time. In 1919 the Mutual Benefit had 615 additional influenza claims, making a total of 1,489 for more than $4,750,000.

The most shocking influenza casualty for the Company was William Winton. He had not spared himself in adding patriotic services to his heavy schedule of Company work and travel during the war years. His hosts of friends looked upon his death in the epidemic as almost a war casualty. The great affection and honor they felt for him found expression in an educational fund raised for his two little boys. Those children justified the generosity of their father's friends and today hold high positions of business responsibility.

This terrific death toll of course was shared by all companies. Mutual companies generally passed their dividends, but the Mutual Benefit was able to keep paying regularly according to the scale established in 1915.

The effect of the war on the Company's investment program was large and far-reaching. The series of Liberty Loans began very shortly after the war started and ended with the Victory Loan in 1919. The Company subscribed heavily. To do this it was necessary to curtail new investments in Western and Southern mortgages and even to borrow nearly $15,000,000 in the fall of 1918.

At the end of 1918 the Company held $38,000,000 of Liberty bonds. At that time the market price of the bonds was below par "by reason of great quantities being placed on the market for realization purposes." That affected the Company's statement, but not the Company's essential stability. Mr. Frelinghuysen commented to policyholders:

> The bonds being obligations of our Government are, of course, absolutely good. . . . We do not, however, sell our bonds* and their earning power is as good and their stability as good as ever. We do not have to realize on the depressed values, the inflow of cash being always more than sufficient to meet all demands—and the depression in values in no way reflects on our selection or the superiority of our securities.

In the year 1919 the Company did its largest volume of new business to date, one-third of the total being purchased by old policyholders. Summarizing seventy-five years of Mutual Benefit Life history Mr. Frelinghuysen reported, in round figures, $621,000,000 of premiums received from policyholders. Net interest earned amounted to $198,000,000, enough to pay all taxes and expenses with a balance of $90,000,000. Payments to policyholders had been 74% of their premiums or $462,000,000, leaving a fund still on hand for future contract payments of nearly a quarter of a billion dollars. He concluded with pride:

> More striking results, perhaps, might have been secured through less regard for economy of management, through a less careful selection of risks, through the adoption of other forms of policies, through harsh forfeitures imposed upon those who were unable to continue their insurance, and through a less conservative investment policy than has been consistently practiced. We, however, take a just pride in the size of the Company, but a greater pride in the knowledge that in the course of seventy-five years there has been no sacrifice of ideals.

* Referring to all bonds, including Liberty Loan, which also were depressed.

CHAPTER NINE

The Twenties

THE DECADE AFTER WORLD WAR I
brought three new personalities into Company leadership, saw the
building of a new home office, and witnessed further substantial
progress of the Mutual Benefit while withstanding the crowd
psychology of the business generally in regard to unsound disability
underwriting.

The first of the new personalities was Oliver Thurman, who in
1919 succeeded Mr. Drew as superintendent of agencies. Mr. Drew
left the home office to become the Company's general agent at
Chicago. Mr. Thurman was a Tennessean by birth, a Texan by
adoption. While he was teaching school in Texas he first became a
representative of the Mutual Benefit at Dallas. Later he was associated for seven years as salesman and supervisor with his older
brother who was the Company's general agent in Baltimore. For
eight years before his Mutual Benefit Life home office appointment
he was with the Phoenix Mutual of Hartford, first as officer in
underwriting and agency work at the home office and then as Boston
general agent.

Mr. Thurman was a connecting link between the old and the
new in life insurance agency management. He shared the old-time
evangelistic zeal for the Company and devotion to its ideals. He
was a persuasive and eloquent speaker in promoting the Company's
cause and inspiring the field forces. He was a great-hearted friend
and a Southern gentleman. He loved horses, playing the 'cello and
good talk with congenial companions.

Mr. Thurman was a pioneer in scientific sales management. He promoted psychological studies of salesmanship and the first organized sales processes for Mutual Benefit salesmen. He was the chairman of the first executive committee of the Life Insurance Sales Research Bureau (now the Life Insurance Agency Management Association) when it was organized in 1921. He was also one of the early trustees of the American College of Life Underwriters organized in 1927 to administer the educational program leading to the professional designation of Chartered Life Underwriter. His leadership gave the Company the early start in C.L.U. promotion which resulted in Mutual Benefit Life's pre-eminent rank* twenty-five years later for proportion of C.L.U.'s among full-time representatives.

The second newcomer to Company leadership was John R. Hardin who was elected president January 9, 1924, following Mr. Frelinghuysen's death on New Year's Day. Mr. Hardin was not unacquainted with the Company for he had served as a director since 1905. As Mr. Hardin was fond of relating, he was a New Jersey farm boy. He was born in the North Jersey hills and maintained a home there all his life. He was graduated from Princeton and lived to become a trustee of his Alma Mater, an honor which he cherished. Those who knew him as the honored and handsome Company president found it difficult to picture him as a coxswain in a Princeton shell, or even as the young law student beginning his career in Newark in 1881.

When he was elected president of the Company, Mr. Hardin was one of Newark's outstanding lawyers. He had served as a member of the Newark Common Council and the State Legislature and on many state, county and city boards and commissions.

The third important addition to the Company's official staff in the twenties was John S. Thompson. In October 1926 Mr. Thompson was appointed mathematician to succeed Mr. Percy C. H. Papps who, having come to the Company in 1907, had served well in that office from 1919 until his sudden death in May 1926.

Mr. Thompson was already recognized as a hard-working and brilliant actuary. He was a native of Canada and was graduated from the University of Toronto in 1905 as gold medalist in mathematics. Mr. Thompson was a fellow of the Actuarial Society of America, of the Institute of Actuaries of Great Britain and of the Faculty of Actuaries of Scotland. For years he had been active as

* Reported in one research study to be first in the country.

council member, editor of its *Transactions* and secretary of the Actuarial Society of America whose president he was to become in 1932. Before coming to the Company, Mr. Thompson had been associate actuary of the Mutual Life of New York.

Mr. Thompson's outstanding professional qualifications fitted him well to carry on the Mutual Benefit tradition of sound actuarial leadership. His personal characteristics of friendliness and consideration for others, of humility and even temper, and of fairness and integrity soon won him a place in the hearts and high regard of his new Mutual Benefit associates in the home office and field.

One of the earliest problems of this decade was one now most familiar—taxes. The federal income tax had been collected first in 1914. From the beginning, the manner of taxation of mutual life insurance companies, and all the life insurance business, was under dispute.

The Mutual Benefit Life paid taxes for certain early years under protest and entered suit against the Government. The taxes eventually were refunded with interest.

Vice President Edward E. Rhodes became a leader for the life insurance business in this matter. A basic difficulty was lawmakers' unfamiliarity with the life insurance business. It was early recognized that life insurance companies could not properly be classed with ordinary commercial corporations for the imposition of income taxes. The Treasury Department and the companies together turned their attention to developing a plan that would take into account the special technicalities of the business.

A major question was: "What is the income of a life insurance company?" Premiums paid, especially in a mutual company, surely are not comparable to regular income in other kinds of corporations.

Legislation was finally framed based upon the concept that the tax should fall on the income from investments. The report of this historic decision for American life insurance, given in the history of the American Life Convention, ends with the statement:

> Thus the principle of federal taxation first proposed by E. E. Rhodes and approved by the representatives of the American Life Convention in 1919 was written into the federal tax law.*

* The tax imposed was based on a formula which gave special consideration to the fact that policy reserves and a certain yearly increase in them through interest earnings are required by law. The exemptions related to such interest earnings have varied from time to time, but the Revenue Act as it exists today still reflects the original thinking.

John R. Hardin

THIRD HOME OFFICE BUILDING

Mr. Rhodes commented that this Revenue Act of 1921 was particularly noteworthy in two respects. It recognized life insurance as a peculiar business, and it demonstrated the successful cooperation between the companies and the Government in formulating a reasonable and consistent plan of taxation.

In 1922 the Company again revised the form of its policy contract, further liberalizing nonforfeiture values, offering the accumulation plan for the use of dividends and providing for dividends on paid-up and extended insurance. These benefits were generally extended also to old policyholders.

Following the years of the influenza epidemic the Company experienced very favorable mortality. This "may have been caused by the deaths during the epidemic which would have otherwise occurred during the intervening years." Also the death rate on policyholders insured in the Company for large amounts was more favorable than for the policyholders as a whole. Therefore, in response to considerable demand from policyholders and agents, the Company's limit was increased to $200,000 in May 1924. This action brought increased business from old policyholders. The proportion increased to about 50% of new production, and it remained at that level for many years, until the era of pension plans brought in large groups of lives mostly not previously insured in the Company.

An aspect of underwriting that was given considerable attention at this time was the relation of body measurements to weight. A home office underwriter, of course, generally must judge a case simply from the written facts as given on the application. The weight as shown is an important factor in acceptance or declination. More often than desirable, there may, for various reasons, be inaccuracies in the weight as given. This means some applicants appear unacceptable who actually are all right, and vice versa.

Dr. Charles P. Clark of the medical board became interested in this problem and conceived the idea that there might be a constant relationship between other body measurements and weight. Working with the mathematical department, a study was made of ten thousand cases, and tables were developed for underwriting guidance. Dr. Clark's tables on the theoretical chest and waist measurements for various heights and weights, and for the theoretical transverse diameter of the heart are still used throughout the life insurance business.

For many years the Company had been insuring lives from ages 14 to 20 rated at age 21. This was due to the unfavorable mortality of young people. Now with improved health for that age group, the Company adopted graded premiums for those ages. Under the retroactive principle policies in force issued at ages under 21 were rewritten at the new premium or future dividends were increased to equalize the experience, whichever the policyholder wished.

The dividend experience was very favorable during the period, due especially to the good mortality. The dividend scale adopted in 1915 was continued, with special dividends for 1916, 1923 and 1924. Successive increases were adopted for 1924, 1925 and 1926.

In their annual report for 1925 policyholders received important news of another change to their advantage, namely that

> . . . after elaborate calculations which showed that the Company had on hand surplus earnings attributable to the old policies in an amount to warrant the appropriation, . . . the reserves on policies written prior to January 1, 1900, heretofore on a 3½% basis, could be placed on a 3% basis. The directors authorized the change, and dividends and surrender values on the policies affected will be hereafter computed accordingly. The increased surrender values will be available in 1925, but the change will not affect dividends until 1926. This change was not made because of any doubt of ability to maintain the reserves on the higher basis. It will give the old policyholders increased equities and increased dividends, and will greatly simplify the work of the Home Office. With this change made the Mutual Benefit will be in the strongest possible position with respect to its policy reserve. It will hold the highest reserve permitted by law.

The initial cost of this change was nearly $2,000,000.

Of course investment experience played its part in these gratifying results for policyholders. For several years net interest earnings for the Company ran over 5%.

For some forty years the Company had been an active investor in farm mortgages. From time to time, with fluctuating agricultural fortunes considerable numbers of foreclosures were necessary, but generally the record was good. At the beginning of 1924 the Company owned no foreclosed real estate. Farm investments reached an all time high in 1927. Some troubles had already begun, however, resulting from the collapse of the World War I boom. The Company, therefore, started a shift to city mortgage investments

The Company had never invested in industrial or railroad stocks. Stock ownership and manipulations were one of the abuses prior to the Armstrong Investigation and the subsequent new legislation in New York prohibited stock investments for life insurance companies. The growing popular interest in profitable stock market operations made many people feel that this was too stringent a rule. As a result of great pressure the law was changed in 1928 to allow investment in preferred and guaranteed stocks under certain conditions and limitations. New Jersey also passed similar legislation.

The Mutual Benefit's first stock investments were in that year. Reporting to the policyholders Mr. Hardin stated:

> The Company during the year varied its investment policy by the purchase of a limited amount of high grade preferred and guaranteed stocks. The stocks purchased were of seasoned investment type and suggest no departure from the conservative principles which have been and will be dominant in the control of the Company's funds.

The investment in a new home office was a major interest at this time. In 1924 it had finally definitely been decided that a move from the handsome marble building was inevitable. Business was increasing, work space was crowded. Some clerks were forced to have their desks in the corridor before the new quarters became available. Various plans for adding floors to the present building or acquiring adjacent property for other expansion proved impractical or impossible. At this point some protest was made at the very thought of leaving the historic location occupied for over sixty years. To this there is a memorandum to the board of directors filed in answer: "Sentiment in this connection is not worth a row of pins and should not be allowed to operate to the detriment of the Company." So eyes were turned elsewhere.

A new site on the western side of Washington Park was regarded with general approval.* Legal difficulties made that property finally unavailable. At last after many months, the present Broadway and Second Avenue location in North Newark was chosen.

Plans for the building were developed, taking into consideration generous estimates of Company growth and a long range view. Again there were differences of opinion. One of the directors wrote:

> I find that some of the Directors feel that fifty years is too long a time for us to look forward to. It may be a long time ahead for any human being to visualize, but I now feel that it would be safe to

* Opposite the new Mutual Benefit Life home office now under construction.

figure on fifty years on the idea that we would come nearer to getting accommodations for twenty or thirty years. I have undertaken many times to provide accommodations for steamship and railroad business for a period of years, and have found that the mistake is generally made in under-estimating rather than in over-estimating.

Mr. E. E. Rhodes was the chairman of the building committee. John H. and Wilson C. Ely of Newark were the architects. Starrett Brothers, the builders of the then recently dedicated Lincoln Memorial in Washington, were the contractors.

Ground was broken for the new building in June 1925. Less than two years later, on the day set before construction was begun, April 18, 1927, the staff was at work at 300 Broadway.

In moving the Company lost only one-half of a working day. The transfer had been most carefully planned in every detail. Very important help was given by the Veterans Club. That organization had been started in September 1922. Its membership included home office men with twenty years or more of Company service.

Dr. Ward gave a vivid report of the big event:

> The officers and members of the Home Office Veterans Club . . . numbering at that time about seventy-five . . . cooperated enthusiastically and efficiently with the employed movers in this task. The Veterans signed up for eight-hour shifts. Some were on duty in the old building and others in the new. Every article of furniture and every filing cabinet had been indexed and labelled, and when taken to the new building they were placed without confusion in their new and proper positions. A train of armored cars, well-protected by armed guards, conveyed the securities amounting to many millions of dollars from the old vault to the new one. In this entire process nothing was lost or misplaced, a most gratifying evidence of efficient planning and cooperative activity.

The new home for the Company cost nearly $6,375,000, including real estate, construction, equipment and fees of architects and engineers.

The building was built as a first unit with opportunity for additions. Experience then indicated that it might be adequate for seventeen or eighteen years. The executives then were thinking about numbers of employees to be accommodated. The spectacular developments in air conditioning and in use of electric-powered machines which did so much to bring this building to obsolescence were still not envisioned by most people.

The institution-type building with its broad, ascending steps and its tall-columned pediments on Broadway and on Second Avenue is familiar, at least through photographs, to most readers of this book. The wide terrazzo-floored central corridor stretching from the front door through the building formed, with the cross corridor from the side entrance, a rotunda flanked by marble pillars in the heart of the building. Imbedded in the floor beneath the gold-embossed rotunda ceiling was a great bronze representation of the Mutual Benefit Life pelican seal. The design included the traditional motto, "I live and die for those I love"; and the dates 1845 for the Company's founding and 1927 for the occupancy of the new building.

The pelican seal soon was nicknamed "the penny," and became a familiar rendezvous: "I'll meet you after work on the penny." The rotunda was the location of the great annual Christmas tree whose first days' balsam fragrance curiously enough was always carried up and down through the building in the elevators opening nearby.

The auditorium opened from the central corridor at the left of the first floor. This beautiful room, paneled and pillared in ivory and gold, had an emerald green stage curtain. There were a Skinner pipe organ, Steinway grand piano and extensive stage equipment. The auditorium seated carefully just fewer than one thousand people, since going beyond that mark would require additional fire precautions.

The new building stimulated group consciousness and activity among the home office staff. In 1927 the Pelican Club was started, the organization for all home office people, devoted to social, athletic and service activities. One of the Club's first projects was a Company paper. This was at first a book-sized, four-page leaflet edited monthly by volunteers under the title *The Junior Pelican*. In 1929 this became the *Mutual Benefit Life* which eventually acquired a newspaper format and a professional editor working with a representative group of reporters throughout the building.

The new auditorium was the scene of many enjoyable home office events. In the early years the Pelican Club often promoted amateur plays, minstrels and variety shows. For a while there was a Company glee club. Choruses and choirs of home office people were brought together for special occasions.

One of the most beautiful events for many years was the annual Christmas celebration. This was generally a combination of a short play or tableaux and Christmas music with carol singing also by the assembled staff at the end of the day before Christmas. Former employees were welcomed back and many babies and children were proudly introduced to their parents' old associates.

The new building brought a minor revolution in the arrangement to have one dining room for men and women together. This was much criticized by the men who felt that there would be too much noise of conversation for their comfort. A compromise settlement was a grouping of tables, a "men's side" and a "girls' side" with a wide gulf of polished floor between. The prestige of the men was also maintained for some years by their use of water goblets while the girls were given ordinary drinking glasses. Measures of economy eventually reduced all to the common tumbler level.

The executive offices and the directors' room are on the Broadway side of the second floor. In accordance with Mutual Benefit tradition, the doors of the officers' rooms always stand open. Visitors taking a tour of the building always are cordially received by the officers for a greeting or a conversation.

The directors' room is much admired. Paneled in rich Circassian walnut, carved at the cornice, with Georgian chandeliers and plaster ceiling ornamentation, the room is rectangular. At one end is a dark Italian marble fireplace, beautifully carved with a design of fruits and flowers. Along one side are leaded glass casement windows. "Family" portraits look down from the walls on the long shining mahogany directors' table and leather high-backed chairs. Here the twelve directors of the Company meet each week at noon on Wednesday, a matter of much interest to visitors who generally assume that directors would meet much less frequently. They are impressed to learn also that Mutual Benefit Life directors are still all New Jersey men. The charter requires only a majority to be New Jersey residents.

Visitors viewing the directors' room often commented that it was an appropriate symbol of the Company, obviously first quality in every respect, but without ostentation and display.

When the Company first occupied the Broadway building work was still scheduled for a five-and-a-half-day week. Many people remember the excitement one Saturday morning, May 21, 1927, when Company business was often interrupted by comment concerning Charles Lindbergh then in the midst of his historic solo flight to Paris.

The full Saturday holiday was first adopted for the summer. Then office hours on Monday were extended to six o'clock so that the weekend backlog of work could be handled. The five-day schedule for summer only was followed with various adjustments until 1941.

The new home office was the occasion in June 1927 for the first Company-sponsored general agents convention. The first convention of Mutual Benefit general agents had been promoted and organized by James H. Glenn, then general agent in Philadelphia. The meeting was held at Atlantic City in 1914 with Company officers invited as guests. Nearly all of the Company's fifty-nine general agents attended. At least one subsequent such meeting was held.

Agents conventions for Mutual Benefit representatives also had their beginning in the field. Charles G. Monser, partner with A. S. Johnston in the general agency at Buffalo, gradually expanded their excellent annual agency meetings to welcome guests from other areas. The first large meeting was held in 1925 and the next year a general invitation was extended to Mutual Benefit salesmen across the nation to attend the "Buffalo meeting." Several hundreds responded, and a Mutual Benefit convention of salesmen with national participation resulted. Again, the home office officials were welcomed as guests.

The inspiration of the Buffalo meetings and their value to the whole Mutual Benefit Life field force were incalculable. An illustration which has become legend is the experience of Wallace H. King of Lima, Ohio. Young Wallace, a second generation Mutual Benefit salesman, went to Buffalo. There he sat at the feet of the giants and his ambition was sparked to do great things himself. Others were selling the Company limit. Asked how it was done, the master salesmen challenged, "Own the limit before you sell it."

Wallace took that advice and used his personal program in subsequent selling. He led the Company's field force in 1930, 1932, 1933 and 1934. In 1933 he wrote more business than anyone who qualified for the Million Dollar Round Table and he has qualified for the Round Table twenty times. In 1939 he completed a thousand weeks of consecutive weekly production. He now has over $25,000,-000 of business in force.

With such members of the family to meet and know, an agents "housewarming convention" in the new building was inevitable. An enthusiastic meeting was held in Newark in March 1928. Agents and Company officers appeared as speakers.

The twenties were a period of great development in life insurance selling in which the Mutual Benefit Life had a creative and important part. The experience of War Risk Insurance made available by the Government in World War I dramatized the importance of substantial coverage. The offering of $10,000 on a single life, as a reasonable standard for the young men who were being called to the army, lifted the sights of buyers generally.

The idea that a salesman could be made as well as born was gaining acceptance. The literature of life insurance selling began to take substantial shape. The School of Life Insurance Salesmanship of the Carnegie Institute of Technology led the way for company training courses.

As has been noted, the Mutual Benefit Life entered this period with agency morale high, with a superior quality of field man due to the self-selection which had attracted practical idealists and solid citizens.

Mr. Thurman found an agency force responsive to his leadership in the new era. The goad of militant principle again was present, for the disability insurance race was beginning. Mutual Benefit leaders saw the unsoundness of the current program and held firmly against it, as will be related later.

When Mr. Hardin became president Mr. Thurman enlisted him in a program of extensive traveling throughout the agencies. They encouraged cross-fertilization of ideas among Mutual Benefit salesmen. The creative sales philosophies which came to full bloom in those days influenced the whole field force. The men who have become legend in the Mutual Benefit (Clay Hamlin, Sam Sturm, William H. Beers, and many others) then, as their successors today, shared their ideas freely. James S. Drewry in Cincinnati developed a group of millionaire producers which is unsurpassed even in these days of inflation. The life insurance sales services and magazines quoted Mutual Benefit salesmen in measure beyond those of other companies. The Company was recognized as having idea salesmen, not just policy salesmen. The life value idea was expounded and exploited, and resulted in multimillion dollar sales records in those days when low tax rates left successful men generous margins for life insurance premiums. Good property ideas were preached and practiced with understanding and enthusiasm all across the country.

Mr. Thurman's eloquent reporting of the Mutual Benefit sales plans and his inspiration of Company sales forces kept them ahead of the parade as scientific life insurance selling developed. Mr. Thurman realized the motivation which salesmen find in recognition and appreciation, and had great skill in dealing with what he liked to call "human chemicals." Many who worked with him in home office and field speak even yet of his belief in their highest ambitions for themselves and of how he helped them do better than their best.

A Company officer who often traveled with Mr. Thurman and

who also in a different way had a large part in building Company spirit was Dr. William R. Ward, a member of the medical board for forty years. Dr. Ward was a native of Newark and a descendant of early settlers who purchased their land from the Indians. He lived all his life in the family homestead where he extended gracious hospitality to hundreds of Mutual Benefit Life men and women from Newark and all over the country.

Dr. Ward was a deeply religious man, active in the affairs of the Presbyterian church, locally and nationally. He was keenly interested in history, especially American history, New Jersey history and the history of the Company.

Dr. Ward participated wholeheartedly, with time, money and unselfish devotion, in innumerable civic, welfare and religious organizations. In 1942 he was honored as the First Citizen of Newark by the Newark Advertising Club and in 1954 was made an honorary life member of the Newark Chamber of Commerce, an honor accorded to only eight* men in that organization's long history.

Dr. Ward loved to travel and made many trips abroad. His travels for the Company took him back and forth across the nation, always carrying an inspiring message for Mutual Benefit Life men and women. He had a genius for friendship, and for a generation bound the field people to himself and to the Company by ties of personal interest and understanding.

These were the years when Mutual Benefit men were breaking records and it was still the day of personal, individual sales.

In September 1924 R. Keith Charles of Timmonsville, South Carolina, a town of three thousand population, set a new world's record writing 235 applications in one month (of twenty-six working days, for he did not work on Sunday) for a total of over $400,000.

A majority of the cases were prepaid and very few were rejected. *The Pelican* explained that his success was due to careful planning and hard work plus "a wide circle of satisfied policyholders, carefully built up over a period of twenty-seven years."

In 1925 Harry Glatz of Jamestown, New York, inspired by Mr. Charles, made the astonishing record of 516 cases written in thirty days (again no Sunday work) for $578,350. All but one of his cases were prepaid. His drive was opened with a dinner given the outstanding citizens of Jamestown, and the first case was written

---

* W. Paul Stillman, chairman of the Mutual Benefit Life board of directors since 1946, is also one of the eight.

on the mayor roused from his bed to sign the application at seven o'clock on the first morning of the drive.

Five hundred and seven of those cases became effective. Ten years later, after the crash of 1929 and the depths of depression, Mr. Glatz reported concerning this group of policyholders.

Not a single person among the 507 could possibly foresee that he or she would be obliged to use their cash values or hidden assets in their policies during the depression years 1930–1934.

I am glad however, that when unexpected, unlooked for acute emergencies came to 117 of these clients, that the cash they had created and built up in the life insurance they had purchased from me meant for them in a number of cases the retaining of their business, their homes, the supplying of food, raiment and shelter to those who were unemployed, and the conserving of other investments which had so terribly depreciated.

Here is a summary of the 507 policies issued from January 5th, 1925 to February 5th, 1925:

Policies still active	335
Taken by death	14
Policies lapsed	90
Policies surrendered	68
Total	507

118 of these people have purchased additional insurance. Another interesting fact is this—16 policies were issued to people, who, for some physical reason could not obtain standard policies. Every one of these 16 has kept his policy paid up to this date—and all are in good health.

In 1925 Clay W. Hamlin representing the Mutual Benefit Life in Buffalo sold nearly $12,000,000 of life insurance. This business was in personal sales to individuals and it was developed through creative sales ideas with low pressure selling. Mr. Hamlin used simple, penetrating questions which helped a client get to the heart of his own problem. One of his favorite approaches was: "Men tell me that they make money in their own business, and lose it in someone else's. How does that square with your experience?"

Samuel W. Sturm of Cincinnati was another Company force during the twenties. He came to the Mutual Benefit in 1912 and until his death in 1948 averaged over a million dollars a year production. Ten times he was the Company leader. He was identified in the minds of the field men as the life value salesman.* He used that idea constantly in his selling and shared his experiences freely with other Company representatives. His influence on uncounted numbers of Mutual Benefit men for a generation cannot be measured. Sidney Weil, a contemporary Company leader, repeatedly today ascribes his multimillion dollar success to the teachings and personal inspiration of Sam Sturm.

In 1926 Company new business exceeded $240,000,000, a level that was not reached again for twenty-five years. In that year also the Company crossed the two billion dollar mark for insurance in force.

During these years William H. Beers developed an organized sales talk based on his famous pendulum chart. This recognized the psychology of the negative swing in the sales interview, combining sales ideas with effective techniques of presentation. This sales plan was the first standardized procedure generally promoted by the Company. Mr. Beers during 1931 was a special assistant on the agency department staff and conducted the first Company sales schools throughout the agencies.

The twenties brought emphasis on selling directed toward specific life insurance needs. The School of Life Insurance Salesmanship at the Carnegie Institute of Technology stimulated thought for business and social uses for life insurance. At this time one of the sales services requested information from the Mutual Benefit Life about policies issued for college endowments, church gifts, hospital funds, charitable foundations and such purposes. The Company replied that it was willing to write such business, but kept no segregated record "because of the small amount done."

One of the first Mutual Benefit college endowment cases was to provide a twenty-fifth year reunion gift for the Vassar College Class of 1924. Ten members of the class were insured with premiums

---

* They said the life value idea was what Sam Sturm discovered and Dr. Huebner made hard to understand. Of course, Benjamin Franklin expressed the life value idea long before Mr. Sturm was born, and others had recognized it also, but he dramatized its effectiveness for life insurance salesmen. The reference to Dr. S. S. Huebner, who had long expounded the life value idea, was to his currently published very excellent book on the subject, *The Economics of Life Insurance.*

paid by class assessments. The program was carried through in spite of various vicissitudes which required some changes made possible by Mutual Benefit Life flexible nonforfeiture provisions. The result was a gift to the college in 1949 of $41,000, the largest group gift ever made to Vassar up to that time.

Competitive pressures from other companies were increasing with the promotion of disability business. The idea of disability insurance in connection with a life insurance contract had become quite common by 1920. A rider or special clause provided that if the insured were totally and permanently disabled he became entitled to monthly income, usually $10 for each $1,000 of his policy. What conditions constituted "total and permanent disability"? What experience was available for the determination of rates? The answers to both these questions were vague. How near dead must a man be before he was totally disabled, unable to do *any* work for pay or profit? A cartoon appeared showing an old man using his body warmth to hatch a setting of eggs. He was doing useful work. Therefore could he be considered totally disabled?

Vice President Harry W. Jones, in his review of the cycles of life insurance history in which the Company took a stand in the face of popular unsound developments, presents a vivid picture of this disability era.

> The actors and the props were different, but the plot was the same. The "something-for-nothing" aspect was supplied this time in the form of disability coverage. With its low premium rate and its benefits that looked substantial by comparison, it appeared to meet that requirement, and disability income benefits became the door-opener for the agent in what developed to be the third great race for business. Underwriting precautions went out of the window, benefits were written without regard to their amount and appropriateness, and "disabled" bellhops went into retirement on disability income equal to twice their previous earned income. But the race was on; life insurance had to be written to stay in the race, and the public could be induced to buy the life insurance if it could be tempted with the "come-on" item. Disability premium rates were raised from time to time, but they were always inadequate because usually each increase in rate was sugar-coated with an "improvement" in the benefits. Contracts were issued that actually induced a man to remain disabled by increasing his benefit the longer disablement continued. One company issued a policy providing for benefits so long as the insured could not resume his original occupation, no matter how else he might succeed in earning an adequate livelihood.

The officers of the Mutual Benefit Life and other disinterested observers realized that this unsound operation surely would end in trouble. Throughout the later 1920's steadily increasing losses in millions of dollars annually appeared. Real disaster came with the crash of the stock market in 1929, the subsequent depression and bank holiday. Financial distress brought actual disability to many. Loss of jobs, discouragement and fear made others subconsciously or consciously seek help in their disability protection. In the years following 1929 the companies generally lost millions of dollars on their disability business. The total for 1931–1938 for only those operating in New York State was $370,000,000. All stopped writing disability income protection, and only a few have recently resumed that service. Again, the conservative course of the Mutual Benefit Life was proved an advantage to policyholders.

During the development of this disability promotion the Company had not been blind to the need which disability insurance meets. Much creative thought, well-sustained by deep understanding of the problems involved, was given to the subject. Finally, late in 1928 a solution was worked out. Early in 1929 the Mutual Benefit Life offered to the public, and also to old policyholders, unique disability protection. This original approach to disability coverage was very largely the work of Mr. E. E. Rhodes. First, the protection was provided in a separate contract, not a rider or clause in a life insurance policy. It was a contract supplementary to a life insurance policy. Second, the Mutual Benefit definition of disability was completely new, depending upon facts of earned income before and after the occurrence of disability. Third, the concept of prorating claims with disability in other companies was established to guard against over-insurance.

Time has proved the soundness of this plan. Adequate premiums have prevented loss to policyholders. Careful administration has not meant undue severity for claimants. A study of 608 cases on which notice of possible claim had been received, and for which claim forms and instructions were furnished, showed 170 making no claim and 438 returning claim papers. Of the 438, the Company approved 396. On 36 others, the Company rejected the claim, stating its reasons, and heard nothing further. A further group of five were compromised and settled. During the entire period only one case went to suit, and the verdict was rendered for the Company.

An outstanding feature of Mutual Benefit disability has become apparent as interest in rehabilitation has grown. The Company's contract encourages efforts toward rehabilitation as other contracts cannot do because of their definition of disability.

A typical case was of a middle-aged man who hurt his back while unloading his car. The injury proved so serious he had to quit his job, and after four months he began receiving $100 a month Mutual Benefit Life disability income.

After a couple of years and a couple of operations he is able to take a few light jobs occasionally. He makes less than 25% of his previous earned income, so his Mutual Benefit Life disability was continued also. Thus the modest sums he earns, plus his disability income, enable him to get along. His disability contract has never encouraged him to become a helpless, useless cripple. It has always been a source of security and left the door open to efforts toward rehabilitation. The Mutual Benefit Life disability policy was born at a time of destiny for the nation. The year 1929 stands forth as the beginning of a great testing period for life insurance and for the whole American economic system.

American ownership of life insurance reached $100,000,000,000 in 1929. This was hailed by the companies with plans for the Second Hundred Billion on a curve of ascending prosperity. President Hoover recognized the achievement, and his statement reflects also how well the institution of life insurance had regained public esteem in the years since the Armstrong Investigation.

> No one interested in the progress of the American people could fail to be impressed with the significance of the achievement which is marked by the distribution of one hundred billions of life insurance among them.
>
> There is no single device in our whole economic system which is greater in its importance in safeguarding the welfare of our women and children than is this. The great institutions which have been builded for this protection against disaster rank with the highest forms of our national achievements. You, the men and women who have helped to build and now carry forward this great structure, have performed a great service and one which the whole country acknowledges with pride.

CHAPTER TEN

Depression Years

THROUGH THE SHATTERING TIME
of the stock market crash and subsequent depression years President
Hardin was a rock of stability in Company management. His own
service to the Company as a member of the board dated back to
January 1905, before the Armstrong Investigation. He used to tell
that in those early days his seat at the board table was next to
Mr. Amzi Dodd. Mr. Dodd had retired as president but continued
as general counsel and director up to his death in 1913. From
Mr. Dodd Mr. Hardin learned much about the history of the
Company and how the old ship had ridden out many storms. He
analyzed the depression of the thirties as most like the period after
the great panic of 1873. That panic had followed a period of inflation after the Civil War. A spectacular crash in stocks and securities
was followed by a prolonged deflation of all types of property.

When younger members spoke with emotion about some difficulty in the contemporary picture Mr. Hardin would say: "Now,
don't get excited. This is like ———." Then with perspective of
experience he would explain some past episode and how the
Company came safely through that trouble.

The market crash of 1929 was on October 29. Ten billion dollars
in values disappeared. The speculations which led to this debacle
were shared by all kinds of people all over the country. School
teachers and taxi-drivers, housewives and salesmen, as well as finan-
ciers had had a wonderful time running up their profits, talking

happily about "my broker" and giving each other hot tips.

An immediate result of the crash was frantic appeals to the Company for "the maximum I can get on my policy." In the eight days following the market break the Company paid out in loans almost $3,000,000. Tragic, too, was the increase in suicide claims, as is expected in time of severe business troubles. For several years, the number of suicide deaths rose sharply with a large proportion of cases involving insurance above $50,000.

There was some drop in volume of new business in 1930 but more policies were sold in that year than in 1929. Some young men who previously could not "see" life insurance, because they were doubling their money in stock investments, now were most thankful to be able to create a life insurance estate for their families.

The acute production down trend began in 1931 and continued with some fluctuations to the low point of $107,000,000 in 1942, less than one-half of the pre-crash level.

As the country gathered itself together after the stock market crash, the life insurance business took the opportunity to emphasize such ideas as these expressed by Vice President Oliver Thurman:

> For the millions of policyholders, the financial and moral effect of being on a sound insured basis goes beyond estimation. They have no doubt but that the safety which they have contemplated for themselves at retirement age, or for their families at a time of premature need, is secure. The building of a life insurance estate is free from the hazards which attend the building of a general estate, two of which have appeared with appalling frequency in recent months, namely, the failure of the plan or the failure of the individual to live long enough to complete his plan. During this last year when savings of a lifetime have been wiped out in the violent fluctuation of investment values, men with adequate life insurance protection have had renewed reason to feel satisfied with their financial programs. When so many apparently successful men have "died at the wrong time," others, who have underwritten their life plans through life insurance have a double comfort in the knowledge that, financially speaking, disaster could not overtake them. Those whose fortunes have been impaired will find courage to carry on as they purchase life insurance to make certain their plans for the restoration of their fortunes.
>
> Life insurance makes possible aggressive, constructive activities. The statement has been made frequently in recent months that now is the time to lay the foundation for big things in the future, to improve machinery, to renovate factories, to invest in raw material for production in the days ahead when business will again be

flourishing. Men who have subscribed to this theory in principle, but who would otherwise have been loathe to draw on their reserves for an investment from which they must expect no immediate returns, have felt safe in going ahead when they have underwritten future profits through life insurance. Now, whether they live or die, their families may be sure of financial security through their business.

During these years the statement was frequently quoted that "no well-established mutual legal reserve life insurance company has ever failed with loss to policyholders."

New business was definitely hard to get. The Company extended the age limit down to age 10 for children in 1931. In 1932 the Company introduced the retirement income bond, a deferred annuity with cash values, for both men and women. The same year it introduced the first contract combining life insurance with a guaranteed annuity income, $10 a month for each $1,000 of face amount with $1,490 as the cash option. The policy was issued on male lives only, with retirement at age 65. (Later coverage was broadened.)

Many old-time agents found the conditions particularly difficult. New men in the business, knowing no easier days, often did amazingly well. *The Pelican,* apropos of this situation, quoted the old story about pelicans at Monterey. Along the California coast there, fishermen gutted their fish and local pelicans found life so easy that they forgot how to forage for themselves. Then the fishing banks changed, fishermen no longer provided food without work for the big birds. They were on the point of starving to death when strange pelicans, unspoiled by an easy existence, were brought in. The newcomers began to catch fish, and soon the hungry natives learned again how to feed themselves.

And the moral was pointed:

> In practically every agency of every company, new men are coming into the business. Like the imported pelicans, they have been used to foraging for themselves. And their production records offer incontestable proof that there is business enough to satisfy any man who will go where it is, then do the amount of work necessary to close it. But, unlike the native pelicans, comparatively few of the old guard among life underwriters have seen the light of day. They have failed to realize that, while prosperity inevitably arises out of the ashes of every depression, it seldom, if ever, wears the same clothes or answers to the same name.

One of the new sources of business beginning to be emphasized at this time developed because of growing federal estate taxes. The Revenue Act of 1926 taxed estates above $100,000 and of course much life insurance had been sold to prepare for that tax bill. The 1932 tax law brought the tax down to the level of $50,000 estates, which widened the market. The 1932 law also included a new gift tax which gave opportunities to alert life insurance salesmen.

During these difficult days Mutual Benefit agents continued to emphasize Mutual Benefit Life superiorities in publicizing claims which would probably not have been paid by other companies. For example, there was an Iowa farmer who bought a $10,000 policy in March 1930. In 1931 he could not pay his second premium and the Company loaned him the full amount. In 1932 he again could not meet his premium and did not borrow the $110 of remaining loan value. The next month he died suddenly after an illness of four days. His insurance was in force under the extended provision although he had paid only one premium in cash. Stories like this were particularly impressive in the atmosphere of hardship and losses from other kinds of investments.

By 1933 the financial difficulties had generated an underlying fear that suddenly grew and spread like a forest fire. People all over the country began to withdraw bank deposits and hide gold and cash in safe-deposit boxes and other confidential places. Their mad rush overwhelmed the banking system.

The paralysis of the banks began early in February in Michigan, and in a month had spread across the nation. All companies faced the situation which came to the Mutual Benefit Life. Transfer of Company funds from accounts throughout the country was interrupted. Policyholders could not pay premiums. Yet cash demands upon the Company were increasing, as many policyholders sought needed funds, or in fear tried to liquidate their life insurance assets.

The Company met all demands in full to the end of the business day, March 3, 1933. Then New Jersey declared a bank holiday, confirmed by the following national holiday.

Franklin Delano Roosevelt's first Inaugural on March 4, 1933, challenged the country with his statement, "The only thing we have to fear is fear itself," and in that spirit he led the country into the years of the New Deal.

When the banks reopened, life insurance companies renewed operations under emergency restrictions imposed by special legislation in the various states. Legislators acted upon advice of state commissioners of insurance who through their national association had agreed upon principles to follow. Thus, for the first time in the history of American life insurance, emergency restrictions were imposed upon solvent companies. Life insurance companies are not organized to conduct a banking business, yet since the market crash they had served millions of policyholders as a very dependable bank of deposit from which to withdraw vast amounts of cash on demand.

The restrictions imposed on the life insurance companies were therefore on the banking features of their business. No delay or interruption was required in the payment of death claims, maturing endowments, or income payments under annuities or supplemental agreement contracts.

The restrictions required that applicants for loans or surrender values above $100 must prove hardship or extreme need for the funds. Many businesses were saved by the use of such life insurance money to meet payrolls. Doctor bills and college expenses were paid, homes were purchased, new business opportunities were seized by people who were able to justify life insurance payments for such purposes. Every agency office and the home office were besieged by policyholders with their stories.

In the Company's history file there is a memorandum dated June 1933 reading as follows:

> Although these facts cannot tactfully be given printed publicity at this time, they will probably be of great interest to future historians of the Company.
>
> At the time of the banking difficulties and moratoria in the spring of 1933, all companies and the institution of life insurance were faced with many problems. Insurance commissioners and company executives held frequent conferences. Following the general conference in New York upon the basis of which the insurance commissioners in this part of the country were going to enunciate state regulations, the New Jersey commissioner invited Mr. E. E. Rhodes to formulate in appropriate phraseology the ideas for control which he had discussed in conference and asked him to confer about his document with the officers of the Prudential. Mr. Rhodes wrote his plan of regulations as requested and after discussion with the Prudential sent it with their approval unchanged to the insurance commissioner. That document promptly reappeared over the commissioner's signature as his regulation for New Jersey insurance operations.
>
> After two months of experience with this plan of regulation in this state, the insurance commissioners met for their annual meeting in Chicago with the primary purpose of making recommendations for

EDWARD E. RHODES

300 BROADWAY BUILDING

the further and uniform regulations of insurance operations under the continued emergency conditions. The commissioners adopted as their proposition for all states a plan that was the New Jersey plan practically unchanged.

In other words, the Mutual Benefit through Mr. Rhodes again demonstrated constructive industry leadership.

Restrictions were relaxed after about six months with variations in different states, and were completely removed within a year after the banking holiday began.

There is no way to measure the good to individuals and the value to the nation of this great life insurance reservoir of emergency funds, tapped at a time of terrible need. In the four years 1931–1934 the companies paid out over $4,500,000,000 in cash values alone.

The Mutual Benefit Life stepped into the depression-time market in 1933 with a new contract—again a unique policy, and again largely the work of Mr. E. E. Rhodes. This contract was designed to meet the current need for low cost insurance. It maintained the traditional Mutual Benefit Life emphasis on cash value insurance. This contract, the ordinary life increasing premium policy, is essentially the same as the contemporary form, popularly known as Olip. The eventual level premium when it was written on the American Experience basis of mortality was the same as for an ordinary life policy written at an age five years older. That was changed to the present three years with the change in mortality assumption.

A town crier ringing his bell was the symbol used in publicizing the new contract, "designed to fit depression budgets in anticipation of better times." It was important news for the life insurance buying community. The *Pelican* announcement shows the sales appeal of this new policy:

> The Mutual Benefit has good news for insurance buyers who need to get the maximum of permanent protection for a limited available premium outlay. As Mutual Benefit men you are now equipped to go out with an unusual answer to the insurance problems developed by the depression. You can show many prospects how they can set up for themselves now a lifetime program of protection on an economy plan of purchase.
>
> Men have been brought to realize as never before what it means to have literally no money available, a bad enough situation when everybody was in the same boat. But what might it be for a woman bereft of her husband's support and companionship, burdened with full family responsibilities, and also faced with the problem of a

personal bank moratorium because her husband owned insufficient life insurance?

Response to the new policy by salesmen and buyers alike was good. Soon about three-quarters of new business was being written on this form. The Company experimented with advertising of the policy in the New York newspapers, the *Times* and the *Tribune,* and in *Time* magazine. This *Time* advertising was the first national magazine advertising done by the Company.

The first claim under an Olip policy was paid in July 1933. A young man in Michigan, who had lapsed his insurance several years previously, bought $2,000 to make their little home safe for his wife if anything happened to him. He paid $18.96 in May and died less than three weeks later from causes not brought out by the medical examination.

Enthusiasm resulting from the new Olip tool was one factor that brought the Company a temporary up-turn in business in 1933. The year showed about $50,000,000 increase above 1932 or 1934.

A plan for substitution of new insurance for heavily loaned old policies, introduced in the fall of the preceding year, also influenced that record. The Company recognized that much of the business with heavy loans stood very little chance of ever being cleared by repayments. At the end of 1932 policy loans represented 27.8% of the Company's assets. This reflected a very serious practical problem for policyholders. The psychological factor was important, since generally people felt that a policy loan "increases the cost and decreases the amount of insurance." However, it is not always true that cancelling old encumbered insurance and buying new is to the advantage of a policyholder.

Recognizing policyholder needs, the Company's substitution plan offered a new start to a policyholder who had borrowed as much as half of the policy's cash surrender value. The plan was changed from time to time as to administrative details. In general it provided for issuing new insurance in place of heavily encumbered old insurance with adjustment of commissions to agents on the new insurance.

With the depression of incomes generally throughout the nation, a home office pay cut was inevitable. In April 1933 a plan was announced that did not affect at all salaries under $2,000 or the first $2,000 of other salaries. The higher salaries were cut by 15% of the excess over $2,000. Also the working day was increased one hour. This in effect increased the pay cut. No home office employees were laid off during all the depression years.

In spite of the salary reductions and increased hours, when the famous NRA program was promulgated a few months later the Mutual Benefit Life was one of the first life insurance companies to cooperate. The Company wired President Roosevelt in part:

> Directors and officers of the Mutual Benefit Life Insurance Company of Newark, New Jersey are heartily sympathetic with your campaign against unemployment. Our employee group has been maintained at full strength. . . . All compensations exceed your minimum wage. Hours of work are less than your maximum except for some non-clerical employees whose hours because of the character of their work are somewhat in excess of your maximum. We shall continue to do everything within our power to promote economic recovery.

President Hardin was drafted by the Government to serve on the seven-man District Recovery Board for the New York District comprising New Jersey, Eastern New York, Western Connecticut and the City of New York.

Symbolic of America's will to recovery, the Chicago World's Fair was hailed as marking the beginning of "A Century of Progress." Life insurance was represented there by an animated exhibit designed by Tony Sarg. The Mutual Benefit Life was one of the twelve original companies underwriting the display.

The exhibit was a diorama of a typical American community, sixty feet wide by fifteen feet deep, and was seen by a million people in the Fair's first year. Among its miniature homes, factories, office buildings, stores, public utilities and farms, people and automobiles were on the streets, children were playing, farmers were at work. Action with illuminated captions and recorded voice described the flow of life insurance dollars into business, industry and family life.

A slightly different life insurance event of world interest was the Tenth International Congress of Actuaries at Rome in 1934. Mr. John S. Thompson was then president of the Actuarial Society of America, and of course a delegate to the Congress. He was asked by the United States Department of State also to accept appointment as official representative of the United States Government. The honorary president of the Congress was shown in the official report to be "His Excellency, Signor Benito Mussolini." About twenty nations were represented at the Congress, which was conducted in four official languages—Italian, French, German and English. After a paper was presented in one language it was summarized successively in the other three. "In consequence," as Mr. Thompson stated with characteristic mildness, "the program moves rather slowly."

Because the events of the depression years had greatly stimulated policyholder interest in Company affairs, President Hardin decided in 1934 to send the annual report for 1933 to all members. Previously the report had merely been available on request. Already in 1934 there were more than half a million policies in force. Envelopes for the reports were run off mechanically on the Addressograph from plates used for premium notices. But at that time there was no system of running only one envelope for a policyholder with several policies. To eliminate duplicates, the whole mass of envelopes was hand-sorted into alphabetical order. For reduced-rate postage further sorting and bundling were necessary. That job required ten to forty workers from the middle of December until early in March. In these days of mechanized operations, such a chore seems impossibly laborious.

In addition to this direct policyholder education, at the urging of the agencies the Company again gave consideration to national advertising. Although the returns from the one-shot advertisements of the new Olip policy in 1933 had not been impressive in quantity or quality, the Company felt that national advertising might help support the hard-pressed field forces. Therefore the first national campaign was launched in 1935.

Full-length half pages were used in the *Saturday Evening Post*, *Time* and *Collier's*. The campaign featured photographs and testimonials by Mutual Benefit Life policyholders then prominent in the public eye. Each advertisement also carried a "tail" section emphasizing some life insurance idea, such as good property, life insurance for college expenses and so on. The series ran about a year with some variations.

Other efforts to increase business at this time included the monthly budget plan introduced in 1935 and the retirement endowments for women offered the next year. The monthly budget plan is a monthly premium plan handled through employers by salary deduction for employees. The expansion of retirement contracts reflected the increased demand for investment policies. The thirties brought an interesting market situation. On the one hand there was the need for low cost contracts. Many people wanted as much protection as possible for the available premium dollars. On the other hand life insurance had proved dramatically safe and stable in contrast to many other kinds of property. That brought a big demand for guaranteed life insurance investment plans. People had learned to depend on life insurance.

The problems of this decade after 1929 gave many women, who had developed specialized skill in Company affairs through long years of service, the opportunity to demonstrate their ability. For example, the emergency demands upon the mathematical department in the floods of requests for loans and surrenders could not have been met without the experienced women clerks. Unusual responsibility was thrust upon them and they gave a splendid account of themselves.

The Company's willingness to recognize the qualified work of a woman appeared at this time in the election of a woman officer. Mildred F. Stone was named agency field secretary in 1934. This is believed to be the first such official recognition of a woman by any of the major life insurance companies.

The Women's Club was organized in 1940. Like the older Veterans Club for the men, membership is open to all women employees with twenty years or more of service. The Club has no schedule of stated meetings, but carries on a varied program of welfare, educational and social events. Very delightful tea and supper parties have been organized for visiting agency cashiers and many happy personal associations established among business acquaintances.

In the midst of the thirties the Mutual Benefit Life became ninety years old. In observance of the Company's ninetieth anniversary and as a stimulus to the field force, the first national agents convention at a resort hotel was planned. An invitation to "a sales conference on the self-entertainment basis" was broadcast for the first ninety men to write $90,000 of business in the first ninety days of 1935.

The location chosen was The Greenbrier at White Sulphur Springs, West Virginia. The qualifiers were promised honors as the "Pacemakers for the Ninety-Years Celebration." Their program was to be devoted to ways to increase sales for the balance of the year, and reports of the discussions were to be given national distribution. Field response was strong, and 108 men did more than the $90,000 in the first ninety days. All were invited to share the Greenbrier meeting. Many still recall that as a landmark in their experience— a time when their faith in the business and in themselves was restored.

One of the results of the Ninety Campaign Conference was the Company's first nation-wide sales drive. A committee of conventioneers planned and carried through promotion of a unique policyholders' campaign. Termed Benjamin C. Miller Week (see page 10), the campaign focused on the unique Mutual Benefit Life contract. Facsimile copies of Mr. Miller's policy were supplied— the form which presented the whole contract on a single page. On the blank inside pages of the folded document was a summary of the development of the contract to its contemporary excellence. Naturally the first year liberal cash values and the settlement options with supplemental agreements were featured.

The committee challenged the field:

> Here is a chance to do something that will demonstrate to us all that the tide is coming in and that business is getting better. It will make everybody feel good and "prime the pump" for other success in production in 1935.

The aim was to beat the best week of the last five years since the depression began, which was the first week in May 1930. The number of cases sold that week had been 1,532.

Using the unique tool of the Miller policy Mutual Benefit men and women all over the country approached Company policyholders and others with heightened activity which brought exciting results. In the Campaign week of May 13–20, 1935, including the anniversary of the issue of the original Miller policy, not 1,533 policies, but 3,205 were written, for more than $8,500,000. This was a triumph and an inspiration for the whole Company.

Sales and sales morale were only one phase of Company problems in this period. Dividend cuts were no surprise in the depression years. The first one was small; it was in 1932. A large one followed in 1933 and still another in 1934. An "adjustment" in 1937 gave some increases to premium paying policies, but there was another general decrease in 1940.

All three factors influencing life insurance costs were hit unfavorably in this decade.

Mortality felt the effect of the large number of suicides and the increased number of claims for larger cases. Both suicides and heart disease appeared in these "jumbo" risks.

Interest earnings fell off. This reflected mortgage foreclosures with loss of interest, of which the Company had a great many; and bond defaults, especially railroad bonds, which also were serious.

Even more important was what Mr. Thompson referred to as the "tide" of interest rates. That is, the whole level of earnings on conservative investments began to sink, in contrast to the "waves" of temporary shifting which may be a normal experience. Of course, Government policy was directed to such a result, for reasons thought to be good, but the effect on the whole life insurance business was difficult.

During the time of heavy demand for loans and surrenders and with uncertainty about emergency needs for cash, the Company had to keep larger amounts of liquid assets than normally. This also resulted in less overall interest earnings. In fact Mr. Hardin reported to policyholders that the whole traditional program of Company investments was disrupted during these years.

The item of expenses was affected unfavorably especially by taxes. The trend was steadily up after the middle of the decade.

Throughout these depression years Mr. Hardin took frequent opportunity to emphasize important facts in life insurance finances. Generally the Company makes investments on the basis of their inherent safety and stability of earnings. Capital gains are not the objective. Therefore when market values were seriously depressed, so long as interest was paid, the Company had no great problem. Even when some bonds defaulted and many mortgages were foreclosed there was still a great stream of money coming into the Company from premiums and interest so that there was no forced liquidation of assets. Bonds and stocks could be held until market values rose. Foreclosed real estate, which had been mortgaged on a very conservative basis, could be disposed of satisfactorily.

The net interest return was affected by defaults and the need to hold large amounts of cash as previously mentioned. Refinancing of high interest bonds at lower rates also was a serious factor. The net interest return fell steadily from 4.85% in 1929 to 3.70% in 1939, and the low point had not yet been reached.

Drastic changes in the Company's portfolio of investments developed during these years. The high point of policy loans was reached in 1932, 27.8% of Company assets. By 1939, that had fallen to 12.8%, largely through termination of the policies with loans.

From 1929 to 1939 there was a marked increase in United States Government bonds, from 1.1% to 14.5%; and in state, county and municipal bonds from 1.3% to 13.2%. The amount in railroad bonds was about halved and in public utility bonds about doubled.

In the period farm mortgages dropped from nearly a third of Company assets to about 6%,* and city mortgages dropped slightly to about 10%. Of course foreclosed real estate increased from about 1% to over 10% by 1934 and continued around that figure.

With thousands of policyholders looking to their life insurance for liquid assets, it is not surprising that some traditional trends were interrupted. For the first time in Company history total assets decreased slightly in 1932, and the next year dropped by more than $17,000,000.

President Hardin emphasized to policyholders that a reduction in assets, though not to be desired, did not reflect any weakening of the Company. Reduction in assets through surrender of insurance eliminated a corresponding liability, and the Company actually closed the year with a very sizeable increase in surplus. His further comments about the Company situation in meeting policyholders' needs at this time reflect a continuing Mutual Benefit philosophy.

Throughout the depression the Mutual Benefit has kept to an ideal well stated in words quoted from an Annual Report of fifty years ago: "The Company's aim and its endeavor is to give to every one of its members a full equivalent for all that is paid to it; and in what form that equivalent shall be given is left as largely as practicable to the option of the policyholders themselves."

This ideal necessarily recognizes the creation of equities in accumulated surplus, and therefore, the right to withdraw (sur-

* The Federal Bureau of Agricultural Economics estimated gross farm income as steadily about $11,000,000,000 during the years 1923–1929. It dropped to the low point of a little over $5,250,000,000 in 1932.

render) on equitable terms. It is not inappropriate to recall that recognition of this right was a feature of Mutual Benefit practice long before it was conceded by other companies and long before it received legislative sanction. . . .

Truly regardful of the sacred character of these equities, we have not changed the terms of our new policy contracts by increasing surrender charges in the hope of lessening, in future experience, cash outlay occasioned by withdrawals. It has not occurred to the Mutual Benefit that this is a sufficient reason for denial of an equitable right. Surrender charges, if imposed contrary to sound principles of equity and mutuality become penalties and their character is not changed by administrative inconvenience resulting from the free exercise of contract privileges. The cash surrender values which have been long maintained by the Mutual Benefit, and which still continue, were originally based on a measurement of policyholders' equities ascertained by the Company to be just and fair to both withdrawing and continuing members. . . . These high surrender values and low surrender charges, *from the Company's standpoint but not from the policyholders' standpoint,* have not been helpful during the depression period in the conservation of insurance in force; and, in recent experience, this positive and distinctive merit of a Mutual Benefit contract has been transformed into a temptation to select this asset for conversion of its accumulated reserves into immediate cash.

Government "interest" in many kinds of financial and business affairs developed greatly during this period. In 1939 a Congressional committee, the Temporary National Economic Committee, commonly called the TNEC, began a study of life insurance. The committee was investigating especially the problem of concentration of economic power. However, it explored all phases of life insurance operation. The investigation lasted for weeks and bales of exhibits were required from every life insurance company. The study was conducted by the Securities and Exchange Committee and the life insurance business felt that the committee's reports to the TNEC were in some respects incomplete and therefore might mislead those who read them. As a result, a group of 151 companies representing over 60% of the life insurance owned and life insurance assets in the United States submitted additional information. The five-man committee which prepared and presented this additional report included Mr. E. E. Rhodes, who for part of the long months of work served as chairman.

When the investigation was all over Senator O'Mahoney, who

was in charge, said to a representative of the business, "You have come through with flying colors." Here was another tribute to life insurance after a searching test, and the Mutual Benefit Life had a large part in the effective presentation of the story.

One of the angles investigated by the TNEC was the frustration of life insurance policyholders. The experiences of the depression with the collapse of many people's financial hopes and plans naturally brought challenges to the life insurance business. Critics, in ignorance and often emotionally disturbed, charged that life insurance policyholders generally were sold under pressure and eventually were frustrated in their life insurance ownership. If such "frustration" were indeed a fact that would be a serious defect in our life insurance system.

One of the interesting points of evidence submitted to the TNEC by the Rhodes committee was a simple chart showing the volume of life insurance lapses and surrenders from 1919 to 1939. On the same chart was traced the *inverted* line of economic activity for the period. The graphs followed very closely the same pattern, emphasizing the controlling influence of economic factors on that life insurance experience.

Inspired by that TNEC frustration charge the Mutual Benefit Life made a study* of a block of Company business—the issues of 1845 to 1865 inclusive. Except for one $1,000 policy all the policies issued in that first twenty-one year period could then be traced to their final conclusion. There were 32,729 policies issued with premiums paid with total protection of $107,005,292. Over 40% of that original total protection was realized as death or matured endowment claims. This included over $1,500,000 of payments made in accordance with nonforfeiture provisions which were not in the great majority of contracts as issued.

Of course cash values were paid for many surrendered policies also. The promise of cash values, although none were guaranteed in the contracts before 1865, and the first one paid, have already been described. The payments in the early years increased from that first 1847 payment to $30,000 in 1851. The Company's outstanding liberality in granting cash values which we know today has been a distinguishing characteristic from the beginning. On this

---

* Reported in 1941 in a paper by James R. Trimble, "A Completed History of Policies Issued in 1845 to 1865 by The Mutual Benefit Life Insurance Company," in the *Transactions* of the Actuarial Society of America, 1941.

twenty-one year block of business cash values were paid over the next eighty years in amounts that have never been tabulated completely. (See page 68 for cash values paid on Southern policies after the Civil War.) Several million dollars of business in this block were term insurance which ended without payments to the insured but having served an important purpose.

In general, the facts of this study justify the conclusion that not only the policies under which death or endowment claims were paid, but a large percentage of the balance, served a much appreciated purpose in the lives of policyholders. Many of the policies on which values were paid before death may have then, as now, been much more useful to policyholders than if they had been carried through to the conclusion at first intended. Being able to change a policy to meet new needs as conditions change is an immeasurable advantage. Such flexibility is a characteristic which has developed most helpfully in Mutual Benefit Life policies.

More Mutual Benefit policyholders spoke of the depression year blessings of their Company contracts than of frustrations. Examples could be multiplied, but one experience which dramatized the stability and security of life insurance was a touching incident reported by a Company representative who was traveling and reached a small Florida city on his Rotary Club day. He attended the local luncheon where, of course, he was introduced as the representative of the Mutual Benefit Life Insurance Company. After lunch, a young man approached with the rather surprising request that the visitor go call on his mother, an invalid.

The young man said that his father had been the founder of the city. He was a wealthy man and long successful in the real estate business. The family felt secure in their future. They had the assurance of growing profits from the father's business transactions and paid no more heed than he to his mention of "a small amount of life insurance."

Suddenly the father died. Almost at the same time the real estate boom collapsed. What was left? Partly developed property, defaulted mortgages, fast-disappearing cash reserves and the "small amount of life insurance," which in fact was a $100,000 Mutual Benefit contract left under an income settlement for the widow.

"Sir," said the son, "my mother has lived and been comfortable on that money ever since. Her check arrives regularly on the same day of every month, or on the day preceding if the usual date falls on Sunday or a holiday. Everything else has failed, but the Mutual Benefit life insurance money isn't even late. What your Company has done for my mother means so much to her that I am sure it would be a great pleasure to her to be able to talk to you."

As the depression years demonstrated the value of life insurance in economic emergencies so also it was tested in new mortality developments. The dramatic value of life insurance was seen in the many, and large, suicide cases which reached 6% of the Company's claims in 1932. Heart death also increased steadily to 38% in 1939 and cancer to 13%. The decrease in death from tuberculosis, beginning in 1915, continued from 7.5% at that point to 2% in 1939.

Especially because of the increase in heart deaths and in claims under large cases the Company felt better information about applicants' heart conditions was necessary. Reports on electrocardiograms and fluoroscopic heart examinations began to be called for in many cases. The Company installed an electrocardiograph in its laboratory in 1931 and a fluoroscope in 1932.

Early in these years automobile accidents accounted for 4% of Company deaths, nearly one-half of all accidental deaths. It is interesting, however, that the percentage of deaths from auto accidents was cut in half by 1939 and has continued at that level, 2%.

Apparently ordinary use of the automobile never gave rise to questions about insurability. When railroads were new there were fears that in addition to accidents it might be injurious to health. In fact in the *Journal* of the Institute of Actuaries a paper appeared in 1863 entitled "Influence of Railroad Travel on Public Health." In that paper the author referred to his times as "a high pressure age . . . an age in which it is too much the custom to sacrifice all considerations of health and safety to a determined and great desire to do in a few hours what our ancestors were content to do in as many days."

An old claim case in the Company files includes a newspaper clipping reporting the death of a young man in Iowa. With it is an editorial ascribing his untimely demise to the unhealthful experience of riding in a sleeping car.

Such being natural reactions to change, it is not surprising that the Company moved carefully in handling aviation risks. The first aviation questions in the application were in 1929—about fifty years after Orville and Wilbur Wright, unknown mechanics from Ohio,

made their first successful experiments on the dunes of Kitty Hawk, with a contraption built in a Dayton bicycle shop.* By the middle of the next year the Company's general standard was to accept an applicant without restriction if he had no history of flying and expected to make not more than four or five flights in the next year. A flight was defined as the time between a take off and a landing. Any one trip might involve a number of flights. Acceptable flying was that done as a fare-paying passenger with a licensed pilot over established air routes.

The handling of aviation risks was subject to almost constant modification, as needs and experience developed. It is interesting to realize that even in 1933 a transcontinental air trip was very unusual. When a Mutual Benefit man made such a trip the news interest was great enough to warrant a five-page play-by-play story in *The Pelican* of meals, weather and landings, and stewardesses and pilots.

Air mail, of course, was being used by the Company. In 1934 a news story in *Mutual Benefit Life* reported an air-mail plane crash out of which fragments of a Company letter had been returned to Newark. The story added:

> For several years the Mutual Benefit has used the air mail service daily. It has been found not only a very satisfactory method of saving time but also a very efficient and safe way of sending mail. In fact, so far as can be ascertained, there have been only three times when air mail, either addressed to us or sent by us, has not arrived at its destination safely.

* Later concerning the first flight of a heavier than air machine with an internal combustion engine, they reported that they flew three miles "over sand hills and waves in the teeth of high wind" and with "no balloons attached to it."

In 1938 the Mutual Benefit had a share in celebrating the twentieth anniversary of air mail in the United States. A Mutual Benefit Life application, complete with medical examination and prepayment, was among hundreds of air-mail letters making a special trip. They all had a mail cachet memorializing the one-hundredth anniversary of the Tahlequah, Oklahoma, post office and the twentieth anniversary of air mail.

The letters were first carried from Tahlequah to Muskogee, Oklahoma, by mail stage, a six-hour, thirty-mile trip. Then they were transferred to planes to go on to their destinations. The mail stage used was the world-famous and legendary Deadwood stage coach. It had been built in Concord, New Hampshire, and shipped around the Horn to San Francisco. There it had made the San Francisco-Salt Lake City routes for some time, then carried the mail over the Black Hill roads to Deadwood, South Dakota. Finally it became part of Buffalo Bill's Wild West Show and was featured both here and in Europe as part of exciting America. Now it was having a little part in furthering the business of one of the biggest forces in the country—privately owned life insurance.

In 1937 occurred the horrifying disaster of the *Hindenburg*, the great German zeppelin. It exploded and burned in mid-air over Lakehurst, New Jersey, just as it was about to land after a transAtlantic flight. Those who have listened to that dramatic part of the recording "I Can Hear It Now" can remind themselves that they so witnessed the death of one Mutual Benefit policyholder. This man had bought his first Company policy at age 25, and with increasing business success he became a very substantial policyholder. For some years before his death he was European representative of a large New York advertising firm. Chancellor Hitler and other Nazi officials were among his personal friends, as was also the commander of the *Hindenburg* in which he had made several previous flights.

Throughout these years the general death rates of the country had been improving. Marked changes were appearing in mortality

among annuitants. Changes in policy provisions to bring settlement option rates into line with current experience became very necessary. For other reasons also it was desirable to modernize the policy in the first major revision since 1922.

An attractive and modern physical design was worked out by Rudolph Ruzicka, eminent American artist. The 1938 policy was set up in documentary style, the first change, except in size, from the 1845 four-page folder.

Important changes in the contract provisions were:

A reduction in policy loan interest from 6% to 5% to comply with New York State law. Because of the cost of handling small loans and the effect on Company financing of standing ready to meet large cash demands, the Company did not feel that this change was to the advantage of the whole body of policyholders. Therefore the change was not made retroactive.

Provision for a ninety-day deferment clause as required in many states. This has never been invoked by the Company.

Reduction of guaranteed instalments under the life income plans of settlement.

Six settlement options, including a joint and survivorship annuity choice. The three new options had been available previously upon request, but were not part of the standard contract.

In announcing the new policy the Company stated that it was continuing practices allowing the broadest flexibility in drafting special settlement agreements, such as the combination of the interest option with the right to a later choice of life income. Earlier Vice President Rhodes had spoken of the Company's established principle that payment of a lump sum of life insurance proceeds was not enough in many cases. He had said:

> Instead of restricting the Settlement Option provision and service as other companies have done, or propose to do, we aim to broaden them. Next to Non-forfeiture I regard our Settlement Option service as the greatest thing that has been developed in life insurance. It has made the purpose of life insurance secure.

The first policy on the new form, 2,000,001, was issued to Mr. H. G. Kenagy. It was on the income endowment plan and its purpose in the Kenagy life insurance program was to provide family Christmas presents.

Herbert G. Kenagy had become Company superintendent of agencies in 1936 replacing Mr. Oliver Thurman who for reasons of health had relinquished those duties. Mr. Thurman continued as vice president, assigned to the underwriting department, an area where he had had experience in a previous company.

Mr. Kenagy had a broad background in sales training work and as assistant manager of the Life Insurance Sales Research Bureau (now the Life Insurance Agency Management Association). He was already well-known and liked by many Company field men.

The Company recognized the need to rebuild the agency forces so weakened by the depression experiences, and began a major investment in that rehabilitation program. The goal of the agency department became: every full-time Mutual Benefit field man earning a good living and having a good time doing it. To develop a procedure that would lead to this goal, methods used in Company agencies with superior production per man were studied. The New Hampshire agency of William E. Johnson was showing unusual results in production and manpower.

From that agency Fern D. Haselton was brought to the home office to develop a distinctively Mutual Benefit sales plan. The result was the Analagraph device and procedure. They were rooted in the good property philosophy and sales ideas already successfully used by many Mutual Benefit representatives.

To get the Analagraph into operation throughout the field, Mr. Haselton was joined in the agency department by three other field service men.* Nicknamed "The Four Horsemen," they covered the nation.

Since 1937 the Analagraph has been promoted as the standard life insurance programming procedure of the Company. The Analagraph device was patented. Its "lines and rules" became a curse, and finally a blessing, to hundreds of field men in scores of schools who sweated to perfect the technique: "These lines and rules enable you to draw a picture of what you want your property to do for you."

A General Agents Advisory Committee was organized in 1937. This operated with rotating membership until the General Agents Association was organized in 1945.

A series of agents conventions, not entirely on the self entertainment basis, was held during these years. That in 1939 at Spring Lake, New Jersey, was notable for several reasons. A member of

---

* One was Bill C. Thurman who later became head of the agency department, as second vice president for 1946–1947.

the three-man agents committee which cooperated in that convention planning was a successful young supervisor from Detroit, H. Bruce Palmer. Mr. Palmer had entered the business in the depths of the depression, but those hard early days were already far behind in experience if not in time.

During this convention a meeting was scheduled for the National Associates under the chairmanship of John D. Hibbard of Grand Rapids. The National Associates had been organized earlier in the year at a meeting at the home office. Invited to the organization meeting were the twenty-five leading agents for the Company in 1938 and three general agents whose personal production was in the same range.

The group was reminded of a small informal group of brilliant and effective life insurance men, mostly from the Mutual Benefit, who met together occasionally during the 1920's to exchange sales ideas and techniques. It was suggested that a comparable program might be useful under the present conditions.

The idea found favor. The old group had called themselves The Associates. The new group adopted the name "The National Associates." They also became an autonomous organization, independent of home office direction. It was decided, however, that membership should be limited to Mutual Benefit men and determined by rank in the Company leaders club. At the beginning and for many years the National Associates paid all their own expenses. Company officers attend National Associates meetings by special invitation.

The National Associates membership in the first year included twenty-one members whose entire life insurance career had been in the Mutual Benefit. The average age of all members at joining the Company was 30.6 years, and their average service just about seventeen years.

The National Associates have become recognized as the top honor group of the Company. Members say that the meetings are the most profitable business discussions they attend. The sessions are real round table discussions, informal, specific and completely frank. At the 1956 meeting not only Mr. Hibbard but eight other charter members were present: John Welburn Brown, C.L.U. of Louisville; Paul W. Cook, C.L.U. of Chicago; Mervyn A. Hedgcock of Detroit; Wallace H. King of Lima, Ohio; Max M. Matson of Cleveland; N. Earl Pinney of Detroit; Lawrence G. Singer of Milwaukee and Sidney Weil of Cincinnati.

At Spring Lake for the first time at a Mutual Benefit convention, social security was an important subject on the program. Earlier in the year the social security law had been revised, bringing into existence the equivalent of $50,000,000,000 of new life insurance. The new income benefits for widows and for school children under age 18 gave Analagraphers and all life insurance salesmen who talked about family protection entirely new ideas for discussion.

The Spring Lake convention was advertised to Mutual Benefit qualifiers as "next door to the New York World's Fair." The trylon and the perisphere and all the suggested wonders for the "World of Tomorrow" were much discussed. Mostly there were dreams and not nightmares about the world of tomorrow. But already during the convention Hitler's panzer divisions were rolling over Poland and World War II had begun.

CHAPTER ELEVEN

World War II

THE RESULTS OF WAR IN EUROPE were felt in a number of claims before Pearl Harbor, December 7, 1941, that "date that will live in infamy." One was a young college professor who had become interested in the Royalist cause in Spain and was killed in the Spanish Civil War in 1939. Another was a civilian on board the *Zam Zam* who died of wounds received when that ship was shelled by the Germans in April 1941. There were also a few other cases of accident and disease in the training camps.

In the year following Pearl Harbor there were ninety-eight war deaths among Company policyholders for slightly more than half a million dollars of insurance, with twenty-five more policyholders insured for $112,000 reported missing.

The matter of "missing" policyholders imposed problems quite new with this war. There were many cases especially from the Pacific theater, because the Japanese Government was very slow in reporting prisoners. Also many small islands in the area of sea battles increased the chances for survival. Proof of death and cause of death (needed in case of aviation restrictions) in many cases were difficult to get because of necessity for military secrecy. This was particularly true of merchant seamen on torpedoed ships.

The United States Government in its various departments co-operated most helpfully within necessary limits. Laws provided that "missing" status would be continued for a year if no definite proof otherwise developed. At the end of the year, if facts warranted, the War or Navy Department issued a Finding of Death. Upon that evidence the Company paid claims. Similarly the Maritime War Emergency Board or the War Shipping Administration provided evidence on the basis of which the Company made settlement.

The effect of the war in number of policyholder deaths was not serious. Through 1946 there was a total of 1,332 claims (including thirty-five civilians) for $4,800,000.

The first member of the Mutual Benefit Life sales force* to be killed in action in World War II was Lieutenant Irving Van Gilder Perine, Jr. He was lost fighting with the Marines in the Solomon Islands in August 1942. Only 34 years old, he was a graduate of Princeton and had been a member of the Company's Newark agency for nine years. In 1941 he had won his place among the top twenty-five leaders of the Company, qualifying as a member of the National Associates.

The only death among servicemen from the home office staff was Sergeant Daniel Mugler of the correspondence department. He was killed in an automobile accident on the West Coast in December 1942. His wife, a former Company employee, was also severely injured.

Of course limitation of acceptance of war hazards became necessary even before the United States entered the war. In May 1940 the Company began using a war and travel clause for policies apparently involving extra risk. Full coverage was provided only with extra premium for such policyholders in case of death in the following circumstances:

1. While serving in military, naval or air forces of any other country than the United States which is at war, declared or undeclared, or in a noncombatant organization (such as the Red Cross or Y.M.C.A.) accompanying such forces, or
2. While traveling or living, temporarily or otherwise, outside of the United States or Canada within two years from the date of issue of the policy.

Immediately after Pearl Harbor restrictions were adopted generally in connection with all men between the ages of 16 and 45, and for others in the armed forces or related civilian services. The clauses limited liability from war, foreign travel or residence and

---

* In all, there were four agents lost in World War II.

aviation hazards. Amounts of insurance even with the war clause were also limited. For the draft-liable men this was generally $50,000. For others the limits varied from time to time. There were some variations also because of the requirements in different states.

By 1943 the National Association of Insurance Commissioners had agreed upon recommended principles for war coverage for all companies. This introduced the idea of judging the limitation of risk according to location. A "home area" was defined as the States of the United States, the District of Columbia, the Dominion of Canada and Newfoundland. The Commissioners recommended that within the home area there be no restriction on coverage because of service in the armed forces, but that outside of that area there be complete absence of coverage while the insured was in active service.

The Mutual Benefit Life adopted the recommendations of the Commissioners, except that it continued protection outside the home area for deaths not due to war service.

This meant, for example, that a draftee killed in an automobile accident going to the movies in the United States was fully covered with all companies accepting the Commissioners' principles. A service man killed in an automobile accident in Egypt going down to see the Pyramids was not covered by companies which followed the Commissioners. Such a man *was* covered by the Mutual Benefit Life.

This Company endeavored to be as liberal as seemed wise during all the war problems. Review of the twenty-five largest companies in 1943 showed that most were limiting all ages and both sexes, and also excluding non-war deaths outside of the "home area." The Mutual Benefit Life was still making its insurance available without war or aviation clauses for women and for boys under age 16 and for men over age 45. The Company also was recognizing coverage for non-war deaths abroad.

By the fall of 1944 the war commentators were talking about an early end of the conflict, "by Thanksgiving," or "surely by Christmas." The Company relaxed restrictions for new insurance for older ages. It was not until August 17, 1945, however, that the agencies received the welcome telegram: "Beginning immediately war riders will not be attached to new policies unless there appears to be a definite extra risk of death from war, travel or aviation."

Home office personnel and procedures of course bore their share of war burdens. When employees began to enlist and to be called into service in 1940 the Company softened the economic blow. For any whose income was reduced because of that service, the Mutual Benefit Life for one year paid the difference between service pay and the Company salary.

The price level increases generated by the war were reflected in home office salary increases, especially for the lower-paid group. There was a general raise for those under $7,000 in 1941, and again in 1943 for all except management and professional staff members who were making under $5,000. The second increase was allowed by the Wage Stabilization Board only with increase of work time to a 42-hour week. In 1943 Newark was declared a critical manpower area and no replacement of employees was allowed. With the normal turnover and the continued drain of men and women going into service this created many difficulties.

In early spring of 1945 there came a demand to the Company to still further release a quota of employees for essential war work. The Company gave the staff members an opportunity to volunteer to fill the quota with the promise of getting Mutual Benefit jobs back later. Fortunately the course of events developed so that this release of employees was not serious. By the fall of 1945 the 42-hour week was discontinued and a 38-hour week adopted.

From 909 employees in 1941 the home office staff contracted to 653 employees in 1945. Naturally in such circumstances many jobs valuable in normal times had to slide. All sorts of operations were affected—from painting the walls to keeping certain records in the mathematical department.

To make best possible use of manpower available the Company encouraged active suggestions from the staff about "ways to speed up the work" or about "rules that might be discarded or changed to advantage." A beginning of an organized suggestion system had been made in 1929 and this was expanded in 1943. During the war the summertime Saturday closing became a year-round schedule. Eliminating the extra day's travel was an overall efficiency in use of gasoline and community work hours.

Home office employees carried many extra responsibilities in volunteer war work as well as in paid defense jobs. There was generous response to war drives of all kinds. At Christmas in 1940 the Company officers and employees raised funds for a mobile kitchen which became attached to the Salvation Army in the Lancaster area in England and served many of the American forces coming in from Northern Ireland.

In 1942 the Mutual Benefit Life became a 100% Company for payroll savings purchase of war bonds.

In spite of special war problems there were opportunities to try some new ventures. In 1941 the first cashiers conference was held at the home office. This brought to Newark for a week's orientation and instruction a group of ten women with long service in the agency offices in the field. Several had worked for the Company for a lifetime and had never seen the home office. The devotion of women agency office employees and their hard and efficient work is an immeasurable asset to the Company. Cashiers conferences have been held many times since with different groups of participants, bringing increased understanding between home office and field.

The home office women have cooperated personally far beyond the requirement of duty to this desirable project. The Women's Club particularly has been especially helpful. As has been mentioned, they have entertained the visitors and in many thoughtful personal ways made their visits memorable.

In 1943 the Company gave a leave of absence to its general agent at Flint, Michigan, H. Bruce Palmer, to serve as president of the United States Junior Chamber of Commerce. That organization was an important force for good on the home front. Part of Mr. Palmer's comments on that year's experiences, as reported in *The Pelican*, are significant. The presidential schedule involved 60,000 miles of travel through thirty-nine states with five trips into Canada, and some two hundred fifty talks, sometimes two or three a day, before audiences ranging from fifty to five hundred people.

This past year I have been privileged to confer with seventy-five of the country's top-notch business executives. To sit with the president of General Motors or of DuPont for an hour, exchanging ideas and opinions, develops a confidence that should last through the years. I also interviewed many government leaders, including most of the governors. I had an opportunity to see the full scale of our nation's productive efforts—in itself an education. It seems, too, as if I visited nearly every army camp, airfield and depot in the country. Almost every large city was included in the itinerary.

Notwithstanding the rigors of my duties, this year has been the greatest experience a young man could have, and I would not exchange it for many thousands of dollars. It was greater than a college education with all its post-graduate studies wrapped up in one year. It is unfortunate that so few young men realize the full concept of the executive training in such activities. When considering the principal attributes of business success—stimulated imagination, toleration and cooperation with one's fellowman, a sense of humor, ability to express oneself on his feet, the demand for intelligent opinions and decisions, and the development of the power of doing the greater tasks in life through ability to do the small things—it is not difficult to realize how my Junior Chamber of Commerce experience has helped me.

Many members of the home office staff shared in camp and hospital shows. A musical event within Company walls was the recital given by John O'Fake on his forty-fifth Mutual Benefit anniversary. "John," as he was known to all, was messenger for the executives on the second floor. He had entered the Company in the days of Amzi Dodd and was very proud of his association with the outstanding institution of Newark. He came of a musical family well-known in the city for several generations. He played the piano, violin, viola and 'cello, and composed and arranged music also. For some years he was an officer of the New Amsterdam Club of New York, an organization of colored musicians. A standing-room-only crowd enjoyed his noon-time anniversary recital. What a picture he made—the gray-haired little man at the big Steinway. His final number was his own composition, words and music, entitled "My Girls, My Men." They were the second floor executives and secretaries whom he served with smiling courtliness.

For Company representatives outside the home office life was anything but a pretty melody in the early forties. As Mr. Hardin said, "They had hard sledding, to take a word from my country boyhood, but they did not give up the sled."

The war years made selling harder for many reasons. There was tremendous pressure on everybody to put at least 10% of earnings into war bonds. Prices were rising which psychologically was bad, even though incomes for many were rising faster. There was much talk and fear of inflation. The public suffered from "tax anticipation nerves" at some periods when increased tax rates were not yet definitely known, and other tax pains when they did know. Moreover they discovered that a tax objection was a new one before which many salesmen easily wilted. Of course when war actually came millions of men between the ages of 18 and 45 were largely taken out of the market.

New business in 1942 fell to the lowest point since before World War I, $107,000,000. The increase in insurance in force that year, because of a great improvement in lapses, was however the largest since 1934, $22,000,000.

That year there were already 142 field men in service. War industries of course were draining off others. For many men who remained there was a personal morale problem. They needed to keep themselves sold on the patriotic value of the life insurance job. A statement by Marriner S. Eccles, chairman of the Federal Reserve System, was much quoted at that time:

> I feel that next to the purchase of Government Savings and War Bonds and Stamps by the public, investment in life insurance is particularly to be encouraged at this time.

By the end of 1944 about two hundred field men were in service and probably as many more in full-time war industry jobs.

President Hardin expressed in a scholarly way in his 1943 report to policyholders facts and ideas which every successful life insurance man needed to remember.

> The real lesson of life insurance history is that our business offers no conflict in war or peace with the patriotic response of a free people to the highest duties of citizenship . . . Life insurance conserves the savings of policyholders and makes them available for the national needs in peace and in war. In time of peace, by wise investment in type and diversity, we make the savings under our administration available not only for our policyholders but for com-

merce and navigation, for trade and agriculture, for production and distribution, for the purposes of enlightened civilization and the advancement of human happiness.... In time of war, life insurance also furnishes the sinews of war to the government which defends us. And, in either war or peace, the . . . great cooperative enterprise, its mutuality uninterrupted, goes on responsive to all contract requirements, a warehouse of national resources, partner in the promotion and preservation of the American Way. . . . Every producing life insurance agent is a participant in that service. In this troubled time, requiring every effort for the protection of the national life and of the ideals for which our fathers fought, life insurance is of vital importance to the war program.

Mutual Benefit Life agents and good salesmen from all companies were the backbone of war bond sales, fund drives, civil defense programs and similar war-supporting work across the country.

From the beginning, life insurance agents cooperated in publicizing the National Service Life Insurance. That was available on a pay-deduction, minimum cost basis, $10,000 to every service man or woman. As discharges began, lapses in National Service Life Insurance mounted. It was the life underwriters of the country who did most effective work to stem the tide. To their own disadvantage they explained that the cost of that insurance was lower than for most private insurance. The Government's heavy subsidy accounts for that. The taxpayers of the nation, not the National Service policyholders, bear the losses of service-connected deaths and all expenses of administration.

Beginning in 1945 the Mutual Benefit Life required with every application that showed ownership of National Service Life Insurance a written statement about plans for keeping it.

The attitude of the life underwriters of the country toward National Service Life Insurance was constructive and patriotic. It made news for the life insurance business as was illustrated one day when General Omar N. Bradley spoke at a New York City Life Underwriters all-day seminar on veterans' affairs.

A newspaper reporter was overheard at the noon recess telephoning his story to his paper. The point of his story was that the life underwriters were preparing to conserve National Service Life Insurance policies. Judging by the conversation, the editor could not believe that a life insurance agent would not try primarily to sell his own insurance, regardless. Finally the reporter shouted into the receiver: "But they are not; they are learning how to help the G I's keep their army insurance." That concept of service was so contrary to the layman's idea of agents' actions to make it "news" for a big New York editor.

War conditions and increased taxes brought opportunities for new kinds of selling. Outstanding was the development of employee benefit plans funded through life insurance. The emphasis on social security and on added benefits to employees in place of restricted salary increases turned attention to pensions. The tax situation made employers feel they were getting a bargain with their dollars spent on pensions.

The Company moved toward cooperating in handling this business for groups of employees who were generally the type acceptable for its standard rates. In 1941 a new retirement annuity with cash values and death benefits was introduced for uninsurable lives under pension trusts.

In 1944 the Company restricted pension trust business to full-time Mutual Benefit Life salesmen. Limits for cases were indicated as 200 lives and $1,000,000 of insurance the first year with an eventual potential of 600 lives and $3,000,000. In that year pension trust business amounted to 26% of the Company total.

These years also saw a great increase in emphasis on all kinds of business insurance. The business pocketbook, not the personal pocketbook, became recognized as the source of large life insurance premiums.

The pension trust sales were a door opener for work with blue-collar men who had previously been neglected by many Mutual Benefit Life salesmen. The rising earnings of this part of every community brought them everywhere into the limelight as prospects for standard ordinary life insurance.

Another newly cultivated market was women. The great increase in the number of working women during the war naturally made alert salesmen recognize their life insurance needs. The Mutual Benefit Life published its first sales material for women with independent incomes.

The following anecdote features a typical woman policyholder, though not a typical sales experience.

A member of the Norfolk agency one day was driving, not too slowly, along a Virginia highway. He heard a siren whine behind him, was overtaken by an officer and pulled over to the side of the road.

"You seem to be in a hurry, Mister," said the policeman as he pulled out a summons book. "What's the rush?"

"I have an appointment to deliver a life insurance policy to a client of mine and I was afraid I would be late," said the agent as he reached for his license.

"Life insurance, eh," said the officer. "You don't know Milton Ames in Norfolk, do you?"

"Yes, he's my general agent. Do you know him?"

"Sure. He's an old friend of mine. Mutual Benefit, right?"

"Right."

"Say, maybe you can help me out," continued the officer amiably. "I lost my son in the war and now my daughter-in-law has a job and extra money from life insurance. I told her she should put some of it away for the future. Would you go and talk to her about it?"

Result: $10,000 twenty-year endowment prepaid. No summons.

In 1942, in line with contemporary developments the Company inaugurated the Veterans Service Allowance Plan. Sixty-one full-time salesmen who were 65 years of age or older and who had twenty continuous years of Mutual Benefit service received their first monthly life income checks. The amount of the income was based on the last ten years of earnings. The plan is noncontributory. It is also *not* a retirement plan, for the salesman may keep on working as he receives the income.

The difficulties in getting medical examinations made during war years, when so many doctors were in service, led to the nonmedical plan. This was adopted in the summer of 1943.

As a further cooperation with the field the Company in 1943 also entered upon a new advertising program. The Mutual Benefit Life had done no national advertising since 1936. The new series of advertisements was run first in the *Saturday Evening Post,* and in 1944 the campaign was extended to *Fortune* and *Good Housekeeping.*

It was a public relations campaign, not aimed toward direct sales results. Its purpose was to build public identification of the Mutual Benefit Life as a sound, friendly and distinctive company, spotlighting things about the Mutual Benefit that are different from other companies.

One of the advertisements in this series was headed "An Unexpected Legacy," a phrase frequently used in describing Mutual Benefit claim payments. The heart of the copy was the following paragraphs:

> A farmer in Kentucky failed to pay the sixth annual premium on his policy, but, according to the terms of the policy, the insurance was continued for a period of nearly seven years.
>
> After the insurance had expired, the farmer died. . . . If the policy had been issued on a *later form* the insurance would have continued beyond the date of his death. Following our established practice of applying the more liberal provisions of a *new* policy to *old* policies, whenever practical, the Company paid the insurance to the surprise and gratification of the widow, *who thought the policy was worthless.*
>
> Perhaps that may help to show you the kind of Company we are.

The effect of the war on Company investments was as drastic as the depression, although in another way. In World War II, as in all previous wars, the Company responded strongly to the call for war financing. Holdings of Government bonds rose from 16.6% of Company assets in 1940 to 47.7% in 1946. In the Seventh War Loan in 1945 the Mutual Benefit Life subscribed for $100,000,000. This was one million dollars for every year of Company history and was made a feature of the centennial observance. Later in the year the Company bought $56,200,000 in the Victory Loan drive.

During this period the Company sold many other bonds, especially municipal bonds with certain tax exemptions. The tax exempt feature was for technical reasons not valuable to a life insurance company, but raised the selling price because of desirability to other investors. The amount of mortgage investments and holdings of foreclosed real estate also decreased steadily during the war years.

The policy loan account shrank with increasing general prosperity. The anti-inflation campaigns of the Government and others interested in national economic health urged the repayment of debts, including life insurance policy loans. Also, banks began seeking loans on the collateral of life insurance cash values. Many policyholders refinanced their policy loans in this way, with a dollar savings and advantage to their life insurance programs. Commenting about this trend, President Hardin said in his report to policyholders for 1941 that it was "a practice which banks did not follow until recently."

The swing to Government bonds for nearly half of the Company's assets brought a continued decline in interest rates. This was the major factor in the decision to reduce dividends in 1940 and again in 1942.

Mindful of the Company's hundred-year-old principle, "The first object of a life insurance company is safety," the Mutual Benefit Life strengthened reserves at this time. With net interest earnings of 3.34% in 1944 and still sinking, the 3% interest assumption used since 1900 did not seem as conservative as desirable. Therefore as of the end of 1944 all reserves were increased to the $2\frac{7}{8}\%$ basis, and again at the end of 1945 they were increased to the $2\frac{3}{4}\%$ basis. Each change required about $9,000,000 addition to the reserve fund. As in similar previous changes, higher cash values and other benefits were thus made available to old policyholders. What this meant is reflected in just one case.

A policyholder in Spokane, Washington, had the frightful experience of seeing his only daughter killed before his eyes. When the next premium on his life insurance was due he ignored the notice and all follow-up efforts. The protection was extended under the Company's nonforfeiture provisions.

The shock of his daughter's death steadily undermined his health, he neglected his business and seemed not to care that all family resources were disappearing. Finally he died on April 4, 1946.

The local Company representative had been following the case and immediately wired the home office to find whether any insurance was still in force. By the terms of the contract with its 3% reserve, the insurance would have been continued to March 27, 1946. That was eight days before the policyholder died. But under the change to the $2\frac{3}{4}\%$ reserve the insurance actually had been continued to April 14. That was ten days beyond the date of his death, and his widow received $11,658.

During the war years, Mr. John S. Thompson and other members of the actuarial staff were working on a project of major importance to the whole life insurance business. The American Experience Table of Mortality which the Company had been using as the basis

John S. Thompson

W. Paul Stillman

of its business since 1870, and which was standard for ordinary business in most companies, was developed from mid-nineteenth century statistics. The progress in sanitation, immunization and care of infectious diseases had brought spectacular improvements in the death rates especially at the younger ages. For instance, Dr. Richard Connolly, mentioned earlier as the young doctor who supervised the Company's first laboratory, was also Newark's first public health laboratory doctor. He told that the first year he came to Newark a family in his neighborhood lost five children in one winter from diphtheria. The year of his retirement, there was not one case of that formerly dreaded disease reported in the city.

Of course in mutual companies dividends could adjust the cost of life insurance with equity regardless of the mortality table used in original calculation of premiums. But there were a number of technical disadvantages and some other problems involved in giving equitable treatment to policyholders in other respects. Moreover, the public often questioned why life insurance should continue using such an outmoded tool.

Therefore the National Association of Insurance Commissioners felt that corrective steps should be taken. In 1937 they appointed a committee to study the need for a new mortality table and related matters. The seven-man committee was made up of five State Department actuaries, and one representative each of the Actuarial Society of America and the American Institute of Actuaries.* Once again the Mutual Benefit Life made a notable contribution to the advance of life insurance because its vice president and mathematician, Mr. John S. Thompson, was appointed the committee member representing the Actuarial Society.

The committee worked for about two years and submitted detailed recommendations. Continuation of the work was authorized with Mr. Thompson remaining a member of the committee. It was called informally the Guertin Committee, for its chairman, Mr. Alfred N. Guertin, actuary of the New Jersey Department of Banking and Insurance.

The second report was made in September 1941 and was in two major divisions. The new mortality table recommended was designated the Commissioners 1941 Standard Ordinary Mortality Table. This was abbreviated to the CSO Table.

* Those professional societies did not combine as the Society of Actuaries until 1949.

Because of Mr. Thompson's membership on these committees much of the staff work—a job for all American life insurance—fell to the Mutual Benefit Life. It was done by members of the mathematical department under the guidance of Harry W. Jones. The available statistics were organized, crude death rates were developed and the results subjected to graduation to smooth away irregularities. Three members of the Actuarial Society had been asked by the committee to be responsible for an acceptable graduation of the data, and, since this required various trials before an acceptable one was discovered, the Mutual Benefit people spent several weeks in constant telephone contact with the three actuaries, who were located in different parts of the country.

Recognizing that the laws of most states would have to be changed in order to permit use of the new table, the Guertin Committee included in its work a second major project—the drafting of a standard valuation law and a standard nonforfeiture law. Not all states that enacted these laws did so in the exact form recommended and some enacted only the most necessary form of statute. However, the way was finally cleared for the use of policy forms based on the new table, and the date at which the use of the new table became mandatory for the new business of all companies was quite generally fixed at January 1, 1948.

Meanwhile it was recognized that if all companies in the country set about computing their own tables of monetary values on the new mortality standard the duplication in work would be enormous. World War II was in progress and the shortage in manpower and machines for normal business operations was acute. Accordingly, the Actuarial Society of America and the American Institute of Actuaries arranged to collaborate through a joint committee of five actuaries in the production of the vast number of monetary value calculations required by the entire insurance business. Mr. Thompson was named as one of the five.

Once again staff in the Mutual Benefit Life was called upon to contribute. The Company having determined to adopt the CSO Table as early as possible, many of its own needs in the matter had already been met. Many machine and punch card methods had been designed and tested, and were now put to more extended use on behalf of the entire industry. To meet the broad and varied requirements of the business, seven rates of interest were used, and the results were published in twenty-four volumes, giving 1,850,000 values. A survey made not long after the last volumes were distributed indicated that nineteen of the twenty-four volumes appeared to be entirely free of mathematical error. Mr. Guertin commented that it was the first time in actuarial history that monetary tables were constructed on such a broad base. The preface to the volumes bears tribute to the Company and to certain of its staff in the following words:

> Much of the work was necessarily carried out by individual actuaries, including, in particular, Mr. Harry W. Jones and Mr. Henry B. Thiessen, whose close supervision, and extensive and intricate planning, much of it without precedent in the construction of actuarial tables by mechanical means, constitute a major contribution to the project. We express our high appreciation of this and of the contribution made through them by The Mutual Benefit Life Insurance Company.

The Mutual Benefit Life was the first major company to issue all of its new business on the new CSO basis. Mr. Guertin asked to have the first contract and became the proud owner of Policy 3,000,001, issued in September 1945. The inauguration of the new series was a part of the centennial observance. Mr. Thompson wrote at that time:

> Insurance history is being made today. Developments of epochal importance to the life insurance business are now being unfolded before our eyes. They involve types of changes which have occurred only a time or two in the century during which life insurance has been developing in America. For example, The Mutual Benefit Life Insurance Company, during its century of existence, before its change of rates in 1945, had changed the basic mortality table used in its premium calculations only once, from Carlisle to American, in 1870; and the basic rate of interest only once, from 4% to 3%, in 1900.
>
> The current changes . . . are the result of the recent important variations in the two socio-economic factors which profoundly affect the cost of life insurance and the stability of the life insurance business:

(1) the decline in the rates of mortality at ages under 50, and

(2) the decline in net interest earnings, especially since 1930.

In addition to the basic changes of mortality and interest assumptions, the 1945 edition of the contract included several very important innovations. A provision was included that guaranteed return of any premiums paid beyond the date of death. Some other companies have a similar provision for the month of death, but none have the complete refund provided by the Mutual Benefit Life. The value of this benefit was illustrated recently in a case in the State of Washington. The policyholder, a banker, died five days after paying the annual premium on his policies. His widow received $545 more than the face of the policies. She and the bank both were amazed and thankful for this unanticipated addition to her funds.

The new 1945 contract also guarantees the right to change the plan on a favorable basis. This advantage had been a matter of practice for some time and is made available to old policyholders also.

Plans for recognition of the Company's one hundredth anniversary had been long in the making. Early in 1944 a committee representing the three home office clubs—the Pelican Club, the Veterans Club and the Women's Club, with a Company officer as chairman, was appointed to plan a program for the home office staff. Mr. Hardin personally took the greatest interest in all plans, and worked closely with the officer assigned to organize the year's special activities. He insisted that the program be designated an "observance" rather than a "celebration." The latter term seemed to him lacking the connotation of dignity and deep significance which he felt appropriate.

A national agents convention was scheduled in hopes that peace developments would make it possible, but that did not come to pass. Each qualifier for the convention, however, received a souvenir of the "hoped for convention," an 1845 penny. The Company quite cornered the market for this large-size old coin in assembling six hundred for the centennial year distribution.

Agencies, such as Albany, Cleveland and Washington, with a hundred-year history staged various centennial events. Frequently there were dinners or meetings for policyholders and friends, with an historical program.

The home office staff centennial program extended over more

than a week. January 30, 1945, marked the end of a century for the Mutual Benefit Life. The closing ceremony came at the end of the office day. The home office staff assembled in the first floor corridors centering toward the rotunda. There were grouped a chorus of Company singers and a quartet of trumpeters. After a trumpet fanfare Mr. Hardin was escorted down the palm-lined east hall from the officers' elevator by representatives of the Veterans and Pelican clubs. The President spoke briefly about the significance of the centennial milestone in Company history. Ceremoniously the great bronze doors at the ends of the corridors were closed. A minute of silence followed. Then the doors were opened again with singing and trumpeting to signify the beginning of the new century.

After the beginning of business on the first day of the Company's second century inquiry was made as to the last policy issued in the old century and the first in the new. Sometimes fate gives a lucky break and this happened to be one of those times.

The last policy in the first hundred years was written by R. Keith Charles of South Carolina, who had represented the Company since 1897. The insured was a young man who was already a Mutual Benefit policyholder and who subsequently became an agent for the Company. The first policy in the second hundred years was written by a successful new agent, an Analagrapher in Minneapolis.

January 31, 1945, was the anniversary of the signing of the special act of the New Jersey Legislature which gave the Company its charter. The Charter Day program began at eleven o'clock in the morning (after some attempt at a day's work). The staff assembled in the auditorium to witness a dramatic portrayal of the century of Mutual Benefit Life history.

The performance was done in the living newspaper technique developed by Hallie Flanagan for the Federal Theater Project under the W.P.A. during the depression. That technique requires very little staging. It is a combination of tableaux, acted episodes, projected pictures, music and narration. Professionals helped with the script, staging, costumes and narration, but the show was essentially a home production. In fast-changing impressions the audience got a factual story of highlights of Mutual Benefit history with a flavor in the presentation that inspired pride in the Company too.

After the performance one of the older women, self-recognized as always critical, said, "That was marvelous. Even I liked the Mutual Benefit this morning."

The historical program was followed by a buffet lunch in the Company's dining room, decorated with spring flowers, palms and ferns. There was music and dancing and just visiting among the office associates, and, most appreciated of all, at 2:30 P.M. the office closed for the rest of the day.

The next week there was still another event for the home office staff. This program was called Family History Day. At the end of the day's work the staff again assembled in the auditorium. They found the stage set as a home parlor in 1845. There were gathered the household, about twenty members of the staff in costume—old and young, fat and thin, male and female, black and white, who presented a delightful half hour of songs of the 1845 era. There were solos, duets, choruses and a little horseplay. Of course Stephen Foster music was featured, and such a gem as, "I wish I was single again," rendered feelingly by a popular member of the underwriting department.

Following the music Mr. Hardin and Mr. Rhodes delivered commemorative addresses, featuring biographical material about Robert L. Patterson, Amzi Dodd and Bloomfield J. Miller.

This day closed with the centennial banquet, also held in the staff dining room on the sixth floor. Special honor was given the one hundred active staff members who were oldest in point of Company service. Their average length of service was nearly thirty-seven years. They sat at special tables with Mr. Hardin and Mr. Rhodes, set apart with golden ropes.

The purpose of the centennial observance in home office and field was to focus thought on the history and principles of the Company as an inspiration to the future. In the souvenir folder of the week of home office centennial activities just described was included a statement by Mr. Rhodes about the aims of the Company:

> The aim of the Mutual Benefit is to keep constantly before it the beneficent character of the business and to regard itself as the trustee of those who are endeavoring to accomplish through life insurance what they could not accomplish in any other way. Accordingly, the

policy contracts of the Company are made as liberal and flexible as possible, the greatest possible amount of service is rendered to the policyholders, the principle of retroaction is applied to the fullest possible extent and the return upon invested funds is regarded as of less importance than their safety. Having done these things, the further aim of the Company is to conduct its business so economically that the net cost of insurance will compare favorably in dollars and cents with the net cost of insurance in companies having other aims.

While the Mutual Benefit ranks in size among the first seven companies whose business does not include industrial insurance, it is not particularly interested in size. Neither is it interested in reducing the cost of insurance, as it might do materially, by issuing a less liberal policy than it now issues, by rendering less service to policyholders and by failing to recognize the principle that in a mutual company old policyholders are entitled, in so far as possible, to the benefits granted new policyholders.

In May the Company had two centennial events for outsiders. The first was a luncheon-reception in the recreation room for five hundred prominent citizens and business leaders of Newark. The second was a luncheon for nearly four hundred members of the Newark Life Underwriters Association on the day of their spring sales congress held in the Company's auditorium.

Throughout the year there was constant mention of the centennial in Company advertising, centennial seal stickers were used on letters and proposals for clients, the postage meter carried a centennial message, and in many other ways the hundredth anniversary was kept before Company members and the public.

A very special feature of the centennial observance was the publication of a book, *The Great Stewardship*. Albert W. Atwood of Washington, a recognized writer often appearing in the *Saturday Evening Post*, the *National Geographic* and similar quality magazines, was the author. The book told the story of one hundred years of mutual life insurance in the United States as reflected in the experience of the Mutual Benefit Life.

The launching of the book was the last event in the calendar of the centennial observance. The Company planned an author's luncheon in honor of Mr. Atwood with the chief librarians of New Jersey university, public and special libraries as honor guests. President Hardin, who had been keenly interested in all the centennial observance and who took a large personal part in the planning, presided at this luncheon. It was his last Company activity. The luncheon was held on Thursday, December 6, 1945. Mr. Hardin died the next day.

Writing to Mr. Atwood about this shocking development, one of the Company officers reported

> . . . feeling a little indisposed he remained home from the office on Friday, and early in the evening suffered what apparently was a heart attack and died just in a few minutes.
>
> After you left on Thursday afternoon I went to Mr. Hardin's room to give him Mrs. Atwood's farewell message. I remained to visit with him a few minutes, gloating over the success of our party. He was thoroughly pleased with the whole performance and spoke with appreciation and admiration about your talk. It can be a pleasant thing for you to remember that you helped make Mr. Hardin's last day with the Mutual Benefit satisfying and happy.

"As when a lordly cedar, green with boughs,/Goes down with a great shout upon the hills,/And leaves a lonesome place against the sky," so fell John R. Hardin. At 85 years of age, still tall and straight, he had been the grand old man of the Newark business community. For thirty-three years until his death he was president of the exclusive Essex Club whose membership included the outstanding business and professional men of the city. He had guided the Mutual Benefit Life through the booming twenties, the great depression and World War II. Through the buffetings of many storms he was wont to say: "We pursue our course."

And thus ended an era!

CHAPTER TWELVE

The New Century

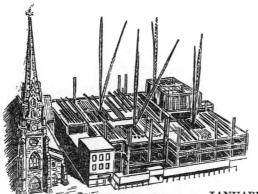

JANUARY 21, 1946, DAWNED JUST like any other winter's day in Newark, and when the home office started its work at 8:20 A.M. (still the wartime schedule), it seemed to be just the beginning of another week. But before the day had ended, action had been taken that subsequent events showed were historic. That afternoon the board of directors took steps that have profoundly influenced the course of the Company in its second century.

W. Paul Stillman was elected chairman of the board of directors, a newly created position in the Mutual Benefit Life. Mr. Stillman was no stranger to the Company since he had served as director for eight years and for six years had been a member of the Company's finance committee. Mr. Stillman was born in Newark and lived most of his life in Red Bank, New Jersey. Upon leaving high school, he started as a runner for the Hanover National Bank in New York City. He advanced through various departments until World War I when he served in the navy as gunner's mate on a submarine. After the war, he returned to banking but left to become a national bank examiner. At only 25 years of age, he was put in charge of all security examinations in the New York banks. Eight years later he became president of the National State Bank of Newark. At that time the bank's assets were $9,000,000. In 1946 the assets had multiplied more than ten times and Mr. Stillman was recognized as one of New Jersey's leading bankers. He was a director and a member of the executive committee of the Fireman's Insurance Company of Newark, a director of the Hudson and Manhattan Railroad and vice chairman of the New Jersey Commission on State Tax Policy. He was chairman of the Newark Clearing House Association, a member of the New Jersey State Banking Advisory Board and chairman of the finance committee of the Hospital Service Plan of New Jersey.

John S. Thompson was elected president. Previous chapters have outlined Mr. Thompson's background of service up to that time. Not previously mentioned were some important facts. From 1937 to 1943, Mr. Thompson was one of the three members of the Board of Actuaries of the Civil Service Retirement and Disability Fund of the United States. For the year 1940–1941, he was president of the Insurance Institute of America. Since its beginning in 1940 he had been a member of the board of governors and secretary of the Medical Service Administration, the parent body of the New Jersey Hospital Service and Medical-Surgical Plans, nonprofit coporations for prepayment of expenses of sickness.

Mr. Thompson was a director of the National State Bank of Newark, a manager of the Bloomfield Savings Institution, president of the Glen Ridge Board of Education and of the Associated Boards of Essex County.

At this same meeting, Edward E. Rhodes was named honorary chairman of the board. At that time, he had the longest record of service of all members of the Mutual Benefit staff, having joined the Company in 1886 at the age of 18.

The Company's management group for the new century swung into action without delay. The first decade witnessed many changes in Company affairs, with a new tempo of activity. The times allowed a vigorous approach to problems. New personalities appeared. New areas of insurance service were entered. Retirement and pension plans were adjusted. A new approach to investment policies was developed. The onerous and confiscatory city tax that had for so long plagued the Company disappeared after an involved legislative struggle. New merchandising methods and an expanded agency program were begun. A new home office building broke the Newark skyline. The story of these years reflects aggressive leadership and sustained purpose—and hard work.

One of Mr. Stillman's first moves was to strengthen the home office team through bringing H. Bruce Palmer from his Flint general agency to the home office. Mr. Palmer had qualified for that year's Million Dollar Round Table and was recognized in life insurance selling as well as in management. He was elected executive assistant to Mr. Stillman and Mr. Thompson in May 1946.

Mr. Stillman promptly began to make known to home office and field the principles and objectives of the new century. Speaking to an agency group in February, he said:

> The institutional roots that have so long sustained us remain the same strong foundation which we have known for a hundred years; and from which for the next hundred we shall continue to receive both vitality and stability. The sound tradition of business methods, the respect for financial integrity, the loyalty that have marked our Company associations are the essence of Mutual Benefit strength; and under no circumstances are they subject to qualification or review. While great age in itself is no guarantee of abnormal success, there is *assurance* in established principles that have won the respect of generations before us, and which are the richest heritage of our Company today. Conservatism, to me, is a policy that, while sticking close to the side of fidelity, fosters a full measure of confidence and is readily compatible with a sound, aggressive, forward-looking program. Growth, initiative and liberalism are not confined to a new order of things nor are they identified only with youth. They go hand-in-hand with the background of our great Company, without impairing or even questioning its basic structures and traditions.

At the big Welcome Home convention in the fall of 1946, the first gathering of agents since the war, Mr. Stillman reported:

> I should like to summarize briefly, a few of the major attitudes and policies which seem to me to be milestones throughout this most progressive year:
>
> *First,* it was fundamental to all our decisions to continue the principles and policies that have made our Company great, and to inculcate those principles and policies into the thinking of those who will assume responsibility for our business in the years ahead.
>
> *Second,* it was a basic personnel policy to provide for the full utilization of the brains, vigor and mentality of everyone associated with our business. May I emphasize that the adoption of this policy has made Mutual Benefit a young man's Company in respect to its top personnel; and has resulted in a timely and fortuitous combination of vigor, initiative and vision, with the experience and maturity of men of greater years.
>
> *Third,* there developed a greater realization of the effort and importance of our general agents and agents, and extensive efforts were made to create a working environment more favorable to the operation and welfare of the men in the field. There are already several

results of these efforts—the new compensation plan for soliciting agents, operating capital to ease the strains of new agency establishments, and a retirement system which, I believe, is second to none in the insurance field.

The ending of the war had brought conditions and a climate favorable to carrying out Mr. Stillman's plans for Company progress. Specific objectives in addition to the general principles mentioned were:

The strengthening of Company management in home office and field especially through younger people released from wartime responsibilities.

Giving Mutual Benefit Life salesmen "a full market basket" in a variety of new coverages consistent with Company standards, and

Converting Company finances from a wartime to a dynamic peacetime basis.

In July 1946 Mr. Kenagy was elected vice president and assigned the task of developing for the Company a public relations department. This was one of the first public relations departments, as distinguished from mere advertising or publicity, in the life insurance business. The purpose was to make the Company increasingly well and favorably known by policyholders and the public.

Mr. Palmer then became superintendent of agencies. That same summer Mathematician Harry W. Jones was elected vice president and in 1948, director. Mr. Jones had come to the Company as a young high school graduate in 1923 and served a rich Company apprenticeship under Mr. Rhodes for some twenty years. He had qualified as a fellow of the Actuarial Society, had been elected an officer first in 1934 with successive promotions to the highest actuarial responsibility. One of the youngest men ever to be named Company vice president, Mr. Jones was a strong link with the past, and stood for qualities in the Company character which the new administration sought to continue.

In 1947 Mr. Palmer was elected vice president in charge of agencies and the next year a director of the Company. In 1950 he was designated administrative vice president, and in 1951, executive vice president. When in 1953 Mr. Thompson retired as president to become vice chairman of the board, Mr. Palmer was elected president, at the age of 44, thus becoming the youngest president in Company history.

Mr. Palmer is a native of Michigan and a graduate of the Uni-

versity of Michigan. Practically all his business life has been spent
with the Mutual Benefit Life, first for a few months in southern
California, then in Michigan. He knows the business as a salesman,
thrown into the job with a minimum of training, and subsequently
through responsibilities as supervisor and general agent.

His interest in civic affairs brought him recognition as president
of the National Junior Chamber of Commerce, as has been mentioned. When he became Company president, *The Pelican* summarized his local and national interests:

> He continues his interest in the Chamber of Commerce of the United
> States. He has served as director, as a member of the Chamber's
> committee on international, political and social problems, chairman
> of its sub-committee on the United Nations, and is currently a mem-
> ber of its education committee. He is also president of the New
> Jersey State Chamber of Commerce.
>
> Mr. Palmer's civic interests also include philanthropic work. The
> United Defense Fund appointed him a director and chairman of a
> committee to coordinate the efforts of the Fund, USO and Com-
> munity Chest Council of America. He served as chairman of New-
> ark's first combined Cooperative Charities Campaign in 1952 and is
> trustee of the Newark and Madison, New Jersey Welfare Federa-
> tions as well as director of several other charitable organizations. He
> is also director at large of the National Sales Executives Club.

Mr. Palmer's election was welcomed by the home office and
naturally was especially popular in the field. His first Christmas
message to them reflects the qualities of the man and the spirit
with which he entered upon his leadership of the Company:

> The friendships of our business are a rich blessing for us all to
> remember at Christmastime. Those of us who work or have worked
> in the field count among our most treasured personal friends many
> whom we first met as clients. All of us, too, in Company associations
> in Home Office and field have developed friendships which are a
> bright part of our life's fabric. In our business we are especially for-
> tunate that our work gives us opportunities for these congenial
> personal relationships.
>
> The past year has brought me many special messages of friend-
> ship from the field and pledges of loyalty for our great Company
> and its aims. Your words and actions have been heartwarming. I
> have been conscious day by day of your trust and of my obligations
> to work with you to bring a new era of achievement for The Mutual
> Benefit Life.
>
> As we come to 1954, I thank you for your past spirit of coopera-
> tion, I congratulate you for the great production accomplishments

of 1953. We know not what tests the new year may bring. But in all that lies before us, our strength of spirit, our moral courage, the ideals which fire our hearts can be more important than all else. Christmas stands as the triumph of the spirit in a world dominated by materialism. The New Year stands as a beacon for those who would attain greater heights of achievement. For the full enjoyment of both, you have our best wishes.

The Mutual Benefit Life entered this new era as one of the nation's billionaire corporations. For the first time, in 1946 the Company ranked among national corporations with a billion dollars or more of assets. The Mutual Benefit Life passed that mark during the centennial year. The list showed ten other insurance companies and eighteen banks.

Another significant milestone was passed in 1951 when the Mutual Benefit Life attained $3,000,000,000 of life insurance in force. At the home office a day was chosen for special ceremonies. President Thompson entertained at luncheon in the recreation room the eighty-seven people still active who had been with the Company in 1919 when the first billion dollars of insurance in force was completed. Each one through the day wore a red rose as a badge of honor.

Yellow roses were worn that day by 112 other staff members who had been working with the Company in 1926, the two-billion-in-force year.

New products in the Company's market basket contributed their part to the increase in insurance in force. The first new policy made available under the program was a new five-year term contract, in the summer of 1946. The Company had had no such coverage since 1933. Later in the decade additional term coverages were introduced. Most important was the family protection rider. Attached to a basic annual premium life or endowment policy, that rider provides a flexible arrangement of decreasing term insurance. It affords family-income-type protection and serves also for mortgage redemption purposes.

Special class underwriting was begun in 1947 to extend insurance protection to lives with extra hazard from physical impairments or occupation. Such "substandard" underwriting is considered one of the most important life insurance developments of the past generation. It has made life insurance available to a large part of the population formerly considered uninsurable.

H. BRUCE PALMER

WASHINGTON PARK BUILDING

A study by the Society of Actuaries of 725,000 policies issued 1935–1949, in which the Mutual Benefit Life shared, showed that about 10% of ordinary issues were substandard. Insurance on any basis was refused to only 2–3% of people desiring it, instead of 10% or more a generation previously.

Other extensions in coverage and service were initiated during this period. In 1950, insurable age limits were extended downward to babies a month old. In 1953, the Company began the issue of an additional death benefit rider. This gives what is popularly called double indemnity for death resulting from accidental bodily injury. The same year a plan of monthly premium payments for individual policies was made available. Monthly premiums had previously been accepted only on cases handled by an employer for a group of employees.

Through these years there were of course developments in underwriting techniques. The x-ray became an increasingly important tool and the first home office x-ray equipment was purchased in 1948. This is used also for routine chest x-rays of home office employees.

The record of deaths from tuberculosis continued to fall during this period, and reached the lowest point in history, .3% in 1955.

Cancer death rates continued the slow climb, to 17% of all Company claims in 1955. Heart disease and related ailments continued through this period as the greatest killer in the Company as in the whole country. In 1955 these causes accounted for 59% of all Company deaths.

Of course the Korean conflict, beginning with the invasion of South Korea in June 1950, brought again question of war riders. This was no great problem because the experience of World War II was unfortunately fresh. Beginning immediately the Company announced that a war rider excluding death as a result of war service would be used in any cases, for both men and women, where facts indicated special hazard.

Generally during this decade underwriting of aviation risks (except those involving war hazards) was increasingly liberal. At the present time passenger flying over established air routes in commercial planes is practically disregarded as extra risk.

After World War II the average size of policy in the Company rose markedly. From 1946 to 1947 the first sharp increase appeared, from $5,750 to $7,353. In 1955 the average-sized policy was $9,682.

During these years the Company repeatedly increased limits of insurance on a single life. In 1950 the limit was raised to $250,000; in 1951, to $300,000; and in 1954, to $400,000.

In 1956 the Company limit was again raised, to $500,000. Although the Company had never before had such a limit several $500,000 Mutual Benefit Life policies had been issued many years before. This was in the 1920's when the amount at risk under high premium contracts was considered the amount of "insurance." One such policy was issued in 1928 to a man in Ohio who had made very large gains in the rising stock market. He took his profits in time, and put over $400,000 in a single premium ten-year endowment contract. How he must have felt when he saw the losses which came to others in 1929!

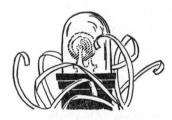

In all the changes that were being adopted, there was one change the Company did *not* make. That was in the quality of the policy contract. In spite of the inflationary spirit of the times and a developing concentration in the industry on size factors, the Mutual Benefit Life reaffirmed belief in basic values. In fact this period saw again lines being drawn between companies which set competitive commercial goals and those whose objectives were expressed in terms of service and stewardship for policyholders. The trends in the business became so strong that Vice President Jones identified the period as a fourth cycle in comparative life insurance history. As in the period of exaggerated expansion after the Civil War, as in the experiences leading up to the Armstrong Investigation, as in the disability race, so again the Mutual Benefit Life felt constrained by principle to stand against what seemed the popular course.

In the summer of 1954 the Agents Advisory Committee, and later the National Associates, by resolution affirmed their belief in the historic principles of the Company. Performance rather than price tags; values to the whole Company membership, not bargains for a class of new customers; flexibility to meet changing needs; and a committal to standards of service consistent with established Company character—these things they were proud to claim as Company objectives.

Time was ripe in the industry for leadership to crystallize on these issues. The Mutual Benefit Life felt that the trends, unhealthy for the whole business, might be slowed or reversed. Therefore, beginning in New York City, full-page newspaper space was taken across the country to present a message in the public interest. The headline was: "What Every Successful Man Should Know about the 'Cost' of Life Insurance."

The advertisement outlined points to consider in judging a company, factors to understand about the differences in life insurance policy contracts, and suggestions about the value of personal service through a trained life underwriter. The emphasis was on quality, not price. The response was impressive—from the business and from the public. But future historians must be the judge of the degree to which this leadership has served American life insurance.

The change in the Company's investment picture since World War II is the greatest change in its 111 years of history, according to Financial Vice President Milford A. Vieser. It reflects the skilled leadership of Mr. Stillman whose financial acumen is widely recognized in the East.

The Company's first objective, of course, is safety of principal with continuity of income to assure fulfilling its contract guarantees to policyholders. The Company seeks prudent management for the members, but also feels a keen sense of social responsibility. Life insurance companies have become the most important single channel through which the savings of individuals are marshalled to meet the long term capital requirements of the country.

During World War II almost all new Company investments went into Government bonds—meeting the greatest current need of our nation. At the end of the war, with nearly half the Company's assets in such low-interest bonds, there was financial as well as social reason to turn as quickly as possible to other kinds of securities.

Mortgage holdings at the beginning of 1946 were 12% of total assets. The booming postwar demand for new housing indicated aggressive developments in that area. Before 1942 when the Company established a separate city mortgage department (when Mr. Vieser was brought into the Mutual Benefit) the Company's urban real estate investments were limited quite closely to the Northeastern states. Now began a movement to all parts of the nation in the arc from Seattle to San Francisco to Dallas. Today the Mutual Benefit Life has city mortgage and real estate activities in 175 major cities in forty states and the District of Columbia.

This period saw also a continued change in mortgages from completely private operations to Government guaranteed loans. Now over one-half of the city mortgage loan account is insured by the Federal Housing Administration or guaranteed in part by the Veterans Administration.

A very important development in 1945 was legislation to permit life insurance companies to purchase and hold real estate for investment income. Previously the Company ownership had been limited to properties needed for Company business and to foreclosed real estate. In 1947 for the first time since 1923 the Company held no foreclosed real estate that was not under contract of sale, but the new type real estate holdings purchased for investment had begun to show in reports to policyholders.

In addition to office buildings and apartment dwellings, the Company has made many investments in retail store buildings such as supermarkets and department stores. With long term leases by merchandisers of demonstrated stability and prime credit these investments are proving very satisfactory.

The low point in Company net interest earnings was 2.89% in 1947. The next year it increased to 2.97% and so began the long climb back. Each point of advance was warmly welcomed. Not only was it progress in the right direction, but also on the volume of assets at that time one-tenth of a percentage point of change in the interest rate meant a gain of over $1,000,000 in income.

By the end of 1948, President Thompson reported a reduction in Government bond holdings of more than $125,000,000. These funds and new money were being turned into a great variety of new uses. Many of the new loans made were handled directly with the borrower, a practice known as "direct placements," not requiring the expense of review and registration of bonds with the Securities and Exchange Commission. New bonds purchased caused increases in the railroad, public utility and especially the industrial accounts. Corporate securities now represent investments in over three hundred companies in about fifty different industries.

An important postwar need for funds related to highway expansion. In 1951 the Mutual Benefit Life shared in financing the New Jersey Turnpike, now carrying the world's heaviest motor traffic.

In 1947 the Company began acquiring bank and insurance company stocks and by the end of 1955 owned $11,000,000. The year 1955 marked the Company's entrance into the broader common stock field. During that year the Mutual Benefit Life bought about $12,000,000 of such investments in three railroads, nine utilities and three industrial companies. However, life insurance companies usually are so regulated by state law that stock investments can never become an important part of their total assets.

An important development of a different kind in Company financial operations was the establishment of the National Farm Loan Office at Ames, Iowa, in 1954. All farm loan operations for twenty-six agricultural states are now headed up there, resulting in important economies and better service to borrowers.

The progress in Company postwar readjustments was not reflected in current cost to policyholders generally for several years. Improving death rates, especially among annuitants, caused the Company to set up a special reserve fund at the end of 1946. This was a first step toward the strengthening of reserves under settlement options in old contracts. Annuity rates guaranteed in policies issued before 1938 were far from realistic under modern conditions. This situation of course was faced to some degree by many companies. However the Mutual Benefit Life, having made a feature of this service, had a greater amount of income settlement plans outstanding than most companies.

Continued decline in interest earnings forced a readjustment in the dividend scale in 1948 for policies based on the American Experience Table of Mortality, the dividends on those older contracts being most responsive to the interest factor. There was some slight increase that year in CSO policy dividends. Those new contracts were most affected by the improving death rate.

The 1948 dividend scales were continued until 1953. Then improving interest earnings and continued favorable mortality allowed a slight increase that affected most policyholders. About $1,000,000 more was distributed in 1953 dividends than would have been distributed under the 1948 scale. Favorable experience resulted in another dividend increase for 1955. During 1955 net interest earnings improved to 3.58%, the best record since the low point of 1947, and the mortality was the best ever experienced by the Company.* Dividend scales for 1956 therefore were increased again.

Following World War II the insurance industry in many foreign countries looked to the United States for guidance in their plans of rehabilitation or expansion. The Company shared with others in much correspondence with companies in Japan, as well as in some contact with companies in India, Africa and Europe.

One most interesting experience was in 1951 when a group of seventeen French insurance executives visited this country. They came under the Marshall Plan for an exchange of ideas and technical information between European and American businessmen. Included in their itinerary was a visit to the Mutual Benefit Life to study the public relations program, gratifying recognition of the Company's accomplishments in that area.

They arrived by chartered bus from New York for a morning of discussions and study of exhibits in the classroom. Most of the visitors spoke little or no English. In the classroom they all wore head sets and were given a simultaneous interpretation of Mutual Benefit speakers' English remarks. This kind of translation has now become familiar through the United Nations sessions, but to participate then in such an operation seemed almost like sharing a miracle. When the speaker made some humorous comment, the words were hardly spoken in English, before the group's smiling response indicated that it had registered in French.

The guests were much interested in what in 1951 was the Company's outstanding public relations project. This was the distribution of a handbook concerning preparation for retirement entitled *Begin Now—to Enjoy Tomorrow.*

---

* Death rates in the United States have been improving steadily, as most people know. The average length of life at birth for the general population was 47 years in 1900. By 1940 it had improved to 63 years, then to 68 in 1950 and 69 in 1955. There does not seem to be much change in the extreme span of life. The average expectancy at birth is affected by the great improvements in child mortality and by the conquest of such diseases as tuberculosis and pneumonia which used to kill many young and middle-aged people.

With the growth of corporate pension plans and compulsory retirement in the postwar years a serious problem was developing in our country—retirement shock. Physicians, psychiatrists and social workers were recognizing this condition as a real physical ailment, bringing disability and even death. Life insurance provides money for retirement under many personal and corporate retirement plans. But money alone is not enough for happiness in retirement. What more appropriate public relations service for a life insurance company than the offering of practical help toward preparing for retirement?

The Company's little book was written by Ray Giles, a popular author long interested in the subject. It was hailed with enthusiasm and many compliments from leaders in all phases of gerontology. In fact, as someone said, it seemed to "hit the jackpot" of favorable public reaction.

Company representatives across the country sparked discussions of retirement problems by service clubs, community leaders and many other groups. The Queen of the Netherlands was in this country and had expressed considerable interest in problems of older people. To her the Company sent a copy of the book and received the following gracious acknowledgment from the Queen's private secretary:

> Her Majesty the Queen of the Netherlands instructed me to convey to you her sincerest thanks for your kind letter and the book you presented to her *Begin Now—to Enjoy Tomorrow*. Her Majesty is very interested in this important social problem.

The book won for the Company the highest award in the field of public relations, the Silver Anvil of the American Public Relations Association. In the first five years over 100,000 copies of the book were distributed through the agencies and directly from the home office.

The Company's continuing interest in gerontological problems was a factor resulting in the 1956 decision by the board of directors to modify the rule for mandatory retirement at age 65 for home office people which had been in effect for a decade. In announcing the plan to give the option for continuing work to age 68 if that would be to the interest of both Company and individual, Mr. Stillman commented:

> A business is composed of many kinds of assets. One of the most

valuable is the human assets, which are the brains, skills, abilities, initiative and loyalties of the people who comprise a business. We found, as a result of our studies, that these human assets were sometimes wasted by forced retirement at an age chosen many years ago in an era of business depression as a theoretical point of retirement. Age 65 is outmoded as an inflexible retirement age . . . the trend is toward advancing retirement, a trend that is supported equally by management and the worker, as well as by organized labor.

This Company's decision was widely applauded by the press, and by leaders in business, education and sociology.

The retirement patterns which crystallized after World War II were partly responsible for a very interesting development in life insurance. The payments to living policyholders became increasingly important compared to death claim totals. In the Mutual Benefit Life the decade after 1945 showed an increase in death claim payments of 25%. Payments to living policyholders increased 120%. This total of "living benefits" included cash values and income payments from cash values as well as proceeds planned originally for retirement purposes.

The development of pension trust business during this decade has already been mentioned. There was increasing emphasis also on many kinds of business insurance. Deferred compensation for executives and various other types of key man coverage, partnership and corporation stock purchase funding became a large part of the service of the Company's most successful salesmen.

Early in 1956 the Company announced its "True Security" group sales program. This bold innovation in life insurance selling, rooted in tested processes of successful Mutual Benefit salesmen, was developed under the personal leadership of President Palmer. It is based on a service to business and industry which at the same time introduces Mutual Benefit Life salesmen personally to groups of qualified prospects. The program uses moving pictures and is a step toward applying automation to time-consuming early steps in life insurance selling. The service offers businessmen and industrialists a complete program for supervisory development, to be used with middle management. Life insurance and money matters form one part of the course, and those discussions are led by a Mutual Benefit Life representative.

The response to the new True Security program on the part of executives has been gratifying. Results for Mutual Benefit Life salesmen in opening doors to rich sales opportunities have been exciting. Again, the long range effect of the program must be judged by a future observer.

The need of Company management to have the help of the field in these years of many changes was met in part by the organization of the General Agents Association in 1945, as has been mentioned. In 1948 the first Agents Advisory Committee was elected, representatives from each of five production level groups in the President's Club.

Emphasis on extension of Company representation through high quality new manpower was recognized in the designation of the Squab Club, and the annual meetings for these most successful new agents each year. The first Squab Club convention was in 1948 and these gatherings of men new to the business and to the Company have proved to be tremendously stimulating and valuable.

The special field activity program in October, now become famous as the Duel, was first scheduled in 1949. In 1955 the field wrote more than $84,000,000 during the Duel, which had a large part in the record-breaking $357,500,000 of new Mutual Benefit Life insurance bought and paid for during the year. A new all-time record of personal sales also was established in 1955. Harold M. Covert, Jr., of Allentown, Pennsylvania, completed $6,884,000 of sales in the Mutual Benefit Life during the year, which was a new high for the Company both in amount of insurance sold and in commissions earned.

During this decade the Mutual Benefit Life had the most unusual honor of having two of its field men serve as chairman of the Million Dollar Round Table: Paul W. Cook, C.L.U., of Chicago in 1949 and William T. Earls, C.L.U., of Cincinnati in 1953. Also in 1953 Robert C. Gilmore of Bridgeport, Connecticut, was elected president of the National Association of Life Underwriters.

In this decade of change for business and industry generally, the

Mutual Benefit took active part in nation-wide efforts to interpret the life insurance business to educators. For the first time in 1949 it cooperated in fellowship programs for college professors. Under these plans college professors spend a month or six weeks during the summer becoming familiar with the Company's operations, problems and management and studying subjects of particular individual interest. These have been mutually pleasant and interesting experiences. The professors generally have left feeling like Mutual Benefit alumni, and many have maintained their contacts with the Company over succeeding years.

Territorial expansion was a factor in Mutual Benefit plans in this decade, with entry or reëntry into several states. The Company for many years had been represented in only forty-three of the forty-eight states. When, in 1953, the Company reëntered Texas, and latei in the same year New Mexico, it made the roster complete for the first time. The Company also began an aggressive program of increasing the number of general agency centers. Since the beginning of 1946 the number of agencies has grown from sixty-nine to seventy-nine.

One of the most important national financial events of the decade was the Revenue Act of 1954. This was the first complete clarification and revision of the country's tax laws since before the turn of the century. The Mutual Benefit Life had a key part in this historic development through John J. Magovern, Jr., vice president and counsel. During the months of work preceding the passage of the act Mr. Magovern was chairman of a joint subcommittee of the American Life Convention–Life Insurance Association of America working with the Treasury Department and Congress. His committee's responsibility was all phases of tax legislation affecting life insurance except income taxation of the life companies themselves. Since 1954 the Committee's work has continued with Mr. Magovern still as chairman. Their responsibility now relates to proposed regulations to be issued by the Treasury Department to implement code provisions, and to proposed additional legislation.

Taxation matters generally have had growing importance for the Mutual Benefit Life as for citizens everywhere during the past generation. State and city taxes were problems from the beginning of Company history. Various federal stamp taxes affected the Company during the Civil War and the Spanish War. Taxes were requiring increasingly specialized clerical work and records before the depression, but it took the advent of social security taxes to add the straws to the load that resulted in a special tax department. That special group was set up in 1937 and Mr. Magovern was brought to the Company to be a part of it.

Some idea of the growing burden which Government places on business may be seen in some facts from tax department history. In 1925 the Company filed only twenty-seven forms relating to federal income tax on income payments to beneficiaries. For 1955 the Company filed 4,300 such federal returns plus thousands more for the thirty-two states which collect state income taxes.

During the war many improvements in work tools and methods, called for by changing conditions and especially by the growth of the Company, were of necessity deferred.

As early as 1937 the Company had made its major decision about mechanizing operations. Even before the war punch card records with modern equipment were being used that did far more than mere sorting and tabulating. As soon as possible in peace time this work was expanded and many new labor-saving and space-saving machines began to be acquired.

One of the first of the completely new equipment was microfilm. The Company's filing space was becoming very seriously overcrowded. So the first step was to copy many bulky files, throw the originals away and have the important records available in a fraction of space on small rolls of film. Later when the Korean War and the associated atom bomb threat were disturbing those responsible for civil defense and Company security, many of the current vital Company records were transferred to microfilm and stored in a bank vault up in the country far from Newark. Some duplicate punch card records were made and stored in a little community in the Delaware Valley. That seemed a very safe course until the unprecedented summer floods of 1955 undermined the warehouse and washed everything down the river. Mutual Benefit Life punch cards were left hanging from the tree tops and spread over the meadows.

Soon after the microfilming equipment was acquired the Company began using several other automatic aids. Teleprinters were installed between the home office and the New York City general agencies in 1947. Dial phones instead of the personal exchange were introduced for the home office intercommunication system in 1948. That same year a specially designed inserting and mailing machine was purchased. This "stuffs" envelopes with several enclosures, seals and prints metered postage, and handles 5,100 such mailings an hour. Several different kinds of duplicating processes were introduced supplementing the mimeograph. The first mimeograph machine had been acquired as late as 1929. When it was urgently requested by some of the supervisory staff, the man holding the purse strings asked, "What in the world would you do with a mimeograph?" That seems unbelievable in view of the one thousand jobs a month now turned out here by the various duplicating procedures.

In 1950 the Company began the job of transferring the premium billing procedures to punch card operations, the direct mailing of premium notices from the home office and the handling of commission accounting by machine at the home office. The change-over on these jobs took about five years.

At the same time the periodical income checks for beneficiaries were transferred to punch cards. These checks previously had been individually typed, one thousand a day, a boring job that must be absolutely accurate, and finished absolutely on schedule. The claim department is justifiably proud of the record of timely deliveries of such income checks. Beneficiaries thankfully report that their checks are received practically 100% on the date due or just before. Using the punch card procedure cuts the cost of this income service in half.

The Mutual Benefit Life was one of the pioneers in the industry to begin using electronic machines. The first IBM 604 machines were used in 1952. On an August morning in 1955 Mr. Stillman and Mr. Palmer pushed the buttons which started the famous IBM 650 on its Mutual Benefit Life career. The machine's potentialities are indicated by several of its jobs. For payroll work it will deliver a file of cards containing all figures on current payroll, including tax withholding, social security deductions, voluntary deductions, overtime and net pay for the home office staff of a thousand people, with cumulative figures for each clerk for the year to date, in half an hour. In dividend work the machine can compute policy dividends from a completely random sequence of cards determining for itself what the description of the policy is and what it calls for in the way of excess interest, mortality savings and margin factors.

The new machines are not displacing present employees. Normal turnover makes adjustments easy. In many ways the machines upgrade employees. They free men and women from many laborious, repetitive jobs. Moreover, though the machines are popularly called electric brains, they are more truly morons. They can do only what they are told. Planning the "orders" for the machines, assembling correct input material and handling output are tasks requiring great skill and extensive training of high-caliber people.

The postwar decade brought not only the opportunity to use new and better tools but also the challenge to improve techniques of management and work. Outside consultants were used to introduce a program of job evaluation in 1946 and 1947, but the work generally has been carried on by Company staff. Analyzing and rating jobs and writing job descriptions were done for several years by a committee of officers and clerks representing all parts of the Company. This work is now a part of the personnel department routine. The job evaluation program results in a much more uniform administration of salary questions than could otherwise be possible.

Home office members always have shown great interest in self-improvement as related to the job. Even before the beginning of the Life Office Management Association Institute examinations, many people attended after-office classes in life insurance fundamentals. The Company was represented in the first L.O.M.A. examinations in 1933. The first man to complete the series of ten L.O.M.A. examinations and the following two minors and the major examination became a fellow of the Institute in 1946. Since then fifteen other staff members have qualified as fellows, including one woman.

Members of the supervisory staff and officers went back to the classroom after the war in the Company's Supervisory Development Program. This also was organized and carried through by members of the personnel department with some help from outside specialists.

The most recent project for improvement of use of manpower in the Company is work measurement, known as O.S.P., the Operational Standards Program, introduced in 1955. Studies leading up to this program began several years previously. Again outside consultants were used only in the beginning.

Greatly increased costs after the war were a problem for employees and Company alike. In 1947 the Company placed the retirement plan benefits on a current funding basis. At about the same time, the Company assumed the cost of hospitalization and medical-surgical protection for home office employees under the New Jersey Blue Cross and Blue Shield plans. The Company paid a Christmas bonus in 1946 and subsequently operated under several extra-payment cost of living adjustment schedules. The last of these was finally merged with the basic salary in 1956.

A change which had the double value of economy to the Company and increased satisfaction to the staff was cafeteria instead of restaurant service for the noon-day lunch, which began in 1950.

The first formal budgeting by departments was undertaken to help control increasing postwar costs. The impersonal ideal of economy which had been traditional and impressively effective in the Mutual Benefit Life has now become personified in the vice president and comptroller, James P. Moore, Jr. Mr. Moore grew up in the Company with extensive experience in field auditing, renewal department and agency finance activities and has been a Company officer since 1946.

As the Company grew, a local tax situation had been revealed as increasingly serious. A franchise tax under the authority of a state statute was levied on Company surplus at a rate determined by the city of Newark. The city received the major part of the proceeds. The Mutual Benefit Life suffered particularly under this levy because it was unable to qualify for special deductions which were not geared to its operations. In 1945 the Legislature revised the tax law so as to limit the percentage of surplus that could be taxed. While this gave some relief to the Mutual Benefit Life, it did not eliminate the basic inequities of the law.

Mr. Stillman and the other executives determined to come to grips with this problem. In 1950, the Company made forceful presentation of its case to the public, municipal officials and the Legislature. The result was new legislation that made deductions available to it which had previously been applicable to others. Thereafter, a court decision involving the constitutionality of similar taxation of other insurers prompted even more important legislation. In 1950 a new basis for taxing domestic life insurance companies was enacted into law in New Jersey. The new tax is a premium tax, although levied as a franchise tax, and provides for sharing of tax proceeds by the city and county. This is comparable to the premium taxes paid by life companies in other states and equalizes the Company's position in the industry.

Vice President Magovern summarized the importance of this tax change: "While the immediate effect of this vigorous program was a progressive but equitable reduction in the taxes paid by Mutual Benefit in its home state of New Jersey, it had much more important and extensive implications. It eliminated a fluctuating tax rate, conformed the tax burden generally to that of other life insurance companies operating in New Jersey, permitted a proper surplus growth without tax penalties and removed local taxation as an important factor in the fixing and carrying forward of our investment policy."

All the second century's studies and new programs in home office operations and expanded service have meant a tremendous amount of additional work by those chosen to hold key responsibility. They have brought disruption of old habits and readjustments to hundreds of staff members, as individuals have been transferred to entirely new work or have learned to do old work in new ways. Through everything the spirit of cooperation and interest has been impressive. The staff generally has adopted the new goals as their own and have felt justifiable pride in progress accomplished.

The Company is now organized in six major divisions. Mr. Jones, Mr. Magovern, Mr. Vieser and Mr. Moore, respectively, head the actuarial, law, finance and accounting areas, as described earlier. The underwriting division vice president is William F. Ward who began his Company experience as an actuarial student newly graduated from Rutgers University. He was first named a Company officer in 1945 and was elected associate mathematician in 1947, a background most valuable for the chief underwriting responsibilities which came to him in 1952.

The head of the agency division is Charles G. Heitzeberg, C.L.U. All Mr. Heitzeberg's life insurance experience has been with the Mutual Benefit as salesman, agency supervisor and home office executive. He has also an unusual army record of service on the personal staffs of Generals Marshall and Eisenhower, and several years ago was released by the Company for a term as special administrator in the State Department. He was elected second vice president and director of agencies in 1953.

President Palmer's philosophy is that the goal of all leadership is the stimulation of individual effort. He and Mr. Stillman believe in the delegation of authority and responsibility. They encourage the officers in charge of the six areas of Company operation to develop new ideas and to stimulate creative activity among their associates. The climate of the Company has become favorable to vision and initiative. Mr. Palmer frequently voices his three-fold objective for Company achievement: to continue giving to policyholders the highest quality of life insurance contract and service, at the lowest cost consistent with that quality, and through the most creative, efficient merchandising programs.

The Company has grown to a multibillion dollar corporation in insurance in force and assets, but the individual still has recognition and is important. About five years ago Mr. Thompson and Mr. Palmer inaugurated a plan of anniversary parties. Each month home office members, officers and staff, retired as well as active, who that month are celebrating quinquennial anniversaries of twenty years or higher, are invited to lunch with the president and several other officers. Complete informality reigns. The reminiscent flavor is strong. People are encouraged to tell of their first day with the Company, why they came to the Mutual Benefit Life, and other interesting experiences.

A fifty-year veteran tells how he was sent home the first day because he had lost his clip-on bow necktie. A woman recalls that on her first day she was repeatedly summoned to the infirmary for blood pressure tests because her abnormally low reading fascinated the medical board. A sober note is often sounded when beginners of the depression years remember with what gratitude they found themselves earning money in those dark days.

One retired veteran communicated his emotion to the whole party when his turn came to speak. He said, "As I got off the bus this morning I noticed the yellow civil defense sign pointing to our building as a shelter area. I thought to myself what a symbol that is of what the Company has been to me and my family for all my life. We found it a good place to work and it has made life comfortable and happy for us in retirement."

With the new century the Company recognized, as many corporations were doing, a new kind of corporate citizenship responsibility. Some Company officers had previously carried Mutual Benefit identification into city affairs. In modern times three had been outstanding. Dr. Ward's activities in philanthropic, civic and church matters had brought him unusual recognition, as has been mentioned. Mr. Hardin's work with the Newark Sinking Fund and the Essex County Park Commission was noteworthy. Mr. Thompson's contribution to the basic planning in our state for a form of medical insurance which developed finally into the Medical-Surgical Plan of New Jersey won him honorary membership in the New Jersey Medical Association—the first layman ever to have been so recognized. He also gave himself generously to the Newark Welfare Federation, the Family Service Bureau and many other worthwhile enterprises.

Now under the leadership of Mr. Palmer the Company actively encouraged participation by many officers and other staff members in all kinds of Newark community projects. Such help is necessary for a city becoming ever more highly industrialized. Moreover Company management recognized that these activities broadened the viewpoint and improved the leadership abilities of people participating. The good work done by Mutual Benefit Life representatives gives the Company a good name in the city. Mr. Palmer's leadership and vision in sparking interest in rehabilitation of the city especially have meant a great deal for Company prestige. To attempt a full report of the many activities of dozens of other people would be out of place, but today as never before, the Mutual Benefit Life takes a citizen's part in Newark.

The Company has always felt a keen sense of stewardship for policyholders' funds. This has been illustrated in many experiences related earlier. Policyholders' money must be used in ways to benefit the whole group of members. Corporate contributions of any kind were not made for many years. In World War I the Company first gave to the national funds of the Red Cross and the various war welfare services. For a long while after the Newark community chest was organized, the Company made no corporate gift. The home office staff, however, always cooperated wholeheartedly in the campaign, and for some years was one of the "Big Four" in an annual chest contest with the Prudential, the Public Service and Bamberger's department store. Promotion featured the pelican with personification of the other groups also, and brought good results in all organizations.

A splendid job of education has been done among the staff with a pattern of generosity set by the executives. The per capita gift now in the United Appeals Campaign (including the community chest, the Red Cross and a number of national appeals) has for several years averaged well ahead of comparable figures for business and industry generally. In this area, too, the Company's concept of corporate citizenship has changed. An annual corporate gift is now made in the city drive.

With the Mutual Benefit Life having become an outstandingly good citizen of Newark, an announcement on October 25, 1954, was big news: the Company had sold its 300 Broadway property and would build a new home office at a location yet to be determined and not necessarily in Newark. Many factors pointed toward the need for a new building. Outstanding were the electric power and temperature and humidity control requirements of the new office machines. The old building was not generally air conditioned and could not be made so at reasonable cost. The Broadway building also was expensive in maintenance compared to possibilities in a new structure.

For nearly two months everybody was in suspense—the home office staff as well as the city. After very definite consideration of outside locations, the announcement was made in December that the Company's new building would be near the center of the city on Washington Park, and would be planned for occupancy in the summer of 1957.

A primary reason for remaining in the city, at least under present conditions, was the employment situation. The Company's new employees are mostly young people just out of high school. Any suburban location would not attract to it a large enough number of such potential employees. Also the Newark location would cause no disruption of residence for present employees whose homes are in fifty surrounding communities. Moreover, although a country location would be pleasant, it would not do what a city environment does for management. Keeping the leaders of this national organization in close daily contact with the whole stream of business activity has great value. What America thinks and does, how America works and lives at home—all are important to the leaders of American life insurance. More than half of the men, women and children in this country own life insurance. Life insurance executives need to keep close to the heart of America.

Welcome to a Stout Ally

The announcement that the Mutual Benefit Life would stay in downtown Newark was hailed with enthusiasm by the whole community. The word that the Company would not only build its own new office but would cooperate in financing rehabilitation for the neighborhood was taken as marking a new era for Newark.

As this is written the new building has already changed the Newark skyline as its promise helped to change Newark community psychology. The structure is a modern tower of white limestone upon a three-story base, twenty stories high in all. The banks of tower windows have glare-reducing blue-green glass above aluminum spandrels. At the top of the face of the tower "Mutual Benefit Life" in twelve-foot-high letters will stand out in shining stainless steel by day and with illumination at night.

The architects for the new building are Eggers and Higgins. That firm designed such well-known structures as the Senate Office Building and the National Gallery of Art in Washington as well as many business buildings. Financial Vice President Milford A. Vieser is the Company officer in charge of the building program.

The Company staff look forward to making the new building a symbol of good citizenship in the city as well as continued service to old and new policyholders. The records so far in the new century give bright promise for the future, with very substantial increases in all measures of progress such as Company assets, insurance owned, new insurance purchased, payments to policyholders and beneficiaries, total investment income, and rate of earnings.

This book, *Since 1845*, has reported the developments and achievements of more than a century of life of the Mutual Benefit Life Insurance Company. One looks back and marvels at the way the Company has come. But looking forward it is clear that in just another decade the changes and progress will be breathtaking. The multimillion dollars of current life insurance purchases and benefits may become multibillions. The processes for issuing and servicing policies will be transformed and incredibly speeded by automation and electronics, and by long-range radio and television devices yet barely dreamed of. New types of contracts and coverage and merchandising will meet new needs. Investments will be made in businesses now still unborn. And beyond that, who knows?

The Mutual Benefit Life of the future will be measured in different dimensions than are known today. The Company's work will be accomplished physically in new ways with new tools of many kinds.

But the Mutual Benefit Life is more than machines and contracts and statistics and physical assets reported on the balance sheet. The Mutual Benefit Life Insurance Company is a stewardship and a service. In the midst of the pressures of physical changes the ideals of equity, mutuality and trusteeship—the spiritual factors which make the Company operations more than a business—will endure. May pride and thanksgiving for the record of the past keep each new generation true in the future to the standards which have made the Mutual Benefit Life the Policyholders' Company since 1845.

Appendix

The Newark Daily Advertiser for Friday, April 18, 1845 carried a nine-inch, single-column advertisement of the Mutual Benefit Life, with heading and text in part reading:

THE MUTUAL BENEFIT
LIFE INSURANCE COMPANY
Newark, N. J.
Chartered January 30th, 1845, by the
Legislature of New-Jersey.

This Company having received subscriptions to the amount of between Four and Five Hundred Thousand Dollars, is now ready to issue Policies of Insurance, on terms as favorable as any similar institution in the United States, or elsewhere.*

Among the most important duties that men owe to themselves and their families, and one, the performance of which, will go far to insure to them the enjoyment of peaceful hearts, in any event of life, is the attainment of means to support the infirmities of old age, or in case of death, to secure those whom they might otherwise leave helpless and unprovided, a certain resource against want. These means are offered to parents and others by the Directors of the Mutual Benefit Life Insurance Company, in the very liberal and accommodating conditions they present to the public in their Prospectus of the terms on which they will insure lives; for not only do they place it in the power of parents to secure an independent support to their families in case of death, but

---

* There is absolutely no record in Company papers of these "subscriptions." The first money appearing in the Company financial records is the $52.25 premium for the Benjamin C. Miller policy. This statement may refer to advance commitments by people to purchase policies. This would explain the large totals of sales particularly by the Lords in New York City.

the possession of such a Policy of Insurance, gives a permanent credit for its amount, to men in business of any kind, and young men can borrow capital on it to commence in trade. Married women can insure the lives of their husbands, (at the age of 30 years, and in like proportion for other ages,) secure from their creditors, if need be, at the small rate of 50 cents per week for $1,000, and after their own deaths, the same may be made payable to their children, or their guardians for them. Also, by an Endowment for their children, parents may secure to them a capital sum on coming to age, with the profit thereon, to be added annually to the principal. Indeed, as various as are the conditions in life, so numerous are the aids, protections and supports to be found in this Mutual Benefit Company, which is confined to Life Insurance and its funds will be applied to fostering the interests of its members—the profits arising from its business, being divided among them in available Scrip Certificates. The By-Laws of the Company, the better to insure public confidence Provide that no policy on any one life, shall be issued for more than $5,000, until the surplus funds amount to $50,000, after which the risks will be gradually increased with the capital.

By reference to the Charter and Prospectus, the several Tables of Rates of Premiums therewith, to be had at the offices of the Company, the superior advantages presented to the community at large, will most strongly commend it to general patronage and favor.

There follows a list of the directors and officers and medical examiners and a table headed "The Rates ot Insurance of One Hundred Dollars on a Single Life, for One Year." The rates are shown for ages beginning at 14 and carrying through 67, for one-year term, seven-year term and life policies.

Notes on Illustrations

Frontispiece

Portrait of Robert L. Patterson, Company founder and first president. The painting was by James Bogle, holder of Policy 403 issued in 1845, and a celebrated portrait painter of the times. Mr. Bogle was a Southerner who had painted many nationally-known men from life, such as John C. Calhoun, Daniel Webster and Henry Clay. The Patterson portrait was commissioned by the Company after President Patterson's death and was painted from pictures and data supplied by the family.

Opposite page 4

Portrait of Benjamin C. Miller, the Company's first secretary. The picture is dated 1858 and carries a signature in an undecipherable, foreign-looking script.

Opposite page 5

Market Street, looking east from Broad Street in 1854. This contemporary picture shows the first home office building owned by the Company, 151 Market Street. The plainly marked 148 Market Street indicates the immediate neighborhood. The flag marks the Company's building. Also, allowing for some slight artistic license in location of foliage in the drawing, an item from an old receipt book is suggestive: "Received from the Mutual Benefit Life Ins. Co. Six dollars on a/c of four trees set in front of their building in Market Street. The small tree is to be taken up and a larger one put in when I am to receive two dollars more. The above trees being warranted the balance is to be paid when the trees are fairly and surely growing."

Pasted into the receipt book is also a city real estate tax receipt totaling $84, including items of $10 each for "Night Watch", "Water Tax" and "Dog Tax."

The architect for this Market Street building was Stephen Grover

Gould, a prominent local citizen and an incorporator of the American Insurance Company. That company became a tenant and, with the Mutual Benefit Life, caused the structure to be known as "the Insurance Building." This building is still standing, housing a miscellany of shops, restaurant and offices in a neighborhood which some day may be restored to former dignity.

Opposite page 14
Portrait of Lewis C. Grover (President, 1862–1881) by Joseph G. Beitl, a native of Newark and a prominent local artist. Several examples of his work are owned by the Newark Museum. Mr. Beitl was also a photographer and conducted a drawing school in Newark. He painted continuously in Newark through 1920 and died in 1929 at the age of 88.

Opposite page 15
Wall Street, New York City, in 1847, looking west toward Trinity Church, from a popular contemporary lithograph. The Company's first New York City office was at the corner of New Street in the left middle distance. This was about opposite the Sub-Treasury Building, completed in 1841 on the site of the old Federal Hall where George Washington had been inaugurated as first President of the United States on April 30, 1789.

On page 16
Representation of the pelican used on the first series of Company policies and in many other publications.

On page 59
The brownstone building which was the second Company-built home office. The drawing is from a faded photograph. The building was designed by a local Newark architect, William Kirk.

On page 66
Sketch of Lincoln statue by Gutzon Borglum on the steps of the Essex County courthouse in Newark.

On page 72
Sketch of Jelliff sofa purchased for the new brownstone building in 1862, and still owned by the Company.

Opposite page 106
Portrait of Amzi Dodd (President, 1882–1902). The minutes of the board of directors for October 10, 1889 report that "President

Dodd be and is hereby requested to sit before some competent artist for an oil painting of himself to be hung in the Directors' Room." This is undoubtedly the resulting picture although it is not dated or signed. Contemporaries considered it an excellent likeness.

Opposite page 107
Portrait of Frederick Frelinghuysen (President, 1902–1924) by Alphonse Jongers, a Frenchman trained in France and Spain, who had won recognition in America following establishment of his studio in New York City in 1897. Works of M. Jongers hang in the Metropolitan and in the National Gallery.

On page 110
Reproduction of the cover of the first issue of *The Pelican.*

Opposite page 136
Portrait of John R. Hardin (President, 1924–1945) by William J. Whittemore, painted in 1931. Mr. Whittemore was an American-born artist who studied and received many awards both in this country and abroad.

Opposite page 137
The marble building which was the third home office structure. The illustration is the architect's drawing.

Opposite page 156
Portrait of Edward E. Rhodes (Vice President, 1908–1946) by William Fiske Noyes, a recognized American artist. The portrait was presented to the Company by the Mutual Benefit Life field forces in 1942 at the time of Mr. Rhodes' fifty-sixth Company anniversary.

Opposite page 157
The Company's 300 Broadway building as pictured in water color by Alan Davoll, an artist celebrated for his architectural paintings.

Opposite page 186
Portrait of John S. Thompson (President, 1946–1953) painted in 1951 by Frank C. Bensing, well-known New York portrait painter. Mr. Thompson sat for the portrait in his own office. In addition to painting men like the president of the American Telephone Company, Mr. Bensing, during World War II, worked through

the USO and other service organizations doing over five hundred portrait sketches of service men to be sent home to their families.

Opposite page 187

Portrait photograph of W. Paul Stillman (Chairman of the Board, 1946–   ) made by Kaiden—Kazanjian Studios.

Opposite page 200

Portrait photograph of H. Bruce Palmer (President, 1953–   ) made by Fabian Bachrach.

Opposite page 201

The architect's drawing of the Company's newest home office building now being completed at 520 Broad Street.

The map on the end papers is based upon one published by the National City Bank of Cleveland, and used by permission, which is gratefully acknowledged.

Comparative Synopsis of Policies in force, and the Amount Insured, for the Year just ended, and Previous Years.

YEAR	Policies Issued	Amount Insured by New Policies	Policies in Force at the end of the Year	Total Amount Insured at the end of the Year
1845	693	$ 2,310,402	624	$ 2,110,717
1846	2,316	6,717,720	2,722	8,265,518
1847	1,847	5,057,910	4,157	12,213,210
1848	1,406	3,818,260	5,063	14,774,060
1849	1,509	3,442,500	5,373	15,025,190
1850	747	2,223,775	5,202	15,004,790
1851	499	1,533,750	5,191	15,335,107
1852	496	1,630,750	5,032	15,188,507
1853	512	1,743,250	5,015	15,538,332
1854	464	1,521,170	5,023	15,829,077
1855	446	1,478,850	5,033	16,069,207
1856	473	1,707,440	5,131	16,702,797
1857	587	2,223,550	5,267	17,477,157
1858	913	3,102,825	5,789	19,108,862
1859	1,366	4,661,100	6,649	22,203,437
1860	1,435	4,932,565	7,575	25,426,538
1861	894	3,208,450	7,026	23,481,353
1862	1,740	5,696,350	7,912	26,140,051
1863	3,511	11,910,392	10,861	36,285,443
1864	7,092	22,387,615	16,931	55,037,168
1865	6,819	24,970,856	21,921	74,178,884
1866	7,193	27,757,037	26,784	92,842,869
1867	6,024	23,413,760	29,858	102,738,027
1868	7,701	31,920,841	34,318	123,528,244
1869	5,361	21,070,631	36,326	129,928,107
1870	3,731	12,997,110	37,298	130,904,083
1871	3,490	10,489,734	38,667	133,137,290
1872	3,121	9,378,240	39,425	133,164,169
1873	3,147	8,739,185	39,938	131,443,818
1874	4,039	10,931,975	41,302	131,938,427
1875	4,637	12,440,560	43,015	134,104,103
1876	3,617	$ 9,528,530	43,307	$131,846,985
1877	3,213	6,767,555	42,796	126,193,045
1878	2,482	5,124,155	41,764	119,179,592
1879	3,325	7,768,310	42,286	117,720,246
1880	5,084	12,909,790	44,350	121,466,979
1881	5,377	14,411,223	46,652	127,411,677
1882	4,355	10,947,229	47,837	129,619,105
1883	4,913	13,171,468	49,178	133,298,768
1884	5,235	13,560,873	50,361	135,463,543
1885	5,608	14,718,957	51,846	139,416,807
1886	6,030	14,706,407	53,633	143,186,656
1887	6,254	15,972,424	55,362	147,189,403
1888	7,355	18,820,772	57,954	153,498,623
1889	8,444	22,057,621	61,327	162,617,014
1890	9,183	23,956,031	65,154	172,840,944
1891	10,543	26,955,758	69,350	183,171,333
1892	11,903	30,350,412	74,346	195,698,088
1893	11,771	28,812,271	77,493	202,276,750
1894	12,469	30,588,996	80,744	209,369,528
1895	13,318	32,451,131	84,916	218,917,716
1896	12,843	30,618,445	87,979	225,417,065
1897	15,032	34,348,190	92,738	234,496,688
1898	15,412	35,586,235	97,884	246,350,788
1899	18,055	41,385,228	106,178	265,266,269
1900	16,178	35,316,369	112,569	278,171,436
1901	18,389	38,387,623	120,869	294,368,513
1902	20,016	42,722,733	130,145	314,256,081
1903	22,691	47,594,210	141,504	337,463,561
1904	26,670	54,483,680	155,009	363,801,084
1905	28,985	61,007,614	168,643	392,548,092

Comparative Synopsis of Policies in force, and the Amount Insured, for the Year just ended, and Previous Years.†

YEAR	Policies Issued*	Amount Insured by New Policies	Policies in Force at the end of the Year	Total Amount Insured at the end of the Year	Percentage (by amounts) of New to In Force at beginning of Year
1906	21,901	$49,499,816	178,089	$ 412,119,264	12.61
1907	21,543	50,055,041	189,602	440,742,990	12.15
1908	22,067	52,641,087	200,819	469,247,427	11.94
1909	24,382	58,246,772	213,571	502,179,900	12.41
1910	26,766	68,006,811	228,591	543,658,197	13.54
1911	28,635	70,804,881	244,047	584,376,714	13.02
1912	32,076	78,743,256	261,851	629,501,147	13.47
1913	32,489	76,768,118	280,142	673,088,683	12.20
1914	32,717	78,066,494	297,170	714,233,070	11.60
1915	34,659	86,353,069	314,763	761,459,167	12.09
1916	41,522	106,901,195	339,608	830,768,806	14.04
1917	41,365	120,424,693	365,249	915,297,422	14.50
1918	32,955	111,619,083	381,507	987,481,787	12.19
1919	51,334	184,438,331	417,215	1,133,144,235	18.68
1920	54,729	221,624,940	456,044	1,311,052,551	19.56
1921	41,085	166,535,095	477,217	1,415,984,749	12.70
1922	41,482	178,338,581	497,611	1,528,749,251	12.59
1923	45,383	194,772,773	521,590	1,653,277,782	12.74
1924	45,324	210,935,136	542,956	1,784,000,311	12.76
1925	47,560	235,757,337	565,313	1,935,188,845	13.22
1926	44,892	242,132,650	583,298	2,082,028,221	12.51
1927	43,837	226,782,549	599,704	2,208,320,123	10.89
1928	41,334	229,254,913	611,658	2,325,527,937	10.38
1929	42,509	233,235,388	622,320	2,435,012,342	10.03
1930	43,210	211,750,011	628,844	2,490,811,762	8.70
1931	37,229	167,287,166	624,407	2,465,136,803	6.72
1932	33,771	135,916,258	604,153	2,334,602,527	5.51
1933	42,729	188,611,748	573,924	2,165,831,398	8.08
1934	36,872	135,740,718	553,310	2,056,941,859	6.27
1935	35,753	$128,062,547	545,080	$2,005,497,838	6.23
1936	34,381	130,109,580	546,005	2,006,774,187	6.49
1937	31,980	129,931,046	549,584	2,032,208,082	6.47
1938	30,970	134,874,138	550,579	2,044,470,484	6.64
1939	26,434	115,294,762	549,604	2,048,726,860	5.64
1940	27,315	121,659,450	550,940	2,068,361,343	5.94
1941	28,997	142,116,575	556,353	2,114,070,806	6.87
1942	23,066	107,224,372	559,497	2,135,966,573	5.07
1943	25,982	138,197,068	568,902	2,205,359,131	6.47
1944	24,532	132,149,007	578,030	2,273,148,501	5.99
1945	28,104	170,758,725	589,664	2,372,337,677	7.51
1946	29,417	169,150,106	601,163	2,461,730,612	7.13
1947	28,338	208,382,906	610,181	2,583,400,609	8.46
1948	30,682	226,231,417	620,439	2,705,486,094	8.76
1949	30,601	224,040,086	629,167	2,818,521,202	8.28
1950	34,114	252,928,218	640,782	2,956,067,256	8.97
1951	33,996	258,987,126	652,689	3,098,126,726	8.76
1952	34,003	267,192,307	663,355	3,239,377,866	8.62
1953	37,517	302,372,644	675,624	3,401,787,319	9.33
1954	35,913	297,914,739	685,767	3,548,837,774	8.76

*Effective for 1906 and later years the Paid-for basis is used.   Effective for 1908 and later years commuted values are used.

†Excluding Group policies issued in connection with the Company's 1947 Retirement Plans.

INDEX

THE MUTUAL BENEFIT LIFE *sends this story of the Company to friends, business leaders, educators and interested citizens, with the hope that it will prove a challenging case history of American free enterprise. The Company came into being to help people build security by cooperative personal effort. We are proud of the record of the past and pledge our continued devotion to the principles which have so long guided our growth.*

President

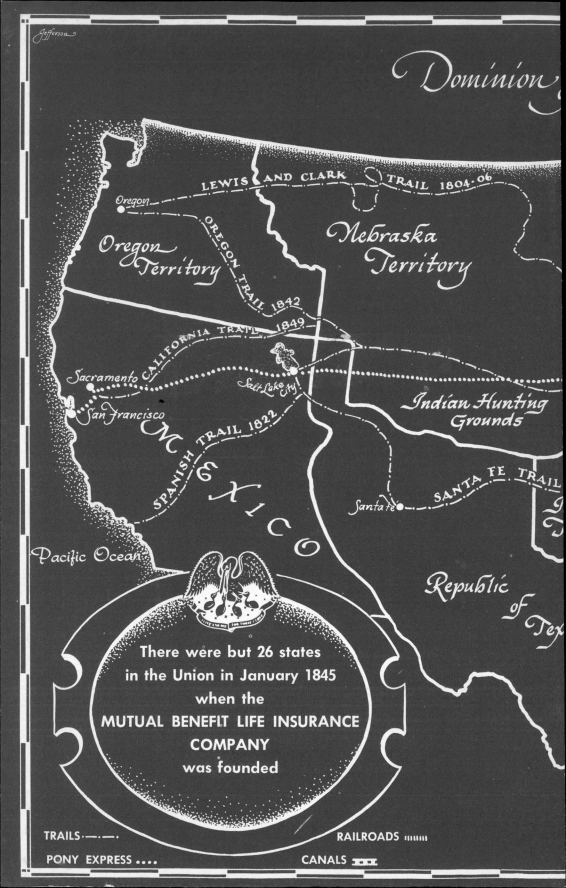